THE
COMPLETE GUIDE TO
PHOTOGRAPHY
TECHNIQUES
AND
MATERIALS

THE
COMPLETE GUIDE TO
PHOTOGRAPHY
TECHNIQUES
AND
MATERIALS

Michael Freeman

PHAIDON

A QUILL BOOK

Published by Phaidon Press Limited
Littlegate House
St Ebbe's Street
Oxford

First published 1982
© Copyright 1982 Quill Publishing Limited
ISBN 0 7148 2249 3

Published in the USA, its territories and dependencies and Canada by
Chartwell Books Inc, Secaucus, New Jersey.

Distributed in Australia by ABP/Methuen Pty Ltd, Sydney, NSW.

This book was designed and produced by
Quill Publishing Limited
32 Kingly Court
London W1

Art director · James Marks
Production director · Nigel Osborne
Editorial director · Jeremy Harwood
Senior editor · Liz Wilhide
Assistant editor · Joanna Rait
Designer · Paul Cooper
Illustrators · Paul Cooper, David Weeks
Picture researcher · Ann Lyons

All photographs by Michael Freeman except where individually credited.

Filmset in Great Britain by Text Filmsetters Limited, Orpington, Kent.
Origination by Hong Kong Graphic Arts Limited, Hong Kong.
Printed in Hong Kong by Leefung-Asco Printers Limited.

Quill would like to extend special thanks to
George Ashton at Patterson Products Limited,
Bruce Coleman, Peter Grant at Gilchrist Studios
Limited, Howard Hopwood at Ilford Limited,
Ernst Leitz, Brian Mead at Keith Johnson
Photographic Limited, Clem Neville at Fox
Talbot Cameras, Polaroid (U.K.) Limited
and Linda Ross at Nikon U.K. Limited.

CONTENTS

INTRODUCTION

One of the unresolved dilemmas of photography is the conflict between technology and image. Producing a good photograph requires both technical skill and creative flair, yet the two frequently seem to be opposed. Technology is rooted deeply in the photographic process, but it can easily drift into gadgetry, which interferes with the clear vision needed to produce good work.

As camera manufacturers and most photographic magazines fully realize, the majority of photographers are easily seduced by the appeal of equipment. In theory at least, no one is in any doubt that the end product of photography is the image, yet the general tenor of advertising aimed at amateur photographers suggests something quite different. The fact that so much camera equipment is so fashionable is a sign that, in some ways, the mere process of taking pictures may be an end in itself – a rather bleak view. Complex cameras, now nearly always produced with an eye to design, can even be a substitute for taking pictures, satisfying a variety of needs – acquisitiveness, something to play with or to display. In a more subtle way, the promotion of technique is a way of reassuring the user that success will flow, that individual skill or insight can in some way be bypassed. The technologically advanced camera – "state of the art" is a popular description – becomes a talisman.

There is not even general agreement among established photographers. Some are strongly influenced by the technology of photography, especially by its innovations, using new equipment as a stimulus. Art Kane (b. 1925), whose distinctive style of colour photography has had a strong influence in New York advertising, talked about the effect that the invention of new lenses had on his work. "My way of seeing changed. It's as if I married each one. Now we're all living together." What some might regard a reverent attitude to technology contrasts sharply with the approach of Irving Penn (b.1917), the American fashion and portrait photographer, who over many years produced his portrait series in a northlit studio with the first Rolleiflex he owned – an undistinguished model by present standards. For other photographers there is a middle ground, where the pleasure of craftsmanship plays an important part and the final result owes much to the careful use of materials. A print by the American landscape photographer Ansel Adams (b.1902) reflects the outstanding control that he exercises over every stage of the process, and is as satisfying for this reason as much as for any other.

Although it is easy, on the face of it, to make a case either for the joy of technology or the purity of the photographer's eye, in reality there is no such clearcut choice. Inventive technique can be used to produce images that are outstanding rather than just intriguing, and many of the simplest and clearest of the world's great photographs are the product of a shrewd knowledge of the potential of both equipment and materials. The solution is to be familiar with all the possibilities and select those that may be useful for your ideas. The following chapters explore the opportunities offered by the range of photographic equipment and materials now available, without neglecting some of the very earliest techniques.

What I have tried to do at all stages is to show how each piece of equipment, material and technique can be put to its best use. To know the technical differences between films, or darkroom procedure, or lenses, is irrelevant unless there is some sense of the value of each. Tinkering with the processes can be a wonderful way of suggesting ideas, but it is hardly an end in itself, and much of this book is taken up with the various influences that techniques and materials have had, and continue to have, on photography's major themes and styles.

Left This photograph, taken by Joel Meyerowitz (b.1938) in 1978, is striking because of its sophisticated use of colour, achieved through extreme care in colour printing from a large-format negative. The contrasting turquoise and shades of orange complement each other easily, and not only suit the art deco style of architecture, but also help to evoke nostalgia in this view of a swimming pool in Miami. The formal composition, with centrally placed horizon and house, gives solidity to the image – a feature of view camera work that is perfectly suited to the stillness of the subject.

CHAPTER 1

THE CAMERA

Out of all the elements involved in the photographic process, it is the evolution of the design of the camera that has brought about the greatest changes in the way photography has been practised in its century-and-a-half history. This history, at least until recently, has mainly been one of problems and solutions, with the inventions and technical improvements acting as catalysts for the development of new styles and approaches. Miniaturization and increasing precision have been the keynotes of camera design, from the first box-like daguerreotype cameras to modern, compact 35mm single-lens reflex models. However, though the effects of these changes have been profound, the changes themselves have made little difference to the principle of the camera. All cameras share some features.

In simple terms, a camera is a light-tight box that allows an image formed by a lens to be projected on to a light-sensitive emulsion. In fact, not even the lens is strictly necessary: a pinhole is capable of focusing light rays into a recognizable image, albeit one that is dim and unsharp. In a darkened room on a bright day, a small hole will project an upside-down image of the scene outside. This simple optical fact is responsible for the development of the *camera obscura* (literally, "dark room") as an artist's aid to drawing from life, used at least as early as the sixteenth century. The *camera obscura*, in its turn, needed only the invention of a light-sensitive plate to initiate photography. Nevertheless, by the time that a practical process for fixing the image had been developed by Louis Daguerre in 1837, the artist's *camera obscura* had itself undergone improvements.

The first recorded use of the *camera obscura* was in 1558, when the Neapolitan Giovanni Battista della Porta (1538-1615) published details of its construction and operation. However, the basic principle behind this camera was described even by Aristotle, and, as Helmut Gernsheim suggested in *The History of Photography* (1955), the projection of an image by a pinhole may have been noticed earlier, in hot countries where rooms are kept darkened for coolness.

From these simple origins, photography developed to quite a respectable level of technology even before an emulsion was invented. The *camera obscura* was first improved by the addition of a lens which gave a brighter, sharper image, by making the length adjustable which permitted focusing, and by miniaturization which made the camera portable and hence more generally useful. The refinement of an angled mirror to throw the image up onto a ground glass focusing screen gave a functioning single-lens reflex. All this was in existence by the eighteenth century; it was the slow progress of photochemistry – the attempts to fix an image on a light-sensitive surface – that held up practical photography.

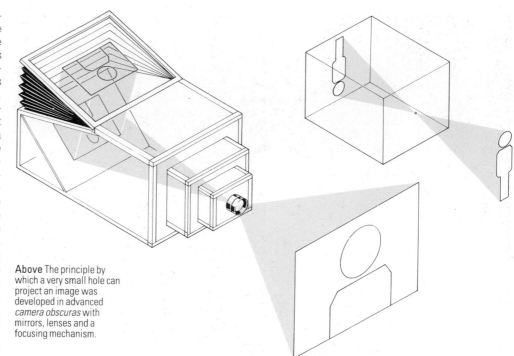

Above The principle by which a very small hole can project an image was developed in advanced *camera obscuras* with mirrors, lenses and a focusing mechanism.

Below *The daguerreotype process* A positive image was produced in a four-step process; although the resulting image could not be reproduced, as a modern negative can, the quality of tone and sharpness was extremely high. The base of the daguerreotype image was a silver-coated copper plate, which first needed to be highly polished *(1)*. This plate was then suspended upside-down in a deep wooden box (over a bowl of iodine crystals in a deep wooden box *(2)*. The iodine vapour rising in the enclosed space combined with the silver on the surface of the plate in a chemical reaction that produced a coating of light-sensitive silver iodide. This, and subsequent steps, were performed in darkness. The plate, loaded into a light-tight holder, was exposed in the camera, and to develop the image, the plate was suspended for a second time in a deep box, but over a bowl of heated mercury *(3)*. The rising mercury vapour formed a highly reflective image on those parts of the plate that had been exposed to light, while the unexposed areas of silver iodide remained dark. This part of the process rendered the photographer liable to the unpleasant effects of mercury poisoning, a danger not appreciated at the time. To prevent any further development of the image, the daguerreotype finally needed, as any photographic process does, to be fixed for permanence. The original method was to soak the plate in a strong solution of salt *(4)*, but this was eventually superseded by the invention of sodium thiosulphate (hypo), which remains the universal fixing agent for all conventional photography. Fixing, in the case of a daguerreotype, dissolved and removed the silver iodide that had not been exposed to light, revealing the original surface of the metal. Because of the highly reflective qualities of both the mercury-deposited image and the bare plate, the daguerreotype had to be viewed at a certain angle. At other angles, the daguerreotype could look like a negative or look half-negative, half-positive.

Right The complexity of early processes, and their lack of standardization, made photographic chemistry one of the photographer's chief concerns. This collodion wet-plate outfit, made by Frederick Cox in 1869, was one of the first processing kits to be produced commercially.

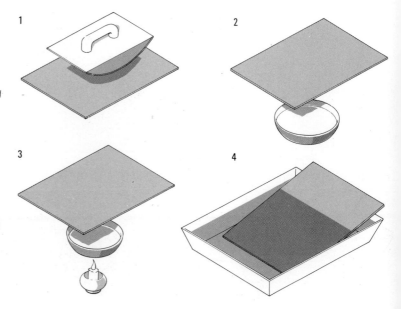

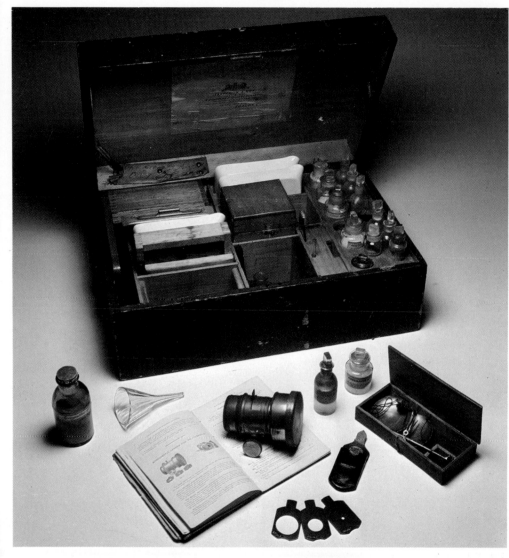

The world's first successful photograph was made by a Frenchman, Nicéphore Niépce (1765-1833), in 1826, using a kind of asphalt which hardened on exposure to light. Niépce later went into partnership with Louis Daguerre (1789-1851), and together they tried to improve Niépce's method. After Niépce's death, Daguerre found that mercury vapour developed a very faint image into a strong one and in 1839 the daguerreotype process was born. The first daguerreotype cameras were essentially *camera obscuras* adapted to a new role. Starting as a fairly crude arrangement of two boxes, one fitting inside the other, with a housing for the plates which could be slid back and forth to adjust the focus, the design of the daguerreotype camera soon improved.

The long exposure times of 20 minutes ruled out certain subjects: at this time, portraits were virtually out of the question, and landscapes or architecture were favoured. Thus, the first modification aimed to shorten the exposure time. One solution to this problem was a smaller camera, needing less light, but as daguerreotypes could not be enlarged, this had limited success. Another method used a large concave mirror to gather more light, but the real breakthrough came in 1840 when Josef Petzval (1807-1891) designed a lens fast enough for portraiture. With a maximum aperture of f3.6, the lens was sharp even when used wide open, and allowed exposure times outdoors of as little as 90 seconds.

Faster emulsions shortened exposure times even further, and new processes such as the calotype patented by William Henry Fox Talbot (1800-1877) in 1841 began to rival the daguerreotype. The calotype process was the first to allow a photograph to be printed onto paper from a negative. After 1851, the collodion

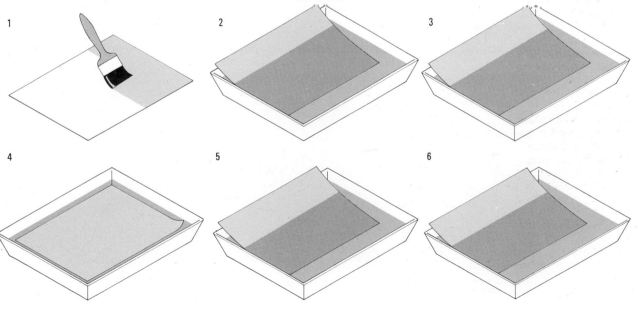

Left *The calotype process*
The calotype process produced a paper negative, from which many positive prints could later be made. Good quality rag paper was coated with silver nitrate solution *(1)*, then allowed to dry and soaked in a potassium iodide solution *(2)*. Just before being used, it was floated on a solution of gallo-nitrate of silver *(3)*, then loaded in a film holder and exposed in the camera. Development was completed by washing in gallo-nitrate of silver *(4)*, after which the paper, with its tonally reversed negative image, was washed in a water bath *(5)*. To prevent further chemical action on the image, the negative was finally fixed in hypo *(6)*.

1

2

Early cameras
The design of the earliest daguerreotype cameras was relatively crude, featuring none of the camera movements that later became common in flatbed field cameras, except for focusing. The basic construction *(1)* was composed of two wooden boxes, the smaller nesting inside the larger. To focus at distances closer than infinity, the rear section was pulled out, and to make the camera light-tight, the fit between the two box sections needed to be very close. The daguerreotype shown alongside the camera is of Louis Daguerre, and demonstrates the difficulties of looking at the developed image. The surface is so reflective that highlights and even surrounding objects are picked out with mirror-like clarity and often interfere with the image. A typical *carte-de-visite* camera *(2)* featured a battery of lenses to produce several small portraits on a single plate. Behind the lens assembly, black painted wooden panels inside the body of the camera prevented the light from one lens from interfering with the images produced by the others. One of the earliest methods of achieving a colour image used the principle of colour separation: taking three images, each through a film of a different colour. This American Tri Color camera of about 1890 *(3)* used three separate film backs, each with its own focusing track and bellows, and an adjustable mirror so that a single lens could be used for all. Slow and difficult to use, this method was quietly abandoned once integral tripack colour emulsions were developed.

3

4

Typical of the many flatbed field cameras that flourished during the late nineteenth century, this quarter-plate Sanderson model in mahogany and brass *(4)* was made in England. The grooved bars with screws allowed the camera to be folded up neatly into a small, portable package – hence the name "field" camera – but, more significantly, allowed the lens panel and film back to be locked into different positions relative to each other. Both the front and back of the camera could be tilted either forward or backward, and the front could also be raised or lowered. With these adjustments, the image could be manipulated in a variety of ways and this control has ensured the survival of the basic design. To reduce weight and bulk, the flexible leather bellows tapers toward the front, approximately following the shape of the cone of light projected by the lens. The aura of novelty that surrounded the beginnings of photography persisted for many decades, and, for a while, so-called "detective" cameras enjoyed a vogue *(5, 6)*. Often excessively ingenious, these cameras were miniaturized and adapted to fit into items of clothing, such as cravats, to look like something else, such as a pocket watch, or even to be concealed in the heel of a man's shoe.

5

6

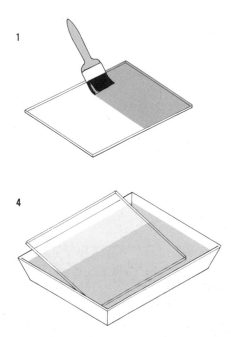

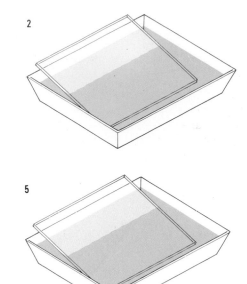

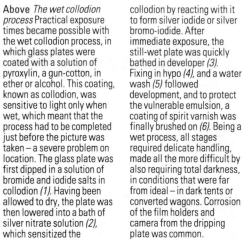

Above *The wet collodion process* Practical exposure times became possible with the wet collodion process, in which glass plates were coated with a solution of pyroxylin, a gun-cotton, in ether or alcohol. This coating, known as collodion, was sensitive to light only when wet, which meant that the process had to be completed just before the picture was taken – a severe problem on location. The glass plate was first dipped in a solution of bromide and iodide salts in collodion *(1)*. Having been allowed to dry, the plate was then lowered into a bath of silver nitrate solution *(2)*, which sensitized the collodion by reacting with it to form silver iodide or silver bromo-iodide. After immediate exposure, the still-wet plate was quickly bathed in developer *(3)*. Fixing in hypo *(4)*, and a water wash *(5)* followed development, and to protect the vulnerable emulsion, a coating of spirit varnish was finally brushed on *(6)*. Being a wet process, all stages required delicate handling, made all the more difficult by also requiring total darkness, in conditions that were far from ideal – in dark tents or converted wagons. Corrosion of the film holders and camera from the dripping plate was common.

wet-plate process gradually became standard, despite the enormous inconvenience of needing freshly prepared plates. The collodion solution had to be applied to the plate just before exposure, meaning that photographers had to travel with cartloads of darkroom equipment. Exposure times were now down to a few seconds for a small photograph, encouraging the invention of shutters – another step towards automation.

In contrast to the daguerreotype, the new wet plates were negatives from which positive prints could be made on paper. However, as photographic printing paper was too slow for enlargement, only contact prints could be made. To vary the size of the print to meet the increasingly varied demands, such as photographs for albums, lockets and exhibitions, the

only solution was to vary the size of the camera. Some monsters were built to take plates up to 4½ x 8 feet (1.4 x 2.5 m) in size, while at the other end of the scale, cameras that could fit into the palm of a hand were made to produce locket photographs. Signalling the growing popularity of photography, the *carte-de-visite* camera used several lenses to produce a number of calling card-sized portraits on a single plate.

The next turning point in photography was the development of a rapid *dry* emulsion in the late 1870s, freeing the photographer from the need to carry so much processing equipment. With the dry plate and then the flexible film, photography suddenly became accessible to a much wider public. The launch of the simple box camera by Kodak in 1888 by George Eastman (1854-1932), a camera which used rollfilm and designed specifically for amateurs, launched the era of the family snapshot, still the most popular use of photography.

From this photographic landmark until quite recently, the camera evolved along two separate paths to meet both professional and amateur needs. Professional camera design grew to meet specific demands, and although innovations in this area set the pace for improvements in popular cameras, only in the last few years has the mechanically complex 35 mm single-lens reflex camera begun to serve both amateurs and professionals.

The view camera, eventually standardized to a small number of film formats, principally 4 x 5 inch (9 x 12 cm) and 8 x 10 inch (20 x 24 cm), has become a more precise instrument mechanically but has not changed very much otherwise. It continues to function as a tripod-mounted instrument for producing highly controlled, large-format images.

By contrast, demand for a "press" camera – a model that was fast yet still produced film large

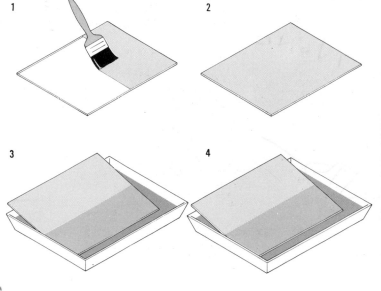

Left *The dry-plate process* An improvement over the wet-plate process was the invention of an emulsion that would remain light-sensitive even when dry, using gelatin as a support for a silver halide. Gelatin was melted and mixed with, usually, silver nitrate, and this emulsion was then used to coat a glass plate *(1)*, which was afterward allowed to dry *(2)*. It could then be stored in darkness until needed, freeing the photographer from the need to combine processing and picture-taking. After exposure and development, the image was fixed in hypo *(3)* and washed *(4)*. Being not only convenient but also capable of greater sensitivity, dry plates quickly superseded the wet collodion process.

enough for engraving – did lead to some new developments. The most famous of the cameras which resulted, the 4 x 5 inch (9 x 12cm) Graflex, was a single-lens reflex with waist-level viewing, allowing news photographers to focus easily and precisely on its hooded ground glass screen. Its focal plane shutter and 45° mirror made it similar in many respects to modern medium-format single-lens reflexes.

Even more influential, however, were the innovations that helped to create true candid cameras, such as the Ermanox and the Leica pioneers. As printing papers became fast enough to allow a negative image to be enlarged, small plates and films became practical for serious use. In 1924 the Ermanox, using singly loaded 2 x 3 inch (5 x 7.5cm) plates, appeared on the market. Fitted with an extremely fast f2 lens, it was used for unobtrusive news photography in poor lighting conditions. The ability to work indoors without flash with a

camera small enough to be tucked out of sight when not wanted, launched photojournalism in the direction it has followed (more or less) ever since – reporting events without artistic manipulation.

The Leica made its first appearance the year following the debut of the Ermanox. Developed over a period of 20 years, the Leica was built around sprocketed 35mm motion picture film and designed for use under almost any conditions. Although at the time its f1.9 lens was capable of producing sharper images than any film emulsion could allow, this camera quickly superseded the Ermanox and eventually had an enormous effect on such photographers as Henri Cartier-Bresson (b.1908) who in turn influenced many present-day photojournalists with his perceptive studies of human nature.

From the 1920s on, many different types of cameras were produced, using mainly rollfilm and 35mm. The Rolleiflex was the first of the

twin-lens reflexes which, although now fading from view, at the time offered both high quality images and mechanical simplicity. The 2¼ x 2¼ inch (6 x 6cm) single-lens reflex Hasselblad, designed to meet the requirements of its inventor's hobby – wildlife photography – found less acceptance in that area than in the field of fashion and advertising, and now has acquired a status that reflects this use.

Today the 35mm single-lens reflex, now virtually an exclusive product of the Japanese camera industry, represents the apotheosis of camera design. Increasingly automated, complex and electronic, it is an instrument whose capabilities often far exceed the demands of most of its owners.

Above Impractical heights of camera design were reached in the 1930s, with the limited production of the Compass camera by the Swiss watch-making company of Jaeger le Coultre. Designed by an Englishman, Noel Pemberton-Billing, to incorporate every conceivable photographic gadget, in a body that could be fitted into the palm of a hand, the Compass contained such innovations as dial-in filters, a depth-of-field indicator, an extinction exposure meter, and attachments for panoramic and stereoscopic views. Although engineered to standards higher than those of most modern cameras, the Compass had a short run, not least because the designer, with eccentric disregard for his market, designed it to be used with non-standard film and plates.

Right The need to load single glass plates for each shot meant that the Ermanox was too inconvenient to survive for long, but its lens had a maximum aperture of f2 – a remarkable achievement for its day. This enabled photographers such as Erich Salomon, who specialized in candid portraits of statesmen in Europe's corridors of power, to work unobtrusively, without tripod or artificial lighting. The camera was fitted with a folding, optical framefinder.

35MM CAMERAS

There are roughly two categories of 35 mm cameras: the viewfinder design, which dates back to the original Leica of 1925, and the single-lens reflex. Of the two, the viewfinder camera is simpler in principle and has fewer moving parts. The light path from lens to film is unobstructed by mirrors or focal plane shutters and viewing is done separately, through a small lens and screen on top of the camera body. This mechanical simplicity is one of the viewfinder's strongest points, and the reputation of Leicas for reliability and longevity is borne out by the large numbers of old models still in use. Viewing and focusing (using the double-image rangefinder principle) is easy even in dim light: the lack of either an instant return mirror or a large prism means that viewfinder cameras are relatively small and light and also quiet to use – qualities which have endeared them to photojournalists for whom a candid approach is important.

Although the latest Leica models have veered towards increasing complexity in order to compete with modern single-lens reflexes, the traditional absence of design frills has been a part of the viewfinder camera's appeal for photographers who choose to avoid complex technique and manipulated images. The cost of these advantages, however, is not being able to see the precise image that will be recorded on the film. At close distances, the viewfinder image is actually slightly different from reality (the parallax error) and special precautions must be taken to adjust this discrepancy. With long-focus lenses, accurate framing becomes too difficult with a viewfinder.

The outstanding feature of the 35 mm single-lens reflex (SLR) is that the image produced by the camera's lens is the one that the photographer sees. A 45° mirror behind the lens reflects the image up on to a focusing screen and then through a five-sided prism to give an accurate eyeline view. Although the mechanics are, as a result, quite involved – the mirror has to flip up before the exposure is made and then return immediately for composing the next shot – the advantages are considerable. There are no parallax errors and no problems with long-focus lenses; the framing visible through the viewfinder is exactly as the photograph will appear. Although the specialized uses have only a limited appeal, an SLR can be attached to virtually any optical system.

The accuracy of the image visible through the eyepiece also extends to focus and depth of field: for clarity, most SLRs employ a system that leaves the lens at its maximum aperture until the moment the shutter is released, but by pressing a preview button on the body, the exact depth of field of a smaller aperture can be examined critically. Furthermore, although through-the-lens metering is now incorporated in the most advanced viewfinder cameras as well, the SLR design makes it possible to see exactly which part of the picture area is being measured.

The drawbacks of the SLR are complexity and noisy operation, but for most people in most situations these are minor inconveniences. The popularity of the 35 mm SLR has made it the focus of innovation, and new design improvements have been applied here rather than to other formats. There are now three subspecies of the SLR: the relatively unadorned non-automatic model, which is the least expensive and leaves most of the decisions to the photographer; the fully automatic model, designed principally for those amateurs who prefer not to worry about exposure calculations; and what, for want of a better description, could be called the professional SLR, the top-of-the-line camera that normally contains both automatic and non-automatic facilities.

Left The Leica, since its introduction more than half a century ago, has always been the leader in non-reflex camera design. The disadvantages of not being able to see precisely the image that will appear on the film have been largely overcome by linking the rangefinder to the lens in such a way that, when the focusing ring is moved, the picture frame visible through the viewfinder alters to compensate for parallax. This modern Leica model, the M4-P, although heavier and bulkier than its predecessors, contains a number of design features, such as built-in metering, that make it more closely competitive with technically sophisticated SLR cameras. Nevertheless, the intense design effort that has been put by manufacturers into SLR systems, and the fact that the Leica, despite its obvious qualities, has no serious rivals, reflect the limited appeal of viewfinder cameras – the Leica remains principally a tool of the photojournalist.

Above More and more camera functions can now be performed electronically – and, as a result, automatically if necessary. Because fully automatic cameras, which demand no knowledge of exposure settings on the part of the operator, appeal principally to amateurs, the range of 35mm SLRs available is now quite clearly divided into three types of design. One of the major manufacturers, for example, produces *(left to right)*: an expensive, lightweight model for amateurs (Nikon EM) that automatically sets an average exposure; a more sturdily built model (Nikon FM) for which the photographer must determine and set the exposure; and an expensive professional model (Nikon F3) that allows the photographer to choose between automatic and manual use, and which incorporates other features, such as interchangeable prism heads, likely to interest professionals.

SLR FOCUSING

Focusing in single-lens reflex cameras depends on the viewing screen, located just beneath the pentaprism. On the better models, the prism head can be removed and a choice of screens fitted. Different styles of viewing screen are designed to ease focusing and composition in different situations and generally make use of at least one of four devices: ground glass, a Fresnel screen, a split prism, or a microprism grid.

Ground glass is the traditional surface for focusing; its roughened texture gives a fine definition. A disadvantage is that the image is not uniformly bright, but this can be cured by adding a Fresnel screen. This thin supplementary screen, with its concentric ridges, acts as a lens to distribute a bright image over the whole area. Even so, accurate focusing still depends on the eye's ability to judge sharpness, and in dim light this may be difficult. The split prism and the microprism are alternative answers: with the split prism, an out-of-focus image appears to be divided into two halves, while the grid of a microprism shows it broken up. In both cases, when the image is properly focused it appears clear and the prisms are no longer visible.

While the simple pentaprism is standard, a variety of other viewing aids can be used either to replace it or to attach to its eyepiece. Most magnify the image; some give eyesight correction; others give an angled view. When there is too little light to see the image clearly, or if it is difficult to hold the camera steady, a framefinder may be needed. A framefinder is usually a simple wire frame which is attached to the accessory shoe to give a direct view of the subject.

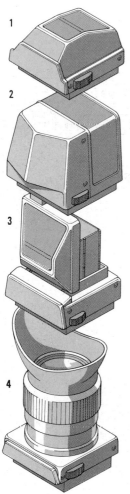

Left Virtually all professional SLR cameras allow the viewing head, which fits over the ground glass screen, to be changed. When the camera is likely to be used for different types of work, heads with specific design features can be very useful. Of the four heads shown here, the topmost *(1)* is the standard fitting, built around a pentaprism that rectifies the image projected onto the ground glass screen to give an eye-level view the right way up. The speedfinder *(2)* enlarges the view in such a way that it can be seen clearly from several inches away, and can be used in underwater housings or when wearing snow goggles, for example. For precise composition, it may be an advantage to look directly down onto the ground glass screen; the waist-level viewer *(3)* is designed for this. When focusing is critical, as in closeup work, a magnifying head *(4)* with an eye cup to cut out extraneous light, can be used.

Right A number of focusing and viewing aids can be attached directly to the standard prism head. These include eyepiece correction lenses for people who normally wear glasses (viewing *with* glasses usually prevents the photographer from seeing the corners of the picture frame), a plain glass protective lens to prevent dust from accumulating in the viewer, and a rubber eye cup to shield the eye from bright ambient lighting. Magnifiers, which either flip up when not needed, or give a right-angled view by means of a prism, are an alternative to fitting the magnifying head shown on the opposite page.

Left For cameras with interchangeable heads, there is a wide range of different types of focusing screen. Even when the prism head is fixed, some manufacturers will fit the screen that the photographer prefers. The basic viewing surface for most screens is a glass screen finely ground on the underside. This gives a well-resolved image, but has the disadvantage of appearing unevenly illuminated, with the corners of the frame darker than the centre; to offset this, a Fresnel screen, which has curved concentric ridges so that it acts as an extremely thin lens, is usually sandwiched with the glass to give a brighter, more even, image. To aid composition and alignment, some screens also have etched grids and cross-hairs, while two additional devices – split-image rangefinder and microprism – can make focusing easier and faster. Both work on the principle of scrambling the image when it is not in focus, and are usually inserted in the centre area of the screen.

VIEWFINDER FOCUSING

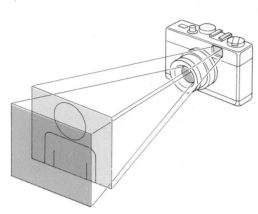

Above *Parallax error*
An inherent problem with any camera which does not allow a direct view through the picture-taking lens is that the viewfinder gives a slightly different image to the one that will be recorded on the film. When the subject is far away, the difference is insignificant, but at a few feet, allowance must be made. Most good viewfinder cameras link the rangefinder to the lens, so that the viewing frame changes to compensate.

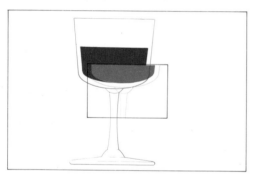

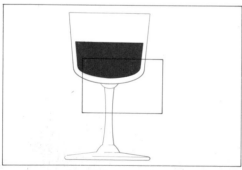

Above *Focusing with a rangefinder*
A rangefinder uses two points of view from windows on either side of the camera body, and calculates the distance of a subject by a form of triangulation, in much the same way that our own binocular vision enables us to estimate distance with our eyes. Although the two windows are only a few inches apart, the slightly different angles of view can be measured, and linked to the focusing ring of the lens. When a subject is out of focus, a second ghosted image appears; only when the correct focusing distance has been set does this double-image effect disappear. Although many photographers prefer the more direct SLR system, one of the advantages of rangefinder focusing is that it works as well in dim light as in bright daylight.

Viewfinder cameras almost invariably have a supplementary viewing system, although for a special check it is just possible to use a makeshift ground glass screen. With cameras that have a single fixed lens, the viewfinder lens is matched to give the same angle of view, resulting in few complications. Interchangeable lenses, however, call for an adjustable view. The simplest way of providing this facility is to have different-sized frames engraved on one viewing screen. The viewfinder system can then be linked to the lenses in such a way that each focal length automatically displays its own frame. Nevertheless, the longer the focal length, the smaller the frame appears on the screen, and the more difficult it is to compose accurately. One remedy is to attach a supplementary reflex housing for long focal lengths, temporarily converting the camera into an SLR. Another is to buy a new optical system for every lens and, although this can be expensive, it is the only satisfactory way of dealing with very wide-angle lenses.

Because the viewfinder lens and camera lens are a short distance apart, they see a slightly different view. At close distances the difference becomes noticeable, and the resulting parallax error can produce photographs that were not quite as the photographer intended. With the camera on a tripod, one slow but foolproof method is to compose the shot before pressing the shutter release and then move the camera so that the picture-taking lens is in the same place as the viewfinder was. Most viewfinder cameras, however, give some indication through the eyepiece of parallax error; advanced models link the focusing system to the viewfinder so that the frame is automatically adjusted.

Rangefinder focusing, which is standard with viewfinder cameras, makes use of binocular vision to calculate distances. The image is split, usually by a combination of prisms and mirrors, so that the angle of view from two different windows on the camera body is measured. In practice, a small rectangle in the centre of the viewfinder shows a ghost image from the rangefinder window, and if this is connected to the lens focusing ring, you can focus precisely, simply by turning the ring until the two images merge into one.

An entirely different focusing technique, which bypasses the photographer's eye completely, is automatic ranging. There are several types of automatic ranging: one measures the contrast along edges in an image electronically; another bounces an infrared beam off the subject and measures the time it takes to return to the camera; and a third, which is now a standard feature of some instant cameras, emits a sonar pulse. Successful automatic focusing depends, however, on having an unobstructed foreground and a subject that is fairly well-centred.

Above *The banks of the Loing (Seine et Marne)* (c. 1965) by Henri Cartier-Bresson. One of the greatest practitioners of candid photojournalism, Henri Cartier-Bresson, uses a Leica rangefinder camera for its unobtrusiveness, simplicity and quiet operation. Cartier-Bresson coined the expression "decisive moment" to define the central quality of his type of work – capturing the precise split-second in which the many potential elements in a situation come together to make an effective image. One of the advantages of a non-reflex camera is that the photographer can judge the complete scene in depth, and change the emphasis of composition or focus accordingly – something that is impossible with an SLR, which in normal use gives a view with shallow depth of field, whatever aperture is set.

SHUTTERS

Most 35 mm cameras use one of two types of shutter – leaf or focal plane. The leaf shutter, with its concentrically arranged overlapping blades, performs better in virtually all respects, but has one major drawback: it does not allow reflex viewing unless a second shutter is fitted close to the film plane. For this reason, the leaf shutter is impractical in an SLR; among 35 mm cameras it is used only on viewfinder models.

The ideal shutter should be consistent, quick to operate, and should expose all parts of the film equally and at the same time. In practice, it is impossible to meet the last requirement perfectly, as the shutter mechanism takes time to operate whatever speed is set. Since the best place for the shutter is where the light rays that form the image are the most tightly bunched, so that the shutter has the least distance to travel, leaf shutters are located next to the aperture diaphragm of the lens. They work on the same principle as the eye's iris, opening out from the centre and then closing again. Leaf shutters are normally very accurate and reliable, but the double action of opening and closing restricts the maximum speed to about 1/500 second. A further disadvantage is cost – every lens needs its own shutter.

For convenience in calculating exposures, all shutters are calibrated so that each setting is twice as fast as the next slowest speed. A typical selection would be: 1, ½, ¼, 1/8, 1/15, 1/30, 1/60, 1/125, 1/250, 1/500 second. Altering the setting from, say, 1/60 to 1/125 second halves the amount of light reaching the film – the equivalent of closing down the lens aperture by one stop. In this way, the aperture and shutter controls can be linked, which is essential when the exposure is set automatically. In addition to the standard speeds, most shutters also have a "B" setting, which allows time exposures for as long as the shutter release remains pressed, and a "T" setting, which will hold the shutter open until the release is activated a second time.

The focal plane shutter, as its name suggests, is situated deep inside the camera body, just in front of the film. In this way, one shutter serves all lenses and does not interfere with the mirror action of an SLR. Just before the shutter operates, the 45° mirror that directs the image from the lens up to the prism and eyepiece flips out of the way, returning immediately after the film has been exposed.

Being next to the film, the focal plane shutter has a greater area to cover than the leaf shutter – nearly 4 square inches (26 sq cm) – and works on a quite different principle. It allows a gap to travel *across* the image, either horizontally or vertically. The normal system uses a pair of blinds that can be adjusted to give a rectangular gap that varies from the full size of the picture to a narrow slit. When the shutter is released, the primary blind starts to move

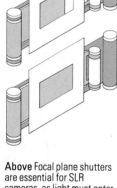

Above Focal plane shutters are essential for SLR cameras, as light must enter the camera body for reflex viewing. In principle, a gap in a tensioned roller blind travels across the area of film to be exposed. Up to about 1/40 second, the speed at which the blind travels is altered, but this becomes difficult to achieve accurately at faster speeds, so that a second system, with a second adjustable blind to vary the width of the gap, is also used.

1 second

¼ second

1/15 second

1/60 second

1/250 second.

1/1000 second

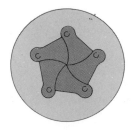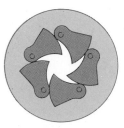

Above Situated close to the centre of the lens, the leaf shutter is a more efficient design than the focal plane shutter, as in this position, the rays of light are more tightly bunched, and the shutter blades have less distance to travel. The principle is that of an iris – several interleaved blades open and close to give an expanding, and then contracting, hole that is roughly circular. For the complete action, the blades open fully, and then close.

Below In this photograph of a South American bullfight, a deliberately slow shutter speed – ½ second – was used with a familiar subject to exploit the flow of motion for an expressive rather than a documentary effect.

across, followed shortly after by the secondary blind. The result is that one side of the image is exposed before the other. Although in most situations this makes no difference, if the image of a moving subject, such as a car, is travelling either with or against the direction of the shutter, it will be distorted.

Another difficulty that this uneven coverage causes is that the highest speeds cannot be used with electronic flash. At speeds faster than 1/60 second or 1/125 second, depending on the make of camera, the gap between the blinds is narrower than the picture, so that any flash triggered at this time would produce a truncated image.

Overall, however, in continuous light, the single action of the focal plane shutter gives it the edge in speed over the leaf shutter, and most SLRs are capable of 1/2000 second. The time it takes for the shutter to be set in motion, though, is longer, and even at its fastest, a focal plane shutter normally takes about 1/30 second to complete its action.

Left and above The shutter has two functions in photography: to regulate the amount of light reaching the film, and to control the way in which a moving subject is recorded. For this sequence of photographs, showing water flowing over rocks, the shutter speed was progressively shortened by a factor of two, but to ensure identical exposures, the aperture was also altered to compensate. At one second, the white water is so blurred that it begins to take on the appearance of mist, while at 1/1000 second, every movement is frozen and the water seems to have a static quality. Neither exposure appears normal: to convey any motion in a still photograph requires a subjective decision on the part of the photographer.

TRIGGERING ACCESSORIES

The ability to change lenses was the first step towards the "system" camera. The most sophisticated 35mm SLRs now fit into, this category. The "system" comprises a wide range of extra equipment (for some models this range would fill a small room), used to put together the instrument of one's choice.

Not counting lenses and closeup equipment, most "system" accessories are concerned with triggering, from a straightforward cable release to a radio-controlled assembly that can expose several photographs each second onto a bulk roll of film, automatically adjusting the shutter speed or aperture and even printing on each frame the time, date and other information.

Automatic and remote triggering systems are invaluable when, for one reason or another, the photographer cannot be close to the subject. In wildlife photography, for instance, many creatures will tolerate a quietly clicking piece of equipment but not a human being. In laboratory work, it may be important to record the progress of an experiment over several days, and an intervalometer, which triggers the camera at preset times, can relieve the photographer of a tedious job. On other occasions, there may be no room for the photographer – when the shot is taken from the wing tip of a glider, for example, or when the camera has to be suspended for an overhead shot of a large hall.

The key to most of these innovations is the motor drive, and its simpler cousin, the motor winder. Publicity and advertising have promoted these attachments from specialist accessories virtually to standard fittings. They have acquired an air of necessity, and not for all the best reasons. Nevertheless, in that they free the photographer's attention from the mechanics of winding on, they are useful, at least in theory.

Right Powered triggering devices are available for all types of work, from general photography to specialized laboratory recording. In the group at right, the box-like intervalometer can be connected to the camera so as to trigger it at preset intervals – from once every 5 seconds to once every 2 hours. In front of the intervalometer is an enlarged film back that will take a roll of up to 250 exposures – essential when recording long sequences automatically. At the right of the picture, three types of automatic film transport show the growing popularity of motor winders *(bottom)* and motor drives. The latter can operate the camera continuously, and the topmost professional model gives a choice of the number of frames per second.

Below To avoid touching the camera when a slow shutter speed might cause camera shake, or when the shutter must be released from a distance, triggering accesories are used. Cable releases of different lengths are widely used, while a broad-topped soft release attachment can be screwed over a standard mechanical shutter release. Electrically operated shutters, and cameras fitted with motor drives or automatic winders, can be operated at a distance by a simple electric lead.

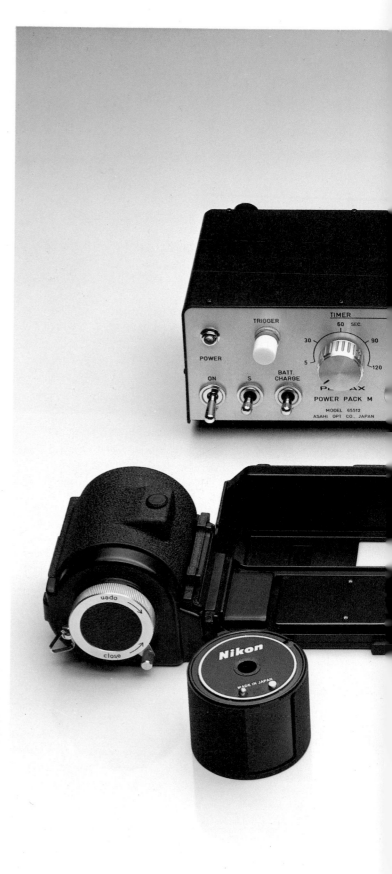

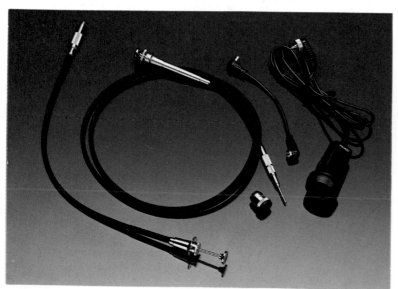

Above Although motor drives are often used unnecessarily in situations where manual operation would do, for short, sharp bursts of action they have no rivals, particularly if a progressive series is the end product. Here, a motor drive operating at six frames per second reveals the flight control of an open-bill stork as it brakes to land on a branch. The pronounced flicker of the mirror seen through the viewfinder makes focusing difficult when the motor drive is in continuous operation, and it is easiest to work with subjects moving *across* the field of view.

CANDID AND REPORTAGE PHOTOGRAPHY

The classic use of the 35 mm camera is in candid photography. Here, the fundamental requirements are unobtrusiveness (sometimes to the point of concealment), fast reaction to changing events, and the ability to work in existing light, however dim. The 35 mm camera meets these demands admirably. It is small, light and simply operated, so that, in the hands of a photographer who knows how to remain inconspicuous, the camera can frequently go unnoticed by its subjects.

The design of the 35 mm, featuring an eye-level view, easy grip, and a cocking and film advancing action that can be performed either by the flick of a thumb or a small motor winder, makes it fast to use. The ability to change lenses rapidly makes it easy to adapt to any new situation. The small film size allows manufacturers to design lenses that give a bright image, and many standard lenses for 35 mm cameras have a maximum aperture wider than f2.

Styles of photojournalism are naturally varied, ranging from the most secretive of candid work to deliberate involvement in the events that the photographer is setting out to record. The doyen of reportage photograph, Henri Cartier-Bresson, prefers to work close to his subjects but without their being aware of his presence. He carries the minimum of equipment, even taping over the chrome bodywork of his camera to appear less obvious, and adopts a quiet manner that enables him to blend in with the scene. Not surprisingly, a simple viewfinder camera – a Leica – best suits his needs. Other photojournalists often have had to adopt more extreme measures to avoid advertising their presence. To photograph the Soviet invasion of Afghanistan, the photojournalist Romano Cagnoni walked around Kabul with his camera hidden beneath a cape, only its lens, prefocused, poking through a fold in the cloth; the shutter was released pneumatically by squeezing a rubber bulb.

Other techniques for being unobtrusive rely on the choice of lens. Long focal lengths, which magnify the image and so can be used from a distance, are understandably popular. With a 150 mm lens fitted to the camera, a standing figure 40 feet (12.2 m) away will fill a horizontal frame, making this and similar focal lengths very useful for street photography. Even longer focal lengths, such as 300 mm or 400 mm, can give close candid views with only a small chance of being noticed, although holding a large lens steady by hand takes practice. At the other extreme, very wide-angle lenses also have their place in candid photography, because the angle of view may be much wider than people expect, and people close to the camera may not realize that they are included in the picture.

Another approach to candid photography is deliberate, sympathetic involvement: making every effort to become a part of the situation and gain the confidence of the subjects. Because of the time needed, the most common vehicle for this approach is the picture essay, pioneered by the original *Life* magazine and exemplified in the work of such photographers as W. Eugene Smith (*b*. 1918), whose work on the staff of the magazine in the 1950s produced many classic examples of this type of photography.

Right Quietly observed moments are a mainstay of candid photography, and if the subject of the picture is engrossed in some activity, as this bush negro girl in Surinam intent on her appearance, the photographer generally has time to select the image without intruding. For this type and scale of photograph, a medium telephoto lens is the most useful – in this case, a 180mm f2.8 lens, a fast but portable design made to almost identical specifications by the leading manufacturers of professional cameras.

Above In what is generally known as "street photography", the opportunities for unobserved, candid shots may exist for only a second or so in any one situation, particularly if, as here in Calcutta, a wide-angle lens is used at close range. There may only be the chance to expose one frame before people become aware of the photographer, and the nature of the image changes. Taking candid photographs demands familiarity with equipment, particularly with the lens, so that the photographer can anticipate the way the image will look before raising the camera. One of the specific advantages of the wide-angle lens is that its inherently great depth of field normally allows the focus to be preset.

PICTURE ESSAYS

Through the medium of magazines, and more recently books, the picture essay has become established as a distinct treatment for photographs. Essentially, it is a way of assembling a number of photographs that cover a single theme, and although picture essays vary a great deal in length, subject matter, and design, they all share one important quality – a consistent editorial idea.

While a skilled designer can work with a wide range of material, the most successful picture essays are usually the result of the photographer, editor and designer recognizing and allowing for each other's intentions and abilities. A picture essay gains its effectiveness from the way in which a series of photographs are arranged to complement each other; even single shots laid out to occupy whole double-page spreads should not seem isolated, because they are located in the sequence of pictures. In a well-produced essay, the sum is always greater than the parts, and there is a sense of unity.

For the photographer, this fundamental requirement has important implications when an assignment is being planned and executed. With the type of story that can be researched and organized in advance, the photographer must have a good grasp of the essential elements of the story, and more importantly, must know which of these are capable of being treated visually. Some aspects are more easily described in words than illustrated, and vice versa. In any case, the copy and the photographs should not parallel each other exactly, doggedly showing the same topics. In good picture essays, the two link together, complementing rather than duplicating each other.

With some stories, it may be possible to do sufficiently detailed research that a short list can be prepared, covering topics that it is known will be important, and in some instances, specifying the type of image. For example, if a picture essay were being planned around a regular ceremonial event, it should be possible, from examining the published photographs of previous years' events, to be specific about which pictures are required. In the same way, if the reason for the picture essay is to treat a familiar subject in an unusual fashion by employing some particular creative or optical technique (for example, infrared view of a city), again, the images can be planned ahead.

Not all stories, however, can be mapped out so thoroughly in advance, and it may be

Right At an early stage in the design, fewer than 40 transparencies were chosen from the original 200 rolls of film, in order to fill 12 pages of a magazine feature on the Pathan tribesmen of the Northwest Frontier. The article is descriptive, with emphasis on the traditional Pathan committment to Islam and the defence of honour. Without a hard news story, the art director is less restricted than usual, but has the problem of a wide choice of picture material. The first step, therefore, is to establish an editorial sequence for the six double-page spreads: a list of subjects that must be covered. In this case, the text will be short and will serve to support the pictures rather than the other way around. The process of reducing the choice of pictures and deciding on their juxtaposition is hardly ever straightforward, and a considerable amount of time is spent experimenting. Here, using duplicate transparencies to avoid damage to the originals, the art director has tried out a few layouts by drawing thumbnail sketches. Several complete changes are likely before any layouts are finalized.

necessary to start work on an idea and hope that something worthwhile will emerge in the end. Some unpredictability can be beneficial in any case. A photographer working on a picture essay should be something of a journalist, following up picture possibilities on the spot.

Nevertheless, even where the nature of the story is fluid or uncertain, the photographer should be aware of the type and variety of shots that the designer or art director will need, and this means being at least partly familiar with the way picture essays are constructed and laid out by editorial and art staff. Beyond normal photographic skills, the most basic requirements are to cover all the likely aspects (and this usually means shooting more than can be used), to deliver a variety of images, and to be able to visualize juxtapositions of pictures. Full coverage is simply journalistic commonsense, but visual variety, which is separate from the content of the pictures, is needed to make the whole sequence of images aesthetically in-

teresting. If all the photographs are similar and look unremarkable, it is very difficult for the art director to structure the essay – the result is almost inevitably little more than a series of pictures. If, on the other hand, the art director has a choice of different types of images – different, for example, in terms of lighting, lens focal length, scale of image, colour, contrast, or composition – it is easier to develop the essay into something that actually *looks* interesting, whatever the journalistic value of its subject.

Finally, by being able to imagine ways in which photographs could be grouped on a page, the photographer can also suggest interesting variations in layout. To choose a specific example: if on an assignment, a photographer notices a number of different design motifs that might be made up into a set – such as paintwork details in a story on custom cars – then these could be assembled in what is known as a mosaic, a page or two composed of many similar images. Placed between two spreads each carrying a photograph, this

Above In preparation for an editorial meeting (which will include both picture and copy editors) the art department has pasted up some alternative layouts. From intermediate negatives, low-cost black-and-white prints have been ordered, and these have been mounted on thin cardboard. The real text has not yet been set, so to simulate its appearance on the spreads, adhesive-backed body copy (a meaningless string of Latin words) is placed in appropriate positions. Because the magazine will be seen by its readers as a sequence of double-page spreads, the layouts are also done in this way, rather than as single pages. A colour swatch selector *(left)* will be used to decide if any background tints are needed.

would give a sharp change of pace to the essay.

Who works on a picture essay depends on the publishing company, but on a magazine with a fairly large staff, the two people most involved would normally be the picture editor and art director. In practice, their work may overlap, but essentially, the picture editor is responsible for defining the needs of the essay and acquiring the material (which, if it is to be commissioned, involves assigning and briefing the photographer), while the art director is responsible for the layout, making the essay work as a unit, giving it continuity, and making it visually interesting. Both are normally responsible for the structure of the essay, and both, from different viewpoints, are usually involved in picture selection.

Each publication tends to have a house style, treating stories in a limited number of ways. Some magazines, such as *National Geographic*, will often take a very general approach to a large subject (there is often no

alternative), and will therefore usually run quite lengthy stories. Other magazines, particularly those that favour news stories, will only do essays on very specific subjects, and these normally run to fewer pages as a result. The text may share much of the weight of the story, or it may be subordinate. Captions may be short, referring the photograph to a fuller description in the main body of the text, or they may be quite full, even acting as substitutes for the text.

There are many different ways of structuring a picture essay, but one convention is to open with a strong image, reproduced large, and to close with one also. What happens in between depends to a large extent on the number of pages; if there are many pages, there is a greater need for visual breaks. Another approach, more suitable for a long, general feature, is to run several very large, minimally captioned photographs as an introduction, before the text begins. Whatever the structure, the material itself will be the strongest influence on the essay's final appearance.

Above The forcefulness, and even aggression, that lies within the character of the male Pathan, surfaces easily. At a weekly livestock market on the northwest frontier, bargaining is tough and serious.
Left One of the essential steps towards manhood is the acquisition of, and proficiency in using, a gun. In a Mohmand Pathan village close to the Afghan frontier, a young boy takes his first instruction in rifle practice from an elder relative.

Above In Pathan society, age confers dignity to an extent since lost in the West. Although tribal elders may lack the physical prowess of the young, in all matters of village life they are deferred to.

Right For all their self-reliance, the Pathan are great traders, and in the late summer months lorryloads of melons from Kabul crowd the bazaar in Peshawar, on the other side of the Khyber Pass.

Left Ultimately, each man takes responsibility for the defence of his own family, property and honour, and the image of a solitary Pathan keeping an armed watch on the rockface above his village is by no means a cliché from a Kiplingesque romance. Throughout a history of feuding at all levels from the personal to the national, one of the principal ways that the Pathan have been able to maintain such a strong cultural identity has been their willingness – and, at times, positive eagerness – to fight for what they believe in.

ACTION PHOTOGRAPHY

The second major area of photography where the 35 mm camera has no rival is fast movement or action. While this hardly qualifies as a distinct field with its own ethos, action photography does embrace aspects of sports, news and even wildlife photography. In any case, it is sufficient of a technical problem to demand special attention.

There are a number of ways of dealing with a moving subject – and not all of them involve freezing the action into a clear, unblurred photograph. Nevertheless, a basic pre-requisite is that the equipment should allow you to produce a sharply defined image if you want to. Two things make the 35 mm camera so well-suited to the task: first, the design makes it easy to handle, reducing to a minimum the time-lag between deciding to shoot and making the exposure; and second, it allows higher shutter speeds, partly because the small format means that the shutter mechanism has less distance to travel, and partly because the faster lenses allow these high speeds to be used.

As with most photography, the equipment provides only a partial answer. An active subject also calls for good timing. The term "decisive moment", coined by Cartier-Bresson, is particularly apt in sports and all fast action. Nearly every rapid event, such as a pole vault or a goal attempt in football, contains certain moments which best convey the special qualities of the action. Some, such as a successful punch in a boxing contest, are obvious, while others need a more discerning eye. With all of them, the skill needed to capture the peak of the movement comes from quick reaction, which can be improved by practice, and anticipation, which can be learned through familiarity with the particular sport or event and with the underlying mechanics of action in general. Well-timed shots are usually the pro-duct of camera dexterity and the ability to recognize that key moment.

Freezing movement depends on the shutter speed, and on how fast the image of the subject appears to move across the viewfinder. If a car, driven at 30 mph (48 kph), fills the camera frame as it moves across the field of view, 1/2000 second will be needed for a sharp photograph. However, if the car's image is half the size, either because the camera is farther away or a wider angle lens is fitted, then a shutter speed that is twice as slow – 1/1000 second – will do the job. Equally, if the car were photographed coming diagonally towards the camera, the shutter speed would not need to be as fast.

What a frozen image lacks is the *sensation* of movement, and although it meets one of photography's most conservative traditions – sharpness – it does little to recreate the impression of activity. The standard technique with continuous movement is panning – following the subject with the camera to keep its image centred in the frame. By choosing a shutter speed just fast enough for a sharp image, and no more, the background is converted into a blurred streak, which makes the subject stand out and emphasizes the direction and sense of motion. The same effect can be achieved by blurring some of the subject as well. With a tightly framed subject, 1/125 second or even 1/60 second can give this effect.

Depending on the weight of the lens, it may not always be possible to shoot entirely unsupported, and for the very long focus lenses used at sports events (600 mm is not unusual for professional work), a monopod, or a tripod with a lightly loosened ball-and-socket head may be the answer. With a fixed camera position, a tripod is no hindrance, and large aperture telephotos, although heavy, are ideal.

Right This photograph of the 1979 Spanish 250cc Moto-Cross Grand Prix was taken by Ray Daniel, a photographer who has been a regular contributor to motorcycle magazines over the last 15 years and is well acquainted with the dynamics of this particular sport. It shows the first corner of the first race in the 1979 world championship season. The photographer deliberately positioned himself at a corner rather than on a straight section of the course in order to capture a better feeling of action. A shot taken head-on would not have conveyed such a strong sense of speed. The picture was one of a series of three frames shot on Tri X using a motor drive at 1/500 second at f11, with a 135 mm lens on a Nikon FM.

SPECIAL OPPORTUNITIES

The features of the 35 mm camera that have identified it with photojournalism have also made it adaptable to virtually any circumstance. Precisely because it is so portable and easy to use, the 35 mm is many photographers' constant companion, and so has become the camera for the unexpected and the unusual situation. A large format camera dictates planning and preparation, but a 35 mm model is often worth carrying on pure speculation – just in case. In this sense, simply through being convenient it creates opportunities for pictures that a photographer might otherwise be unable to utilize. For many people whose interest in photography is mainly in keeping a record of their families' lives, the 35 mm is now a standard accessory, whether on a picnic or travel abroad.

On a more exotic level, the 35 mm camera has opened up possibilities in situations which demand so much concentration and effort that there is little time to devote to anything else. Mountain-climbing, shooting rapids or flying are among a number of activities that have yielded spectacular images in this format – photographs that would, with any larger camera, simply not have been attempted. In aerial photography, for example, although large format equipment is used for surveys and mapmaking, it is the 35 mm camera that has given non-specialist photographers the freedom to look for striking images. Taking photographs through the open window of a light aircraft is a noisy, buffeting affair and the landscape below slips by too quickly for a contemplative approach. A 35 mm camera makes it possible to compose rapidly, to change lenses if necessary and, above all, to make a number of exposures in quick succession.

Left The small size and advanced technological capabilities of a modern professional 35 mm SLR made it the ideal instrument for this difficult air-to-air photograph of the prototype of the new Tornado ADV banking over Lytham St. Annes, near Blackpool, England. Photographer Richard Cooke, who specializes in this type of work, used a Nikon EL fitted in a specially designed camera housing which was attached to the fuselage of another aircraft, flying ahead of the prototype. The housing *(far left)* was designed by Cooke in collaboration with Squadron Leader Alan Voyle and was secured to the fuselage and aerodynamically cowled in. The photographer flew in the camera plane, triggering the camera through the aircraft's electrical supply. The arrangement of the entire shot was carefully controlled and set up with the pilot of the prototype. By means of a special sighting technique, the pilot of the prototype knew when his aircraft was in the picture; it was up to the photographer in the preceding plane to control the background and lighting. Although the focus, aperture and shutter speed were preset, the photographer had the freedom to select the background. To do this, he directed the picture-taking plane into such a position that a view he had selected as a potentially interesting background was in the picture. Technical problems apart, it was this ability to visualize the picture and to direct both aircraft into a position to achieve it, that made the final result so successful. The camera itself had to be windproofed with tape and functioned perfectly well up to 6½G. The photograph was taken with a 20 mm lens at 1/500 second at f5.6.

ROLLFILM CAMERAS

By today's standards, rollfilm cameras are medium-format cameras, between 35 mm and sheet film. Rollfilm gives an image approximately 2¼ inches (6 cm) across its width, but there is not the same complete standardization as there is with 35 mm. Some cameras produce a 2¼ x 2¼ inch (6 x 6 cm) image, others 2¼ x 3 inch (6 x 7 cm), with hybrids such as 1⅝ x 1⅝ inch (4.5 x 4.5 cm), 1⅝ x 2¼ inch (4.5 x 6 cm), and 2¼ x 4 inch (6 x 9 cm) making an occasional appearance, quite apart from the panoramic formats. Rollfilm camera design, like that of 35 mm, has moved steadily towards single-lens reflex; the viewfinder and twin-lens reflex models are now in the minority.

Viewfinder rollfilm cameras are either the descendants of press cameras, characterized by rugged simplicity, or specialist equipment where reflex viewing is not possible. The Hasselblad SWC is an example of the latter – there is no room behind the excellent Biogon wide-angle lens for a reflex mirror. Between-the-lens leaf shutters are standard.

The twin-lens reflex combines reflex viewing with a leaf shutter to give some of the advantages of both viewfinder cameras and SLRs. It also shares some of the problems of each and on balance its popularity has declined. By using two matched lenses, one on top of the other and with identical focal lengths, the light path to the film remains undisturbed and picture taking functions as efficiently and quietly as in any viewfinder camera. The upper lens projects its image onto a ground glass screen, which is normally viewed at waist level by looking down at the camera (although eye-level prism viewers are available for some models). The two-dimensional appearance of the image on the screen helps composition, and makes it easier to preview the way that the photograph will appear. However, the twin-lens reflex is bulky and on most models the lenses cannot be interchanged. Parallax is a problem just as with viewfinder cameras and the image, when viewed directly on the ground glass screen, is reversed left to right, although this problem is not unique to this type of camera.

The 2¼ x 2¼ inch (6 x 6 cm) SLR, of which the outstanding example is the Hasselblad C/M, has many of the advantages of its 35 mm equivalent. Most models use two shutters – one inside the lens and the other at the focal plane – to achieve reflex viewing through the picture-taking lens without having to sacrifice the benefits of a leaf shutter. In operation this camera is noisy and clumsy, but its advantages are considerable. The large ground glass screen can be used either at waist level for careful composition or at eye level for more rapid use, and the focal plane shutter, opening before the main leaf shutter in the lens, protects the film from exposure during viewing. It also makes possible one of the Hasselblad's most renowned features – interchangeable film backs. With the film protected by a detachable metal slide, the magazines can be removed in an instant without losing a single frame, even though the roll may have been only partly used. This makes it possible to move quickly from colour to black and white, or to any variety of rollfilm loaded into a spare magazine (or to Polaroid, 70 mm or sheet film with the appropriate holder). Lenses are also interchangeable, making the 2¼ x 2¼ inch (6 x 6 cm) SLR a versatile piece of equipment. Its disadvantages are bulk, noise and slowness of operation. In addition, compared with the more usable 2¼ x 3 inch (6 x 7 cm) format, the square 2¼ x 2¼ inch (6 x 6 cm) is an unusual shape for a negative or transparency, permitting so few satisfactory compositions that the photographs must nearly always be cropped. Perversely, this is frequently presented by the manufacturers as an advantage, although the loss of film area simply squanders some of rollfilm's superiority over 35 mm.

There are two quite different designs of 2¼ x 3 inch (6 x 7 cm) SLRs. One, using the same principle of reflex viewing, double shutter and interchangeable film backs as the Hasselblad C/M, is very much a studio camera, slow to use but precise and adaptable; the other, made by Pentax, is in essence a scaled-up version of a typical 35 mm SLR. The Mamiya RB67 is similar in many respects to the Hasselblad C/M, but apart from the slightly larger format has the additional sophistication of a built-in bellows that allows closeup photography with the minimum of fuss, and a rotating film back that can be used to change the format from horizontal and vertical without moving the camera. However, it is bulkier than the Hasselblad. The Pentax, although it invites comparison with a 35 mm SLR (and seems unwieldy as a result), can be used more rapidly and comfortably than other SLRs, and is well suited to handheld use on location. It uses a focal plane shutter only.

Right These representatives of the major types of rollfilm camera are fairly similar in bulk, although their handling characteristics and technical performances vary. The Mamiya C330 follows one of the most traditional rollfilm designs, using a matched pair of lenses – one for viewing and one for exposing the film. Mechanical simplicity is one of its strongest points, but it lacks the obvious advantages of the SLR models. Even more basic is the Mamiya Universal press camera. Its large viewfinder and handgrip make it extremely easy to use in uncomplicated situations, but for complex work it is too unsophisticated. Of the three SLR cameras shown here, the Hasselblad (in the foreground) and the Mamiya RB67 have similar waist-level viewing, while the Pentax is built to be used in the same way as a 35mm SLR, with the intention of being easy to handle.

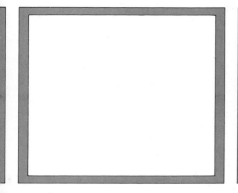

Left Although all the cameras grouped here accept 120 rollfilm, different formats are possible by varying the length of the 2¼ inch (6cm) wide frame. Trimming it to 1⅝ inch (4.5cm) gives a frame that is easier to compose within than the standard 2¼ x 2¼ inch (6 x 6cm) square, and fits more pictures on to a roll. Lengthening the frame to 3 inches (7cm) gives a photograph that more nearly coincides with the 8 x 10 inch (20 x 24cm) proportions most commonly used in printing, while the 2¼ x 4 inch (6 x 9cm) frame gives the same proportions as the popular and familiar 35mm photograph.

LANDSCAPE AND PORTRAITURE

In many ways rollfilm cameras represent a compromise between the highly portable 35 mm with its small image size, and the view camera, which is unsurpassed for image quality but cumbersome. Because these cameras occupy a middle ground, their advantages are not quite so well defined as those of the other two formats, but for the type of photography that needs a degree of spontaneity combined with a reasonably sized negative or transparency, they are ideal. Camera manufacturing nowadays is characterized by frequent innovation, and competition with 35 mm cameras and with larger formats is strong and active: film improvements bring better and better image quality to 35 mm; at the same time view cameras are experiencing a resurgence

Right In landscape photography, the value of a rollfilm camera is its ability to give a picture area much larger than that of 35mm film, without sacrificing very much portability. In the majority of landscape work, fine resolution of detail is important, as is a delicate rendition of smooth tonal areas such as sky and cloud. The photograph of palm trees against mist needed to be enlarged less than 1½ times to be reproduced on this page, with the result that the finest detail of the feathery leaves is retained.

Left The view of morning clouds rising up the foothills of the Andes relies for its effect on being able to reduce subtle variations of tone without the interference of grain. For this , a rollfilm camera was the best compromise – larger image than 35mm, but not as unwieldy as a view camera. Although the Hasselblad *(far left),* with 250mm lens and 70mm magazine, used for this photograph, is no lightweight, it can still be carried easily in difficult country, such as mountains.

of interest among enthusiastic amateurs as well as professionals. Rollfilm cameras, for their part, have retaliated with their own improvements, both in ease of handling and versatility.

A 2¼ x 2¼ inch (6 x 6 cm) image is nearly four times the size of a 35 mm frame and that of a 2¼ x 3 inch (6 x 7 cm) image slightly more. A standard 8 x 10 inch (20 x 25 cm) print calls for an enlargement of not much more than four times. As a result, sharpness and tonal gradation are good, and graininess often not apparent. Because the magnification does not need to be so great as from a 35 mm original, blemishes such as scratches and dirt are not as prominent and retouching is easier. Where image quality is important but the camera also needs to be convenient to use, rollfilm cameras have the advantage.

Formal portraits and landscapes are two fields of photography where detail and freedom from grain are often felt to be important. However, while photographers have taken up Hasselblads, Rolleiflexes and similar rollfilm models because they meet these basic needs, the cameras themselves have influenced styles of photography, notably portraiture, just through their mechanical characteristics.

Portraiture has always been one of the major uses of photography, reflecting our constant fascination with the human face. From the travelling tintypists of the late nineteenth century to society photographers and the thriving portrait studios of today, portraiture is almost an industry in itself. As with many areas of photography, there is some danger in defining too closely the different styles of portraiture – this can encourage a rigid view of an inherently fluid subject. Even the word "portrait" is a little arbitrary; although its meaning is clear enough, it suggests a formal approach, rather than pictures taken with the speed of a snapshot. Nevertheless, the rollfilm camera has imposed certain methods of working on the photographer. Portraits can be, and are, taken with every type of camera, and within certain limits, the equipment can be used casually or deliberately, intuitively or with careful planning. Yet, as a rule, the 2¼ x 2¼ inch (6 x 6 cm) and 2¼ x 3 inch (6 x 7 cm) formats are the ones tied most strongly to the formal approach.

The nuances of expression in a face depend to a surprising degree on fine detail, such as the subtle lines and shading that reveal small movements of the mouth and eyes. The large rollfilm negative can capture this detail with little interference from the grain of the film. With 10 or 12 frames on a roll there is still the advantage of an uninterrupted sequence of shots. In a portrait session, the photographer often tries to coax a particular expression or attitude from the subject, and if this is fleeting, several shots may be needed. For purely practical reasons, it is also safer to make a number of exposures to allow for blinking or other gestures that look awkward.

Used in the traditional way – composing directly on the ground glass screen – a rollfilm camera encourages a deliberate approach. The image on the screen makes it possible to study the composition carefully and objectively (by comparison, the 35 mm camera encourages a *subjective* view). Objectivity is important not only when making full-face photographs, but also for environmental protraits where the subject is shown in his or her surroundings and the composition aims to show a relationship between the two.

Because photographers usually hold the camera at waist level in order to look down at the screen, many portraits taken with these cameras tend to have a slightly low viewpoint. Provided this is not too pronounced there is usually some aesthetic advantage in this approach as a high viewpoint tends to overemphasize the forehead. The square format presents no problems either; the human face is one of the few subjects that actually suits square composition.

Landscape photography is another field that frequently calls for fine detail, at least in the tradition so strongly established by Edward Weston (1887-1958) and other members of F64 Group formed in the United States in 1932. (This group was named after the smallest stop on a large-format camera, an aperture which gives great clarity and depth of focus.) Although this approach, which aims for extreme clarity of vision, really calls for a large-format view camera, some of the most spectacular views are relatively inaccessible and reaching them involves the type of physical exertion which rules out carrying heavy equipment. In mountain areas or where strenuous backpacking is called for, rollfilm cameras are a good compromise. They can also be used with very long-focus lenses to give image magnifications that would be nearly impossible with view cameras: a 300 mm or 500 mm telephoto lens gives the selective view and compressed planes characteristic of a particular type of landscape photograph, but to achieve the same thing with a 4 x 5 inch (9 x 12 cm) view camera, you would need a very heavy lens of around 1000mm, with all its attendant problems.

Right *John Huston* This portrait was taken in 1955 by Norman Parkinson (b.1913) on the set of the film *Moby Dick*. Parkinson likened the photographer's job to that of an engine-driver – he must "get there on time!" He positioned his Rolleiflex camera on ground level to capture the massive presence of the film's director playing cards on set. The versatility of the rollfilm camera gave this powerful portrait the combination of a formal structure backed by interesting detail, and a spontaneous atmosphere shown by the untidy pile of notes and a moving hand.

WORKING TO LAYOUT

The best rollfilm cameras (the Hasselblad, Mamiya RB67 and Pentax 6 x 7) occupy a special place in professional photography. In this field a large transparency is needed for photomechanical reproduction, and the composition comes under close scrutiny and art direction at the time of shooting.

Modern reproduction methods, such as laser scanners, cope quite well with 35 mm transparencies, but larger film is always easier to handle and graininess, which is usually unpopular in commercial work, is less apparent than with the smaller format. As a result, rollfilm cameras are the main tools of the trade in fashion and beauty photography, for the same reasons that they are useful for general portraiture – they provide a good compromise between rapid shooting and detail.

A great deal of advertising photography involves working to a design that has already been decided by the client. Sometimes even the precise layout has been worked out and, in any case, the art director will contribute his or her own ideas from the outset. The planning involved in this type of professional work alters the photographer's approach so radically that photography becomes, in effect, a branch of illustration. The layout often poses problems that may well be technically interesting but frequently threaten to squeeze the life out of an image. For example, if a headline or the masthead on a magazine cover has to run across the top of the printed photograph, the shot will need to be composed so that there is "empty" space at the top; in turn this means balancing the composition to include the typography, and calls for some imagination. This kind of constraint is typical and exerts a major control, although it has nothing to do with the subject of the photograph. To be able to work to a formal brief and yet *still* produce an image of some artistry demands both skill and persistence. The best advertising work displays a high degree of talent, which is highly rewarded.

Although shooting to layout is not as easy with rollfilm cameras as on the large ground glass screen of a view camera, rollfilm cameras still have a large enough viewing area to be able to study the composition carefully and to permit a reasonable amount of cropping. To allow last-minute changes of layout, or to delay decisions, most art directors prefer compositions to have some slack around the edges – it is always easier to crop into a photograph than to try and extend part of it by retouching.

With so much emphasis on planned layouts, the final advantage the rollfilm camera has over the 35 mm is its ability to use Polaroid film, at least in the case of the Hasselblad, Mamiya RB67 and one or two others, which have interchangeable backs. In these cameras, a special holder fits in place of the normal film magazine, carrying a Polaroid film pack. The ability to use Polaroids to check composition, exposure and lighting gives rollfilm cameras a great advantage.

Left The first stage in preparing the jacket illustration for a paperback novel is a rough layout by the art director. In this case, the requirements were precise, both in terms of content and composition.

Right For this type of studio shot, where all the elements, from props to lighting, can be determined in advance, the right-angled view down onto a ground glass screen is ideal – the two-dimensional view makes it easy to visualize the appearance of the shot when printed, and the camera can be mounted on a tripod. A professional model and makeup artist were used.

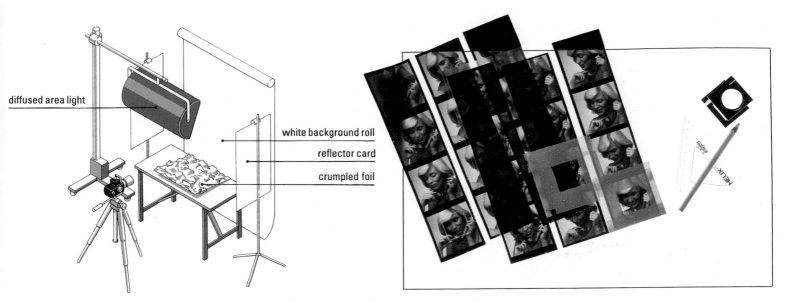

diffused area light

white background roll

reflector card

crumpled foil

Above In a photograph where the model must look attractive in closeup, one of the most effective lighting arrangements is to use a well-defined area light, which throws very soft shadows, from a position in front of the model's face and slightly overhead. This gives gentle modelling to the skin and good definition to the reflective surface of the telephone receiver. Any remaining shadows can then be filled in by reflector cards underneath and at each side.

Below Two standard film backs were used, allowing reloading without interrupting the shooting, and a Polaroid back for testing composition and lighting.

Pan

PIERS PAUL READ
A MARRIED MAN
The highly-acclaimed new novel from 'one of Britain's most intelligent and disturbing writers' NEW YORK TIMES

Above Even with a professional model, accustomed to assuming poses and facial expressions in front of the camera, it is normal to shoot several rolls of film to allow the art director choice. Often, the beginning of a session can be a little "cold", so that one or two rolls may be wasted before the picture begins to work. With transparencies on a lightbox, the art director can experiment with different ways of cropping them.

Left From a studio session in which the actual shooting lasted little more than half an hour, six rolls of film – a total of 72 transparencies – were whittled down to one shot for the book cover. This transparency was marked up by the art director and sent to the printer. A proof of the printed photograph was then sent by the printer to the art director who corrected it for colour, making sure that the printed version corresponded to the original transparency. The proof was then sent back to the printer with the type artwork. All the elements – photograph, type and logo – were stripped together in position by the printer, who makes final film for the printing of the finished cover.

Special uses of rollfilm As it is the largest film format manufactured commercially, rollfilm is favoured for a number of special applications, where good resolution of detail is important. One of its most famous uses has been in the American space programme *(right).* Here, Hasselblad cameras were used with certain adaptations. The controls were simplified for use with thick gloves. Leatherette, which normally covers the camera casing, gives off poisonous fumes in zero pressure conditions, so this was removed for safety inside the spacecraft. A 70mm film back was used to hold large quantities of film – changing film would be impractical in these conditions. Crude line-of-sight viewfinding had to replace the more normal optical system, as bulky space helmets precluded using an eyepiece finder. All picture-taking had to be as simple as possible because the astronauts had so much else to do. A straightforward choice of exposure settings, which would approximate to the light conditions, were marked on the camera. When the astronauts returned to Earth, clips from the film were tested at NASA before the whole roll was processed. Exposure was a problem because the lack of atmosphere on the moon meant that the contrast between sunlit areas and shadow was much greater than in any scene on Earth, Because of the need to bring as much information back as possible, many of the photographs taken served a dual purpose, not simply as a record of the event, but also as an aid to making detailed measurements of the features of the lunar surface. To this end, a reseau plate (made of glass and etched with cross-hairs) was placed in the camera in front of the film. When the film was exposed, the cross-hairs were also recorded, allowing the photographs to be used for mapping.

Above Paradoxically, although the underwater housings for rollfilm cameras are very bulky when compared with 35mm equipment, the extra weight and size are of no significant disadvantage to the diver, because underwater buoyancy makes handling extremely easy. For such richly detailed subjects as this dragonfish, the large film size is also very useful. Underwater housings are invariably tailored to specific camera models and the principal camera controls are usually connected by means of cogs and levers to control knobs on the outside of the gasket-sealed housing.

Because at any depth beyond a few feet, water absorbs sunlight's longer wavelengths, underwater shots taken without artificial lighting invariably have a bluish cast. For this reason, underwater flash is nearly always necessary to record the true colours of fish and coral. Both specially designed flash bulbs and electronic flash units can be used, but the latter are more popular.

Top Although picture formats ranging from 2¼ x 2¼ inch (6 x 6cm) to 2¼ x 4 inch (6 x 9cm) are the most common with rollfilm cameras, there are actually no practical limits to the picture length. Some special panoramic cameras, such as the Linhof Technorama used here, expose long strips. This can be done either by using a lens that has a wide coverage, as in this photograph, or by rotating the lens mechanically, so that the image is, in effect, scanned.

VIEW CAMERAS

In principle, view cameras have changed little over the last century. They employ the oldest and simplest design of any format: lens panel and film back joined by light-tight flexible bellows and a viewing system in which the image is focused in exactly the place where the sheet of film will be placed – on a large ground glass screen. Such a simple design conceals a sophisticated way of manipulating the image, and view cameras are essential equipment for many types of serious and professional photography. They range in the size of film they accept from 2¼ x 3¼ inch (6 x 7 cm) to 11 x 14 inch (28 x 36 cm), with 4 x 5 inch (9 x 12 cm) and 8 x 10 inch (20 x 24 cm) the most popular formats. Shutters are normally in the lenses, although behind-the-lens shutters are available.

A walk through a museum of old view cameras – collectors' items nowaday – shows what at first seems to be a bewildering variety of designs, but underlying most of them is one basic system, consisting of a level board that supports the lens panel and the film back. This type of view camera, known as a flatbed, is still made and used today. There are two forms: the field camera and the technical camera.

Field cameras acquired their name because they were light for their size, could be folded up for carrying and could be used on location. Typically, field cameras are made of wood with metal fittings (mahogany and brass are the best materials) and are focused by means of a rack and pinion that move the lens panel along a track in the flatbed.

A large ground glass screen in the film back gives an inverted image for focusing – being upside-down and dim, this takes some getting used to, although various reflex devices are now available. The screen is usually sprung so that the film in its holder can be pushed into the same place after focusing. Depending on the model, the lens panel, and to a lesser extent the film back, can be moved around and locked in different positions; they can usually be raised or lowered, tilted back and forth and sometimes even rotated to the left and right. These camera movements, as they are known, are an essential part of image control, although on a flatbed camera they are less extensive than on the modern monorail design.

The more recent version of the field camera is the technical camera. With a metal construction and calibrated movements, it is a more precise instrument, although heavier and more expensive. More attachments, such as different film backs, optical viewers and hand grips, are available, and the camera is rigid enough for handheld use.

For studio work demanding maximum versatility, the modern monorail camera is unrivalled. Two things set it apart from the traditional flatbed models: the support is a single metal rail – in effect, an optical bench – and the design is deliberately modular, with a wide choice of components for constructing different cameras to suit different jobs. The result is precision – the best use micrometer drives – and extreme flexibility, with an almost limitless range of camera movements. By adding rail extensions and additional bellows, the camera can take extreme closeups or use very long focal length lenses (view camera lenses themselves have no focusing mounts). Viewing attachments and a multitude of film holders can be fitted to the back; universal shutters and probe exposure meters can be fitted inside. The components of the Sinar P give a fair representation of the possibilities; often, even the format can be changed by altering only one or two elements.

Right A new camera, despite its traditional appearance, this 4 x 5 inch (9 x 12cm) field camera was made by a family workshop that has been manufacturing similar models to order for more than a century, to specifications that have remained virtually unaltered. Its movements are limited to a lens panel that shifts, rises and falls, and a back that can be tilted slightly, but these are adequate for most location work such as landscape and architecture. Moreover, constructed of mahogany, leather and brass fittings, it actually weighs less than some fully equipped 35mm SLRs with motor drives attached.

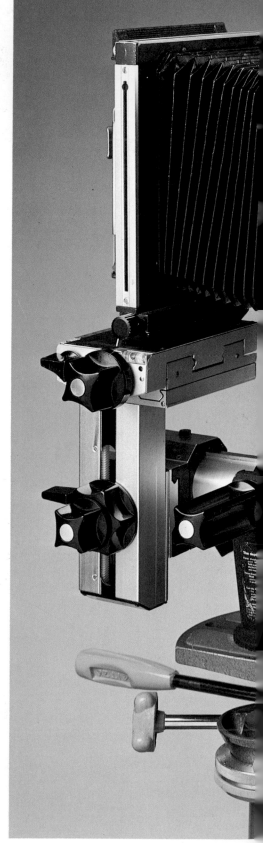

Left The Swiss-built Sinar is the most technologically advanced of all monorail view cameras. The Model P, shown here *(far left)* in its 4 x 5 inch (9 x 12cm) format, allows shifts, rises, falls, swings and tilts in all directions, and all these movements are engineered so precisely that nothing needs to be locked in position – friction holds everything in place. By siting all the controls underneath, the camera panels and bellows are given unusually free movement. The construction is modular, so that a photographer can order, to his own specifications, what is virtually a custom-made camera. Outside the studio, however, a monorail camera such as the Sinar can be a liability, being unwieldy and slow to set up, and liable to damage. For location work, while still retaining a degree of flexibility, a technical camera such as the 4 x 5 inch (9 x 12cm) Horseman *(left),* is more useful. Combining some of the advantages of both the traditional flatbed field camera and modern studio models, the technical camera can be folded neatly for carrying, set up quickly, and even handheld on occasions (by using a built-in viewfinder); at the same time, it has a respectable range of movements, and the facility to take several types of film, including sheets, packs, Polaroid and rollfilm.

VIEW CAMERA MOVEMENTS

Wʜᴀᴛ really distinguishes view cameras from all other types of cameras is their ability to control the image. By altering the positions of the lens panel and the film back, two things become possible – the plane of sharpest focus can be moved, and the actual shape of the image can be changed. In practice, this means that, for example, a flower a few inches from the camera and a distant horizon can both be brought into focus together without using a wide-angle lens and without stopping down to a small aperture. In addition, a mirror can be photographed head-on without the camera being reflected. To anyone familiar only with the fixed bodies of 35 mm and rollfilm cameras, such capabilities are exciting.

With most cameras, the plane of sharpest focus is at right-angles to the lens axis and parallel to the film plane; if you focus on a tree in the middle distance its image will be sharp, but everything behind, towards the horizon, will be increasingly out of focus, as will objects nearer the camera. However, if the film and lens are set at an angle to each other, the plane of sharpest focus is tilted; in an extreme case, by aiming the lens sharply towards the ground this plane can be made to lie horizontally.

Tilting the lens panel does nothing more than

1. *Rise and fall* Having aligned the camera so that the subject appears in the middle of the frame, the image can then be altered simply by moving either the rear standard or the lens panel. Here, by raising the rear standard, the image of the Rubik cube and spirit level is shifted to the top of the picture frame. The succession of pictures that follow show some of the other ways in which the distribution of sharpness, the position and even the shape of the cube can be altered by changing the relative position of lens and film.

2. *Rise and fall* By raising the lens panel, the image that it projects onto the ground glass screen at the back of the camera is shifted up. However, as the image is projected upside-down, the effect is to lower the position of the cube in the picture frame. The limit to which the image can be raised or lowered is only partly dependent on the mechanical movement of the camera – more important is the covering power of the lens. If the circular image projected by the lens only just fits around the picture area, these movements cannot be used; a lens for a view camera should have plenty of room to spare.

3. *Shift* On most view cameras, both the lens panel and the film back can be moved sideways as well as up and down. In principle, these lateral movements, known as shifts, are identical to the vertical movements – they all simply move the image around inside the picture area. Here, the camera's rear standard, where the film is loaded, has been shifted to the left when viewed from above. The result is to offset the optical axis – and therefore the image of the cube – to the left of the picture. This kind of movement is useful either to make small compositional changes, or when the camera cannot be moved.

4. *Shift* By moving the lens panel to the right, and leaving the rear standard in its normal position, the effect on the image seems at first glance to be the same as when the rear standard was moved *(left)*. However, there are some subtle differences, particularly at close distances, due to perspective. Here, because the position of the lens has changed relative to the cube, the alignment of squares on the top surface has been shifted. With distant views, and with irregularly shaped objects, this difference is normally too small to be noticed, but with some formal compositions it can be significant.

alter the plane of sharp focus; tilting the film back has a similar effect but also distorts the image, often in a useful way.

The ways in which the positions of lens and film affect focus are governed by something called the Scheimpflug principle, which is reasonably simple to follow in practice, despite its grand title. This principle states that if the planes of the film, lens and subject can be made to converge, the resulting image will be sharp overall. However, to take full advantage of this principle, the lens has to cover a larger area than the size of the film – these camera movements need space. In general, long-focus lenses for view cameras have a wider coverage than wide-angle lenses; to preserve good definition when using extreme movements, it is sometimes necessary to use a small aperture.

This extra image area makes possible another type of movement – the shift. When moving the lens panel or film back to either side, up or down, no changes are made to the focus or shape – instead, a different part of the image can be brought into view. Apart from allowing changes to be made to the composition without having to move the complete camera, this useful movement makes it possible to straighten converging vertical lines.

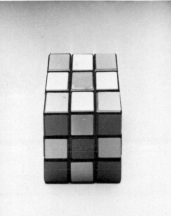

5. *Tilt* The greatest effect on the image comes through using tilts and swings. In these movements, the lens panel or rear standard (or even both together) are rotated slightly. The movement shown above is a tilt, and in this case there is a major difference between tilting the lens and tilting the film. Both have an effect on the distribution of sharpness, but what governs the shape of a projected image is the alignment of the film plane to the *subject*. Here, by tilting the rear standard until it is aligned vertically, the film and the front surface of the cube are parallel. As a result, the sides of this front surface no longer appear to converge, although the overall appearance is distinctly strange.

6. *Tilt* By tilting the front standard rather than the rear standard, the shape of the cube remains unaltered, but the distribution of sharpness is no longer the same. Here, the front standard has been tilted back, and as a result, the plane of sharper focus is no longer parallel to the film, but now lies at an angle that is almost vertical. In the case of a cube, this is no advantage, but with a vertical subject, such as a tall bottle, it enables the photographer to achieve sharpness without stopping the lens down.

7. *Swing* The equivalent lateral movements to tilts are known as swings, and with a professional monorail camera, both the lens panel and rear standard can be swung to the left and to the right. In principle, the effects are similar to tilting: that is, swinging either lens panel or rear standard alters the distribution of sharpness, but only by swinging the rear standard is the shape of the image changed. Here, the back of the camera has been swung quite sharply to the left, so that the sharpest focus runs diagonally through the image of the cube, from back left to front right. The shape of the cube is also distorted, and its position altered slightly in the picture frame.

8. *Swing* Swinging the lens panel sharply to the left has no effect on the shape, but makes the plane of sharpest focus run diagonally from the near lefthand corner of the cube to the far right corner. The exact position of this plane of sharp focus can be calculated by imagining the plane of the lens panel and film back to extend beyond the camera. From where they intersect to the subject focused on is the plane of greatest sharpness. This is the Scheimpflug principle.

ARCHITECTURE

Buildings, like most landscapes, are fixed and formal subjects and so are also suited to the view camera's deliberate approach. In addition, they often pose a specific technical problem – converging verticals – and although this point tends to get laboured, the problem usually does need some special treatment. Viewpoints for most buildings are at ground level, so that usually when we look at a building we look up. Naturally, the effect of perspective makes the vertical lines appear to converge, but because we are accustomed to this effect and know that we are looking up, our eye and brain read the information normally. However, in a two-dimensional photograph the straight-sided borders of the picture accentuate the convergence, and the image looks wrong.

There are a number of ways of avoiding this problem, such as including foreground details in a wide-angle composition so that the camera can be aimed horizontally, or making the convergence so pronounced that it is obviously deliberate. However, the most logical solution is to ensure the verticals remain vertical and the building more or less fills the frame. The vertical shift of the view camera makes this possible.

Convergence can only be avoided by keeping the film frame parallel to the vertical lines of the building. In other words, the frame cannot be tilted, which ordinarily would mean that the top of the building was left out of the picture, while unnecessary foreground was included. However, as a typical large-format lens has

image area to spare, by sliding the lens panel up, the upper part of the building can be brought into view. This is not so much a trick as an essential part of the view camera's controls. Some special lenses are available for smaller format cameras that duplicate this effect, but with a view camera it works with any lens.

Nevertheless, the vertical shift is not a universal panacea for the problems of architectural photography, as there are fairly narrow limits to the movement. At the extreme of the movement, the dark circular edge of the image comes into view and sharpness close to this border is poor. Additionally, even with a lens that has exceptionally wide coverage, the building begins to look strangely elongated when the lens is shifted severely. One kind of

Right Rendering fine detail with extreme clarity is an essential element of architectural photography, and for this, nothing rivals a large format. This formally composed view of the fountain in front of the Library of Congress in Washington D.C. is only one-third larger than the original Ektachrome transparency, and as a result makes full use of the resolving power of the lens, with no sign of grain. Large format lenses are invariably slower than their 35mm and rollfilm counterparts, and exposure times are therefore usually relatively longer; for this reason, running water is often reproduced as a misty blue, which in this case has the advantage of revealing more detail of the figures than would otherwise be seen.

Left This picture of the Louvre Bibliothèque, which was taken in about 1855 by Edouard-Denis Baldus (1820-1882), is one of a series of photographs depicting the renovation of the palace. It illustrates the photographer's ability to match composition to subject: an impressive frontal, it fills the entire page. The textures of the brick and stone, and the sturdy beauty of the whole, are clear at a glance; the combination of interior light and detail, and long depth of field is remarkable. The verticals converge only slightly, juxtaposed against the side of the frame.

distortion – converging verticals – is traded for another – stretching.

With indoor architectural photography, the larger the interior, the more difficult it is to add lighting; there is also a strong argument for retaining the atmosphere of the interior by using only available light. As a result, large-format exposures under these conditions, particularly with historical subjects such as cathedrals, tend to be long in order to achieve the f45 and f64 apertures needed for great depth of field. This inevitably involves the special precautions for reciprocity failure of the film. One occasional bonus of long exposures lasting several minutes is that people walking through the field of view (often unavoidable in public buildings) do not register on the film. Complex shading operations, to reduce the light reaching the lens from a window for example, are also possible when the exposure is long.

Above Decorative details, such as this bronze art deco door panel, are as important in conveying architectural style as the more obvious large-scale view of a building. As exterior details are subject to a wide variety of lighting conditions, depending on the weather and position of the sun, timing is particularly important.

Left Correcting converging verticals is not always possible with interiors, due partly to the proportions, which frequently do not allow the photographer to stand far enough back to cover the whole scene, and partly to the fact that in many palaces and public buildings, ceiling decoration is an integral part of the design. In such cases, as in this photograph of the main hall of the Library of Congress, a pronounced upward view is the only solution. Here, only available lighting was used, to preserve the interior's normal appearance.

Above For the photograph of the clock tower at Hampton Court, near London, the shot was timed for early morning, both to give good modelling to the brickwork and other details of the facade, and to strengthen the tonal difference between the sunlit areas and the shadowed archway, used as a complementary frame.

STILL LIFE

Of all the fields of photography that need a considered and deliberate approach, none demands it more than still life, where maximum control is paramount and speed of working largely irrelevant. The view camera – slow to use but extremely precise – is ideally suited to this application, and little serious still life photography is done with any other kind of camera. The still life image is nearly always produced in an indoor setting like a studio, and the monorail camera is the preferred piece of equipment.

The strong tradition of still life photography derives originally from painting, but more recently has been influenced by advertising work. Advertising uses still life photography very precisely. Because the image can be planned, designed and executed down to the finest detail, and there are large amounts of money to spend, high technical standards are encouraged.

The prime motivation behind still life photography has always been the exercise of skills, chiefly in composition and lighting and, on a more fundamental level, in the choice of subject and setting. At least outside commercial work, where the subject is part of the brief, still life allows the photographer to exercise imagination. Unlike location photography, nearly every element of the still life image can be manipulated in the studio.

The process of constructing a still life photograph is usually painstaking. Even with simple, single subjects, the choices are infinite: setting, camera angle, composition, lighting angle, lighting diffusion, and so on. When the subject is more complex, and draws on juxtaposition or the creation of a set-piece for its effect, then the problems of selection become even more involved. Moreover, because a still life picture is very much the photographer's creation, with very little in the way of chance creeping into it, every element comes under closer scrutiny by the viewer. If a foreground subject in a landscape photograph seems to spoil the composition slightly, at least the photographer can claim that the viewpoint offered limited choice. However, in a still life, if the design or concept is awkward, the responsibility falls squarely on the originator.

Still life photographs are constructed rather than captured – built up from the raw materials of subjects, props, background and lighting. With plenty of time at the photographer's disposal, the process is generally one of refinement. The elements are changed or improved by smaller and smaller amounts until the image is as exact as the photographer can make it. The thorough, even rigorous, attitude that goes hand in hand with still life photography suits the view camera well. The ground glass screen is a large enough area for composing, and the inverted image, far from being a hindrance, actually helps the photographer to see the design more objectively. The camera movements add to the precision. Only the lighting is inconveniently served by the view camera, as a plain ground glass screen always gives an unevenly lit view of the image; practice and Polaroids are the usual solution to this problem.

Left For an essentially straightforward picture of two pistols, simplicity – of composition, props and lighting – was important. The surface of a dark wooden chest was chosen as a background, to give a contrast in both tone and texture with the smooth reflecting metal. The 45° camera angle and use of diagonals gave the composition more interest than would a formal side-on arrangement, and this virtually dictated the relative positions of the two pistols. (Had the smaller been behind the larger, the result would have been unbalanced.) Finally, a single, diffused light source was used, to simplify the reflections in the metal.

Left In this more complex arrangement, still life has become virtually a room-set – the working area of a nineteenth century American pharmacy. Here, a wide-angle lens has been used, and a viewpoint chosen to show the setting of the foreground objects. Diagonal lines are used not only to strengthen the composition, but also to enhance the feeling of depth. By elaborating a still life into a full set-piece like this, the image can be made to seem uncontrived, particularly if a certain amount of casualness is introduced into the arrangement. The directional lighting contributes to the period atmosphere.

LANDSCAPE

Fashions in photography are always changing, often following developments in equipment. The view camera's relationship with landscape photography illustrates these shifting tides in an interesting way. During the first few decades of photography the long exposures required and general inconvenience resulting from bulky equipment made it difficult to find *any* subject bright and still enough to make a satisfactory picture. Portraits were certainly out of the question at the beginning, and landscapes quickly became the most popular subject matter. Later, this tradition of the formal unhurried approach remained with the view camera, while users of the new smaller format cameras hunted more technically ambitious subjects – candid shots of people and things in motion. Large format landscape photography was raised to new heights in this century by

Right In both these landscape photographs, the two principal advantages of a view camera have been exploited: the large 4 x 5 inch (9 x 12 cm) negatives contain extremely fine detail and no obvious grain, and the camera's rear tilt has been used to give foreground-to-horizon sharpness without having to close the aperture to its minimum setting. The shutter speed for the picture at far right was set at 1/20 second – sufficient to give a realistic treatment to the water but slow enough to show movement. For the photograph at right, the speed was set at a deliberately slow one second, to give a more unusual impression.

Below *Setting up a view camera* This takes more care and deliberation than when using a 35mm or rollfilm camera. Experimenting with composition and framing by looking at the ground glass screen is not particularly easy, and most view camera photographers tend to plan their images in advance. The sequence of setting up a field camera starts by setting up

the tripod *(1)*. The camera is then unfolded *(2)*, and the position and focus set approximately (with experience this becomes easy). As the viewpoint is low, and the scene not far from horizontal, the back is tilted slightly *(3)*. The camera is now reasonably well-aligned *(4)*, but for final adjustments the scene is viewed through the ground

glass screen, a black velvet cloth shielding the dim view from extraneous light *(5)*. The lens aperture is set, and the shutter closed and cocked *(6)*, and finally, with the film holder inserted, the dark slide is removed (the black cloth preventing possible light leaks) and the shutter tripped *(7)*.

1

2

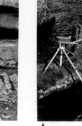

3

4

5

photographers such as Ansel Adams who, from the 1920s on, used all the advantages of the view camera to the full – the ability to capture fine detail, the delicate tonal rendering of sky and clouds possible with a large negative, the discipline of visualizing the image before setting up the camera, and the use of camera movements to bring background and close foreground into sharp focus.

The postwar rise in popularity of the 35mm single-lens reflex seemed to mark an effective end to this special association, although view camera landscape photographers still persisted. 35mm film was used in more and more fields, including landscape, which after all remains one of the most popular themes. The gritty, high contrast images that often were unavoidable with 35mm eventually came to be admired for these textural characteristics. View cameras were largely relegated to professional work, and that meant the studio.

While the view camera can hardly be said to have reestablished its position, there is a revival of interest today in the uncompromisingly sharp and precise images of the large-format landscape photograph. This is largely due to the general boom in photography, which has pushed enthusiasts towards the technical high ground. Some part has probably also been played by the rise of interest in the classic landscape photographers and the corresponding increase in the commercial value of their work.

Even with modern improvements in camera design, films and film holders, view cameras are still rather cumbersome to use on location. The time needed to set up equipment for one exposure discourages casual shots. Flatbed models, either wooden field cameras or technical cameras, are the most convenient. Because of their size, they are more likely to be affected by wind than smaller format equipment and a rigid tripod, carefully set up, is essential. Wind vibration is one of the main difficulties with this type of work, because slow shutter speeds of a quarter of a second or more, are normal (the maximum aperture of large-format lenses rarely exceeds f5.6, and small settings are usually needed to preserve depth of field). It is also one reason why long-focus lenses are not too common, as the magnified image is even more liable to suffer from camera shake, particularly with a long bellows extension.

The most useful camera movement in landscape photography is the tilt – the lens panel or the film back is moved to make the plane of sharpest focus lie almost horizontally. With this technique, a foreground detail such as a flower, and a distant skyline can be brought into focus together without having to use extremely small apertures. This type of image has accordingly become one of the most popular in the repertoire of large-format landscape photographers.

6

7

WORKING TO LAYOUT

The still life taken by a view camera is particularly favoured in advertising and in any commercial or editorial work where the photograph must be tailor-made to fit the design. The large format makes it possible to follow even detailed layouts accurately, which means the typography can be planned beforehand. The still life image has two commercial advantages: it can be guaranteed in advance and designed before the photographer begins shooting and, with its infinite capacity for juxtaposing subjects and settings, it can be used to present ideas.

In such orchestrated work, the camera becomes largely a tool of the designer or art director. The photographer's job changes, but is no less difficult for being determined by a layout. The skill the photographer needs is the ability to solve technical design problems – with flair. These problems may be as obvious as keeping sufficient depth of field or coping with a difficult perspective, but if they affect the layout they are crucial. A designer's sketch, often the starting place, may well not obey the rules of camera optics, and anticipating this kind of difficulty is at least part of the talent of successful professional still life photographers. The other part is to be able to add, even at this late stage, a fillip of visual interest.

Much depends on the nature of the design job, and on the relationship between designer and photographer. Generally, the procedure is as follows: the designer first produces a layout sketch to the format and dimensions of the finished picture, including the position of the typography and any other design elements, such as the masthead of a magazine cover. At this stage, the photographer has to decide what will be involved in translating the sketch into a photograph and if there will be any unanticipated difficulties. On some occasions the photographer is brought into the design discussions before the layout is prepared; at other times the layout is presented as a *fait accompli*.

If any special effects are needed – a multiple image, for example, or retouching – the designer and photographer will have to decide who will be responsible for them. Retouching in particular can be done at any of a number of stages in the production and it may not always be obvious which is best or cheapest. For instance, it may be easier to change the colour of a car by retouching the transparency if the alternative were to respray a real prototype. On the other hand, multiple exposure is simpler in the camera rather than after the photograph has been shot, provided that the background is black.

At the start of shooting, the layout can be transferred to the ground glass screen, either roughly, by masking the approximate area the photographic image will cover, or precisely,

by copying the sketch in exact proportion. Most view camera screens are etched with a grid, which makes this straightforward. Normally a margin is left on the screen around the layout in case of error. A further refinement is to make a Polaroid print partway through the session and sketch the layout onto that, to check that everything is looking as it should. There are 4 x 5 inch (9 x 12 cm) and 8 x 10 inch (20 x 24 cm) Polaroid backs available for view cameras and these are almost invariably used in professional still life work.

The technique of masking the image on the ground glass screen can also be used to make several exposures with a fair degree of accuracy on the same sheet of film. Multiple exposures work most realistically with a black (that is, previously unexposed) background, but graduated or ghosted effects are possible with a tonal background. A view camera is the best equipment for this; the image is large enough to allow reasonably close registration, and by using single sheets of film rather than rolls, the different exposures can be made at any time and in any order. First, one exposure is made and the outline of the image traced on the screen. The second subject can then be exposed accurately in relation to this outline, and so on. The sheet of film must be taped down in its holder so that it cannot shift between exposures.

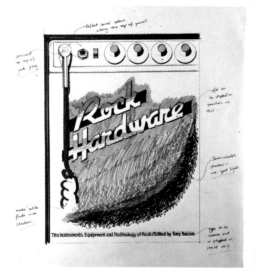

Above The layout sketch. The designer had precise ideas for the final picture: in the margin directions he details the colours and the shape of the shadows, the starburst on the top of the jack plug, and the red cable fading into black; he also specified the technique needed to bring out the red typography from the background.

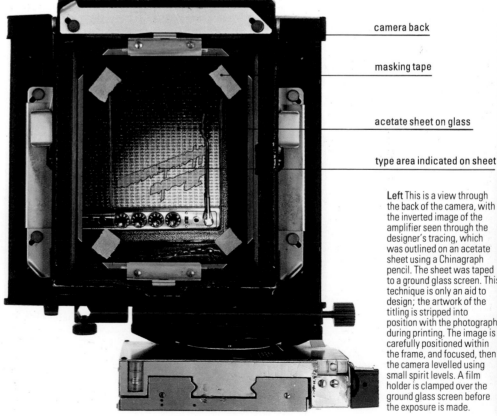

camera back

masking tape

acetate sheet on glass

type area indicated on sheet

Left This is a view through the back of the camera, with the inverted image of the amplifier seen through the designer's tracing, which was outlined on an acetate sheet using a Chinagraph pencil. The sheet was taped to a ground glass screen. This technique is only an aid to design; the artwork of the titling is stripped into position with the photograph during printing. The image is carefully positioned within the frame, and focused, then the camera levelled using small spirit levels. A film holder is clamped over the ground glass screen before the exposure is made.

Left The finished cover. The brown strip over the top half of the control panel, which had a slightly curved surface, was achieved using a coloured strip of acetate and a light above and to the left of the amplifier. The semi-circular shadow at the base of the picture was created by a spot light of an intensity to highlight the texture of the grill cloth, but confined by a snoot attachment which directed the light precisely around the titling. The artwork of the titling itself was painted with an airbrush and stripped in position by the printers. The single star burst was photographed separately to achieve the exact positioning vital to the style of the complete photograph.

SPECIAL CAMERAS

In addition to basic camera formats, there are a number of what could be called special purpose cameras – special either because they have been designed to solve a real photographic problem, such as working underwater, or because they exploit some technical oddity (for example, stereo cameras). The trouble with most of this equipment is that it is only needed on a few occasions, and the cost of photographic equipment that lies outside the mass market is always high. Except for photographers who specialize in particular fields, the usual answer is to hire the camera.

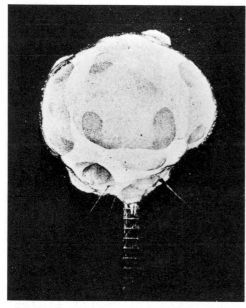

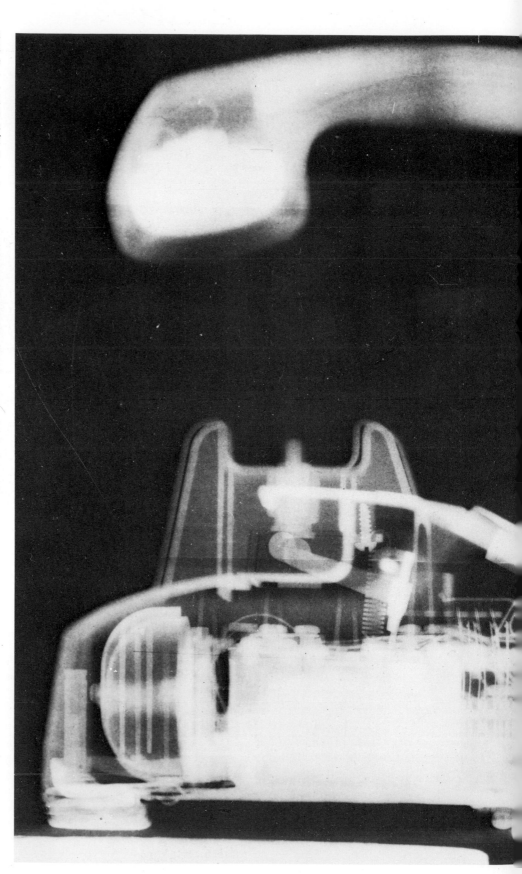

Above Beyond the limits of normal photography, it may still be possible to record images on film by constructing special equipment. The man who has done most to stretch one of photography's limits – its ability to record very fast movement – is Professor Harold Edgerton, who developed a complex triple shutter to capture the first microseconds of a nuclear fireball. A mechanical shutter opened one second before the explosion, then an electronic shutter exposed the film for a few millionths of a second, and finally, to prevent the film from subsequent fogging by the intense radiation, a surge of electricity through a glass sheet vapourized a matrix of lead wires.

Right One of the other limitations of photography is that most materials are opaque to light. For interior views of subjects such as the human body, X-rays have normally been used, but even their ability to resolve details is crude when compared with the more recent neutron radiography, used here to show the structure of a telephone.

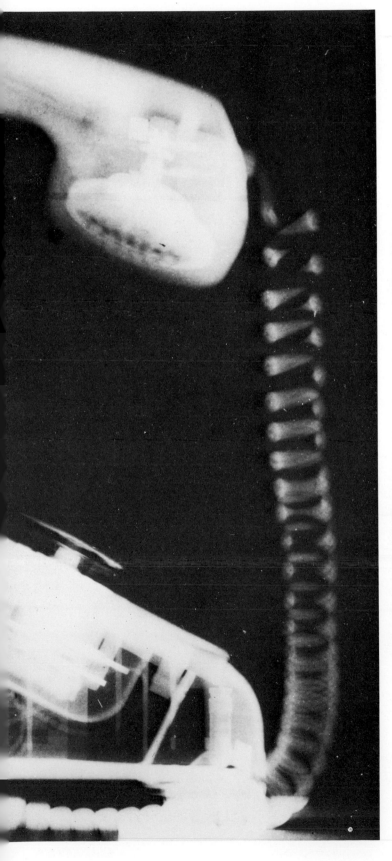

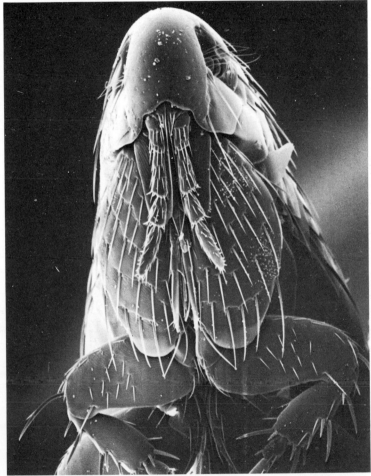

Above A third limitation of photography is set by the wavelength of light itself, and at very high magnifications it is too coarse to be able to record detail. Instead, a thin beam of electrons can be used, in a scanning electron microscope. Although unable to record colour, which is a property only of light, this instrument has exceptional resolving power, and can produce images with such great depth of field, like this 300-times magnification of a tropical rat flea, that they resemble photographs taken at much larger scales.

LENSES

Modern camera lenses give the photographer considerable freedom to control the image. Continuous development over a long period has resulted in a wide variety of lenses, designed not only to suit different cameras but also different situations. From the user's point of view, the most obvious choice is between focal lengths, short ones giving a wide angle of view, long ones a magnified image over a narrow angle, and zoom lenses having a variable focal length. Lenses vary in quality, and some models perform better than others in different respects. Lenses can also be designed for specific uses, such as closeup photography or copying without distortion.

The earliest lenses were designed to produce nothing more ambitious than a reasonable image. Modern lenses are the product of continuous improvement, aided by computer design, multiple coating and rare earth glasses. In performance and the provision of special features, lenses have come a long way from the first simple landscape lens of 1829. A cutaway illustration of any modern lens, showing the variety and number of elements, reveals the high level of technology involved in today's lens design.

Nevertheless, these complex arrays of glass, which at first glance appear to differ widely from lens to lens, conceal an underlying simplicity. The principles of lens design were well understood even in the nineteenth century, and virtually all modern lenses are based on one of three basic designs: triplet, symmetrical or highly asymmetrical. The one exception to this is the mirror lens, which works on the same principle as a type of astronomical telescope.

The simplest lens of all is a single piece of glass, convex on both sides so that it is thickest in the middle and tapers towards the edges. This does the job of forming an image, but it also suffers from a number of faults called, in the language of optics, aberrations. Aberrations limit the quality of the image and also restrict the design possibilities; the elaborate configurations of modern lenses are the result of attempting to overcome these problems.

There are seven main aberrations, two affecting the whole image and the remainder noticeable only towards the edges. The two faults that cause blurring overall are spherical aberration and chromatic aberration. Spherical aberration is really a problem of economics because, although lenses are easier to grind if they have regular, spherical curves, rays of light passing through different parts of the lens focus in slightly different places; chromatic aberration occurs because the colours that make up the spectrum are each bent in a different way by the glass and so do not focus at the same point.

The other five aberrations affect the rays that pass obliquely through the lens, and so are worse away from the centre of the image. Lateral colour aberration gives coloured fringes, coma turns points into comet-shaped streaks, distortion causes straight lines to be bowed inwards ("pincushion") or outwards ("barrel"), astigmatism converts points into short lines, and curvature of field, which occurs because a simple lens does not focus the image into a flat plane, blurs the edge of the image.

All of these faults can be corrected, at least up to a point, and although some of the solutions are highly technical, they all share a few basic principles. The most important of these consists of splitting the lens into at least two different parts (called elements) so that lens designers can balance one error with an equal but opposite one. In other words, if half the lens is crown glass, shaped to make the light rays converge, and half flint glass, shaped to spread

1

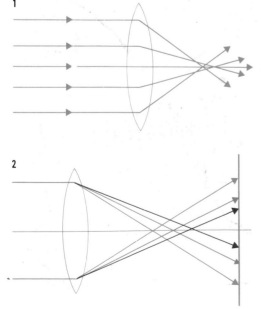

Left 1. *Spherical aberration* Cheap massproduced lenses are ground with curves sectioned from spheres. Spherical aberration occurs when light waves passing through the edges of these lenses are focused at a different point from those passing through the centre, causing a blurred image. It can be overcome by making lenses with aspherical surfaces where the curvature changes.
2. *Chromatic aberration* The different wavelengths that comprise white light travel at different speeds and at slightly different angles through the lens. The result is a loss of definition because the focus is spread. A second effect of this aberration is the colour fringe at the film plane. It is possible to use a compound of lens materials to correct these faults.

3

4

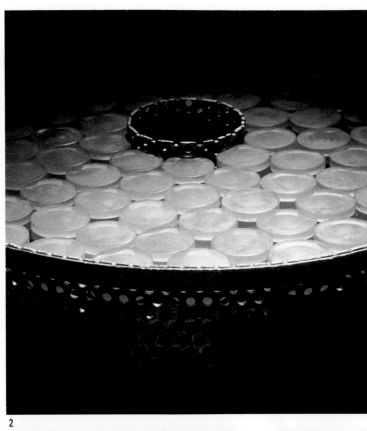

2

5

6

7

Manufacturing lenses
Nikon is one of the world's best-known manufacturers of camera equipment. These photographs show some of the stages in the production of lenses, nowadays a highly technical enterprise, aided in the design process by computers which help to work out the complex arrangement of elements, coatings and other corrective procedures. (The glass in these photographs appears opaque, but is, in fact, clear.)
1. Raw glass, transported on a continuous roller, is melted and flattened.
2. The basic optical lenses are annealed (toughened by heating and then cooling).
3. The lenses are polished by automatic lens polishing equipment.
4. Each lens element is coated with multilayered lens coating – Nikon Integrated Coating (NIC).
5. Each lens is inspected and checked for faults.
6. The lens elements are assembled in the barrel.
7. The lenses are tested for optical performance.

the rays, the two combined will cancel out most of the chromatic aberration. This solution, in fact, constituted the first corrected lens – the chromatic doublet – used in telescopes as early as the eighteenth century.

The chromatic doublet set the pattern for improving lenses. By making elements from different types of glass, shaping them differently and placing them in different positions in the lens barrel, the designer is free to suppress some qualities of a lens while enhancing others. However, this method does not guarantee a perfect lens. It is impossible to correct even one fault completely and when trying to overcome several problems together, design changes to correct one usually adversely affect the others. Any general purpose lens is really a compromise only when lenses are designed for one particular use can a fault be corrected to a high degree. For example, if a photographer wants a lens with the best definition, this will probably be achieved at the expense of a large aperture and wide coverage. Hence the variety of types of lenses now available – each performs best at a particular task.

The most useful lens is the triplet (and its descendants) which still forms the basis of modern general purpose lenses. As the name implies, the triplet consists of three parts: two converging lenses, with a diverging element in the middle. The triplet gives good all-round correction without being expensive and most standard lenses fitted to average cameras are likely to be of this type. Even zoom lenses, complicated though they are, had their origins in this design. The Zeiss Tessar is one of the most famous triplet designs but, like other triplets, suffers from being rather slow – wide apertures are not generally possible.

The second major type of lens is symmetrical, or nearly so. From the lens layout it is possible to see that the elements behind the aperture are virtually a mirror-image of those in front. (This makes it easy to arrange cancellation of faults.) Wide apertures are possible with symmetrical lenses, correction is very good, and because they also give even illumination, they are a good choice for wide-angle lenses and for the wide coverage lenses needed in view cameras. Their disadvantages are that they are costly, and the wide-angle varieties need to be used so close to the film that in small format cameras there is no room for an instant return mirror. The process lenses used in photomechanical reproduction, where definition and high correction are needed, are usually symmetrical. Among regular photographic lenses, the Super Angulon is a classic example.

The third group of lenses are highly asymmetrical, which means that one part converges the light rays, while the other diverges them. Apart from cancelling out faults, this system has one very special advantage: it makes it poss-

Right Some measure of the progress in basic lens design can be seen by comparing these two images, one taken with a lens made more than 100 years ago, the other a modern lens that has been corrected for all the important aberrations. Both lenses are standard for a 4 x 5 inch (9 x 12cm) format camera, with a focal length of 150mm. In this photograph, a Busch Detectiv Aplanat lens, dated 1880, was used in a modern studio camera, under lighting conditions that provided a fairly severe test of any lens' ability to control flare. At this, the lens performed poorly, and the light from the illuminated white background has been reflected from the internal surfaces of the lens sufficiently to degrade the image overall, and reduce contrast. In addition, chromatic aberration contributes to a slight fuzziness, and the limited coverage of the lens causes some vignetting at the corners.

ible to alter the physical length of the lens despite the limitation of the focal length. In this way, a wide-angle lens can be constructed which, even though it has a short focal length, in practice focuses the image much further behind. This makes it possible to use very wide-angle, short-focus lenses with a 35mm single-lens reflex: a divergent element behind the front elements pushes the plane of focus back, so that there is space behind the lens to fit the mirror, meters and shutter. This is known as a retrofocus design and is widely used; it even enables a single-lens reflex to accept fisheye lenses (which allow extreme barrel distortion in order to achieve very wide views, often over 180°). Using exactly the same principle, but in reverse, the length of a long-focus lens can be compressed. The result – a telephoto lens – is shorter and more convenient to use, and again is very common.

Zoom lenses, which are extremely complex, work on the principle of moving some of the elements back and forth inside the lens to alter

the focal length. The earliest were triplet designs, and by altering the distances between each element, the focal length could be shortened or lengthened. The lessons learned from making zoom lenses have been passed on to regular lenses, many of which now have floating elements to keep aberrations to a minimum when the focus is changed, and even to focus the lens itself more efficiently. However, because the optics change as the zoom control is moved, it becomes very difficult to correct the aberrations; consequently a zoom lens needs many elements. With so many variables, only computer-aided design has made it possible to develop high quality, moderately priced lenses; multicoating is needed to prevent the loss of most of the light to flare at the many surfaces.

Zoom lenses, in fact, have benefited most from the three fairly recent advances in lens design – the use of computers, multicoating and rare earth glasses. Because optics involve calculation, and because modern lenses use so

many different elements that the variables are enormous, the computer has an obvious role in lens design. Designs that would have taken too long to work out by slide-rule or calculator can now be attempted; the practical benefits for the photographer are faster, more highly corrected lenses over a range of focal lengths.

The second breakthrough has been the ability to coat the surface of lenses so finely that many layers can be deposited on one piece of glass – in other words, multicoating. The purpose of coating is to reduce flare, which can seriously affect the quality of the image. Flare occurs in a lens when the light passes from air to glass, and not only reduces the amount of light reaching the film, but also scatters light around *inside* the lens and so weakens the image. If the glass is uncoated, something in the order of 4% of the light is lost at each face by reflection, so that in a zoom lens with 20 elements, only 30% of the light would finally reach the film. However, an extremely thin layer of a material that gives a particular refraction, such as silicon dioxide, sets up a second reflection that can be made to cancel out the reflection from the lens.

One suitable coating can help a glass element to pass around 95% of the light. By choosing different coatings to take care of individual parts of the spectrum, more than 99% of the total light can be passed, so that even though a lens may have many surfaces, very little light is lost. Multicoating, with stacks of between seven and eleven layers on a surface, is now common.

Finally, the development of rare earth glasses has helped lens designers reduce some aberrations even further. Glasses that have a high refractive index do not need to be given very strong curvatures, and a very low dispersion virtually eliminates lateral colour. Artificial fluorite is another useful material, especially for long-focus lenses, although its focal length changes very slightly with temperature. All these materials are expensive and add heavily to the cost of telephoto lenses.

A completely different type of lens, but one that can only be used for long focal lengths, is the mirror lens. Its first great advantage is that, by using a surface that reflects light rather than refracts it, colour aberrations are eliminated. Secondly, the lens can be made very short, by bouncing the light between two mirrors. Also, the focus can be changed by only small movements of the focusing ring, which is useful with very long focal lengths. Set against these, however, are some problems: an aperture stop cannot be used so that the only way of altering the amount of light passed is by placing filters in the path or changing the shutter speed; contrast is low; and out-of-focus highlights appear as rings. Also, the fact that mirror lenses are relatively light and compact does not necessarily make them easier to hold, and many photographers find that telephoto lenses allow a steadier grip at slow shutter speeds.

Above In this photograph, taken with a new Schneider Symmar, multiple coating on the different glass surfaces has virtually eliminated flare, with the result that the colours are purer and the tonal range greater. Because the lens is designed to be used with extensive camera movements, it covers a much wider area than the picture format, and there is no darkening towards the edges.

USING LENSES

f5.6

f8

f11

Apart from lenses with built-in shutter mechanisms (for cameras without focal plane shutters), the two important lens controls are focus and aperture. The closer the subject, the further the film needs to be from the lens, so that some arrangement for moving the lens backwards and forwards is essential. View cameras, which have a flexible body, focus in the simplest way of all – by compressing or extending the bellows. In all other cameras, however, the lens needs its own focusing mechanism. The usual arrangement is for the lens elements to be fitted to an inner barrel, which can be moved within the outer barrel of the lens by a helical screw. When focused on infinity, the lens is closest to the film plane, and this distance from lens to film is the lens' focal length, usually measured in millimetres. A more recent and efficient system – internal focusing – moves only some of the lens elements inside the barrel, so that the entire lens does not have to move.

The aperture stop, which is a bladed iris connected to a control ring on the outside of the lens barrel, can be adjusted to give a circular hole smaller than the diameter of the lens. Naturally, this control alters the amount of light reaching the film and so, together with the shutter speed, controls exposure. For convenience, the aperture mechanism is calibrated; stopping down halves the amount of light passed at each setting. This mechanism means that the aperture and shutter controls can be used in tandem – each click stop on either control doubles or halves the exposure.

The longer the focal length, the less light is passed by the same diameter of lens opening, so to standardize exposure calculations, f numbers are used. These are worked out by divid-

ing the focal length of the lens by the size of the aperture. As a result, the f number is a direct measure of exposure, irrespective of the focal length. At f5.6, a 200mm lens allows the same quantity of light to reach the film as a 20mm lens, even though the sizes of the apertures are quite different. Lenses are often designated by their maximum apertures – an f1.4 lens, for example, is considered fast.

In addition to controlling exposure, the aperture also affects the depth of field. Definition is determined by the circle of confusion. (Even the best lenses record points as tiny circles. The largest circle that still looks like a point to the eye is the circle of confusion.) The smaller the aperture, the shallower the angle at which the light waves converge on the film, so the circles of confusion on either side of the film plane are smaller. In effect, this means that more of the subject, in depth, appears sharp. A large aperture opening, such as that in a long focus or very fast lens, gives little depth of field.

Finally, aperture affects the quality of the image. As most of the aberrations already described come from the edges of the lens, there is an obvious solution: make the aperture smaller, and so use just the central part of the lens. However, this only improves definition up to a point, because one important fault – diffraction – gets worse with smaller apertures. Any thin edge – in this case the blades of the aperture diaphragm – tends to scatter light passing close to it. Most lenses perform best when the aperture is closed down two or three f stops.

Using a lens successfully depends on reducing flare. Even the latest multi-coated lenses are not completely immune from this fault, and any light shining directly on the front of the lens will tend to soften contrast and generally

f22

weaken the image. The sun is normally the chief culprit, and the most basic precaution is to shade the lens from its direct rays. However, any bright area outside the frame of the picture is liable to cause some flare, so that the best control of all is to fit a lens shade that masks right down to the edges of the image. Standard lens hoods are circular and although useful are not as efficient as adjustable professional lens shades. Some lens shades double as filter holders, but there is a risk that any filter in front of the lens may add to flare, particularly if it is not spotlessly clean or, in the case of thin gelatin filters, if it buckles. On view cameras, filters are best placed behind the lens, inside the body.

f16

f32

f45

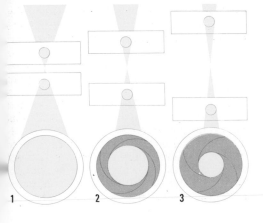

1   2   3

Left From whatever point on the subject that a lens is focused on, the sharpness of the image decreases towards the camera, and away from it. The limits to sharpness are set by the resolving power of the human eye, to which a very small circle will appear as a point. When a lens is used at full aperture *(1)*, the cones of light on either side of the point of focus broaden very steeply; as a result, the smallest circles that the eye interprets as sharp points lie very close together, and the depth of field is, as a result, shallow. With the same lens stopped down, however *(2)*, the cones of light are narrow, the circles more widely spread, and the depth of field greater. Maximum depth of field is achieved with the minimum aperture *(3)*.

Above In this sequence of photographs, taken with a 300 mm lens on a Sinar view camera, the lens was progressively stopped down from f5.6 (its maximum aperture) to f45 (its minimum). At f5.6, the depth of field at this distance measures only 1 inch (2.5 cm), less than the width of a single square. At the other end of the scale, at f45, the depth of field extends from the front to the back of the chessboard, a depth of 18 inches (45 cm). In practical use, a full depth of field is often, but by no means always, desirable – shallow depth of field can be used to emphasize one limited part of the subject.

67

FOCAL LENGTH

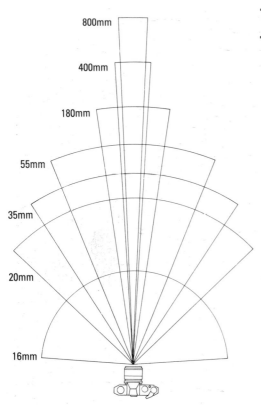

For any particular film format, the focal length of the lens determines the angle of view for the image, and therefore the degree of magnification. Generally speaking, when the angle of view is about the same as the diagonal of the film frame – that is, the maximum distance across the image – then the angle of view is considered "normal", as is the perspective. For a 35 mm camera this would be 43 mm (although by convention, 50 mm is usually sold as the standard focal length), and for the 2¼ x 2¼ inch (6 x 6 cm) format, 80 mm. However, the whole concept of a standard lens is a convention, simply because the eye and brain do not perceive images as framed photographs.

The human eye can resolve a sharp image over an angle of slightly less than 2° without moving, although the whole field of vision is a blurry oval with an ill-defined edge covering an angle somewhere between 180° and 240°. The eye sees by scanning a scene rapidly, focusing on points of interest, from which the brain builds up a composite image. So, while an angle of view of 40° to 50° is, in practice, a fair approximation of a normal view, there are strong arguments for the "normality" of both short and long focal lengths as well. For instance, a 20 mm lens on a 35 mm camera gives a field of view across the longer side of the photograph of 84°, which is very wide. However, if the picture is reproduced sufficiently large for it to fill the view, as the original scene did, then it appears normal in perspective. Conversely, a 600 mm lens on the same camera gives an angle of less than 4° across the horizontal, yet this comes close to what the eye is capable of paying attention to in detail. It is the frame and the size of a photograph that make discussions of normality in focal length rather artificial – these factors inevitably constrict the way we look at the picture.

Different focal lengths also have some definite characteristics, and the images they produce give a range of associations, some of them subtle. Standard focal lengths exert no great graphic influence over the image; they do not distort obviously, and the perspective is unremarkable. Their optics interfere very little with the content of the shot.

The first and most obvious use of a wide-angle lens is to cover a scene that allows only a close viewpoint. It may be physically impossible to move further back to include the whole of a subject, and, for an interior, a wide field of view is essential to give a clear idea of the form of a room. The other attribute of a wide-angle lens that is directly linked to its short focal length is great depth of field. Even when used

Above An angle of view of about 45° to 50° gives a normal perspective and is generally considered standard. In addition to this, however, a considerable range of lenses offers wider and narrower angles of view for most makes of camera, in particular 35mm. Although some fisheye lenses exceed it, 180° is as wide a coverage as most photographers need, while the 2° angle of view of a 1000mm lens (on a 35mm camera) is the normal limit at the other end of the scale.

Right At one extreme of focal length, the fisheye lens produces images that not only cover very wide angles of view, but also have a pronounced and distinctive curvature – a form of barrel distortion. True fisheye lenses, in fact, give a circular image, and have more scientific than pictorial uses. Most fisheyes, however, like the 16mm lens used for this photograph of one of the space shuttle's rockets, cover the full frame. The angle of view – in this example 180° from corner to corner – makes the fisheye useful for cramped spaces, while the curved distortion can be used to add graphic interest.

Left This selected group of lenses from one 35mm manufacturer is representative of the most popular designs of fixed focal lengths (200mm lenses, not shown here, combine many of the characteristics of a number of such lenses). The 50mm lens is generally considered standard, and is the one most commonly sold with a camera body. The 35mm lens to its left gives a rather broader angle of view, and is frequently used as a general lens, while the 28mm at the far right is unmistakably a wide-angle design, useful for cramped spaces and rapid journalistic work. The 16mm lens is a fisheye modified to give a full-frame view, and can be used to introduce graphic distortion for pictorial effect. The 105mm is a moderate telephoto lens, particularly good for portraits because of its slight flattening effect on perspective. Of the two extreme long-focus lenses, the 1000mm f8 is the more compact in design, using two mirrors to compress the light path, but the heavier 400mm has the very wide maximum aperture of f3.5.

at its maximum aperture, a 20 mm lens can be focused so that everything appears sharp from infinity to less than 6 feet (2 m). By stopping down to f22, the close limit of sharpness can be brought to not much more than 14 inches (35 cm). Because depth of field depends on the focal length rather than on the angle of view, wide-angle lenses for small format cameras give more pronounced results than those for larger formats; in other words, a 50 mm lens on a 2¼ x 2¼ inch (6 x 6 cm) rollfilm camera is the equivalent of a 100 mm lens on a 4 x 5 inch (9 x 12 cm) view camera, but it has better depth of field. This is useful not only for images that need to be sharp overall, but also as a safe-guard when shooting very quickly, when there is no time to study the focus. In news photography, for instance, opportunities may appear only briefly, but by setting the focus in advance so that infinity just remains sharp (this is known as the hyperfocal distance), the camera can be aimed and used in an instant, with a good chance that the subject is in focus. The wide field of view also makes it easy to compose shots quickly.

The effect that a wide-angle lens has on perspective is to make objects close to the camera appear more prominent. This, combined with the great depth of field, makes possible a very distinctive type of wide-angle image – one where a relationship is set up between the near and far components of the scene. It is this strong spatial relationship that tends to involve the viewer in the image.

The pronounced perspective also has another use – the diagonal lines and distortion at the edges can be used to strengthen the graphic composition of a photograph. This in turn can be used to bring visual interest to a dull subject.

If the wide-angle lens produces a subjective image, the long-focus lens, at the other end of the scale, gives a cooler, more objective view. Because it magnifies the image, it is a lens that most photographers use at a distance from the subject, and so is a mainstay of candid and wildlife photography, or for any situation where the photographer cannot get close enough. However, because it magnifies the image, it also magnifies many aberrations, and long-focus lenses are costly to correct to the point where they give definition and contrast that is as good as a typical standard lens. Camera shake is also magnified, and even very modern, smaller telephoto and mirror lenses are difficult to use handheld at slow shutter speeds. These problems increase with focal length, and the most powerful lenses, of 600 mm and more, need a solid support. Long-focus lenses for medium and large format cameras are particularly bulky.

Typically, long-focus lenses isolate subjects from their surroundings. The narrow angle of view makes it possible to concentrate on small features from any viewpoint, picking them out from their surroundings. Because the depth of field is shallow, background and foreground are usually blurred and out of focus. In many situations, this limited depth of field is immensely useful for removing distractions that would otherwise interfere with the main point of interest in a shot.

Whereas the perspective of a wide-angle photograph appears stretched, that of a long-focus view is compressed or flattened, so that a scene often appears to be built up from a stack of two-dimensional planes. Size relationships between objects in the shot are truer; for example, mountains on the horizon appear larger in relation to the foreground and middle dis-

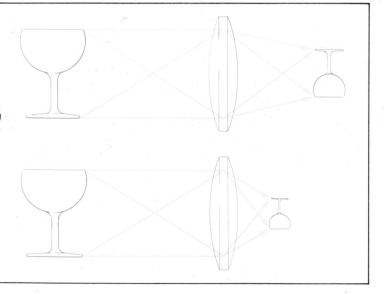

Focal length
Although the actual design in modern lenses is more complex than shown here, the essential difference between focal lengths is in the degree to which the image-forming rays of light are bent. The curvature of the long-focus lens surfaces *(top)* are relatively gentle, with the result that the image of the wine glass is brought to a focus of a greater distance behind the lens than would be the case with a shorter focal length. Consequently, the image is magnified. The short-focus lens, by contrast, is curved more sharply, and focuses the image at a shorter distance, giving a compressed, wide-angle view *(bottom)*.

Above At the other end of the range of focal lengths from the fisheye, the long-focus lens imposes a completely different graphic character on its images. Perspective is compressed, so that the planes of the image often appear to be squeezed together, with the background appearing to loom over closer subjects. With massed subjects, such as this Indian waterfront, the compression of perspective can be used to enhance the crowded sensation.

tance, as indeed they are. This flattened perspective can also be put to good use in portraits. Because we are especially sensitive to the proportions of a face, the slight distortion given by a wide-angle lens – or even by a standard lens used in close-up – tends to look unattractive, with the nose in particular appearing too large. A long-focus lens removes this effect and gives more pleasing proportions.

One answer to the problem of carrying a number of different focal lengths is to use a zoom lens, which has a variable focal length over a range. The advantages are obvious enough – combining several lenses into one for convenience and weight, and very fine control over framing and composition – but there are some disadvantages. Although lighter and less bulky than the group of fixed focal lenses it substitutes, a zoom lens is still heavier and less agile in use, and the maximum aperture is not as wide. Also, most photographers are quite capable of making a good composition with whatever fixed focal length lens they have to hand, and the ability to adjust the frame to an infinite degree is, in most situations, not a very practical advantage. Whether to use zoom lenses or regular ones is largely a matter of personal taste.

Right One of the classic uses of the wide-angle lens is to show a subject in its setting, and therefore related to its surroundings rather than isolated from them. In portraiture, this can be an important role when the photographer wishes to add dimension to the image. Here, J.R.R. Tolkein, Oxford professor and author of the widely read *Lord of the Rings*, is seated among the gnarled roots and trunks of an old woodland. The photographer, Lord Snowdon, has managed to convey some of the qualities of this writer's work without making an obvious statement. Several features of wide-angle imagery have been put to deliberate use – the angle of view and great depth of field places the subject firmly in the landscape, while the low viewpoint, with the camera tilted up, makes the trees tower over the writer, dominating the composition. This is essentially a journalistic approach to portraiture, enhancing the content of the photograph by adding outside elements, and for this the wide-angle lens is well suited.

Right By compressing perspective, a long-focus lens can be used to impose valuable graphic control on an image. A diagonal view of any row of similar or identical subjects, such as these gilded Buddhas in a Bangkok temple, can be made to take on an almost two-dimensional appearance, with virtually all sense of depth removed from the overlapping figures. The effect is strengthened by using a small aperture, to make the most of the limited depth of field of a long-focus lens.

Above and right These two photographs, both taken from exactly the same position, show the ability of a long-focus lens to isolate detail from its surroundings – the opposite quality of that associated with short-focal length, wide-angle lenses. An overall view of this ornate chapel, taken with a 20mm lens on a 35mm camera, reveals pattern and the general design. A closeup of the carving, on the other hand, taken with a 400mm lens, is an entirely different image, focusing attention on an individual piece of work.

The difference in magnification is in the order of 20 times. Although there were very few positions from which the wide-angle photograph could be taken for reasons of symmetry, the telephoto lens offered a wide choice of images, making it possible to refine the composition carefully.

Left Because the perspective effect, which in a wide-angle view causes foreground objects to have exaggerated importance, is severely reduced with a very long focal length lens, elements of the picture at different distances from the camera appear in truer proportions. This has been used here to bring together, in one composition, bank signs and a statue in the City of London. The greatest problem with this technique is achieving sufficient depth of field to render everything sharp; the longer the focal length, the shallower the depth of field at any given aperture, and here, at f32, the depth of field of a 400mm lens has been used to its limit.

CLOSE-UP

ost photographs are taken at distances ranging from a few feet in front of the camera to infinity, and the optics of most lenses are designed to perform best in these conditions. The close-focusing limit of most lenses (which is rarely less than 3 feet (1m), and considerably more in the case of long-focus lenses) is a practical one, for at very short distances image quality deteriorates. For closeup photography, additional equipment and some special techniques are needed. Despite the technical problems, however, it is a popular field, partly because of the possibilities of new and unusual images at a scale that is unfamiliar to the human eye, and partly because the size of subject and close working distance gives the photographer greater control.

Closeup images are normally described in terms of their magnification or reproduction ratio. These are both ways of relating the size of the image to the size of the object: if the image in the photograph is half the size of the original, then the magnification is 0.5x and the reproduction ratio one to two. The reproduction ratio in most photography is less than one to seven, so that closeup photography is generally considered to begin at this point. Beyond life-size reproduction (one to one), the techniques alter

slightly and the term used is photomacrography, while beyond about 20 to one camera optics are not really suitable, and a microscope must be used.

For limited closeup work at a low magnification (up to about one-quarter the size of the original subject), simple meniscus lenses can be fitted to the front of the camera's standard lens. Known as supplementary closeup lenses, they are available in a number of different strengths, measured in diopters, and work on the principle of bringing the point of focus closer. For instance, a +1 diopter, which is quite weak, has a focal length of 3 feet (1m), so that if placed in front of the camera lens (itself focused at infinity), will bring the focus down to 3 feet (1m), to give a reproduction ratio of one to 20. Supplementary lenses are available in sets, normally up to +4 diopters, and can be added together for greater magnification. However, image quality deteriorates noticeably with the stronger diopters. The great advantage of these lenses is that they are simple to use and need no special exposure calculations.

For most closeup and macro work, however, the standard technique is to increase the distance between lens and film. With a view camera no additional equipment is needed, as this is the normal method of focusing – for

greater magnification, only a longer set of bellows is necessary. With other cameras, however, an extension must be fitted between the lens and the body. This extension can be rigid, in the form of rings and tubes, or adjustable, in the form of a bellows. All do essentially the same job, although the type of work and conditions may favour one or the other. For the studio, a bellows generally offers the greatest control and flexibility; some models allow swing and shift movements similar to the movements of a view camera, and this can be very useful in maximizing sharpness. In the field, however, the relative fragility and awkwardness of bellows can be a hindrance, and extension tubes are often more convenient. The better tubes and rings also do not affect the operation of fully automatic diaphragms, unlike most bellows, with which the aperture must be stopped down manually.

Macro lenses are designed for optimum performance at close working distances, and models such as the Micro-Nikkor allow much closer focusing than normal (to give a reproduction ratio of one to two unaided). Other macro lenses, such as the Zeiss Luminar series, are designed specifically for use attached to bellows, and so have no focusing mount of their own. Enlarging lenses, which are designed to

Right The equipment illustrated here, designed for a 35mm SLR, permits closeup and photomacrography up to the magnification at which the optics of microscopy would be a better choice. The supplementary lenses *(below left)* are uncomplicated attachments suitable for up to 0.25 x magnification, but a more convenient alternative is a close-focusing macro lens, which can reach 0.5 x magnification, yet can also serve as a standard lens. For much higher magnifications, the choice lies between an adjustable bellows attachment or a set of fixed extension rings. Both fit between camera body and lens, and vary only in ease of use; generally, bellows are more useful in a studio, while extension rings are particularly suitable on location.

Left One of the special advantages of closeup photography is that its subject matter is frequently interesting simply because it is too small to be noticed under normal circumstances. Insects, for example, offer a wealth of visual material – this white, feathery mass is, in fact, a liana in a southeast Asian rainforest covered with young homoptera, so tightly packed that they are almost indistinguishable from one another.

Left In field conditions, some mechanical ingenuity is often needed. Many closeup subjects, such as flowers, are at ground level, and too low for a conventional tripod; when a long exposure (needed for the small apertures normally used on closeup work) requires a solid camera support, one common technique is to reverse the tripod's column, to hang the camera upside-down.

Above An alternative to a time exposure is to use a portable flash unit – virtually indispensable for photographing small, active subjects, such as insects, at short distances. It is usually best to mount the flash close to the front of the lens, while an angled mirror, or second flash, can be used to fill in hard shadows.

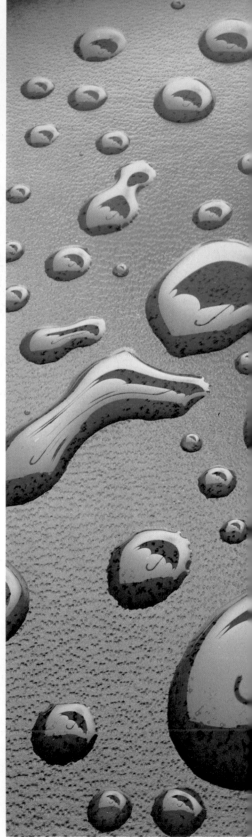

Above For photographing flowers and plants, such as the foxgloves on the opposite page, a tripod is essential unless flash lighting is used. Even with the camera steady for a time exposure, the flower must also be kept still to avoid a blurred image. An umbrella, or even a sheet of plastic, can be used as a windbreak.

magnify the image from a negative up to print size, provide an alternative.

When regular lenses are used at magnifications greater than life-size, the image quality can be improved by reversing them. Special adaptor mounts are available for this.

The major technical problem in closeup work is calculating the increase in exposure; extending the lens forwards reduces the amount of light reaching the film. When using a through-the-lens meter in continuous light, the reading automatically compensates for this, but in other situations, with flash lighting or when only a handheld meter is available, adjustments need to be made. The increase in exposure is proportional to the extension and to the magnification and reproduction ratio, so that tables and formulae provide a straightforward, if sometimes laborious, means of calculation.

A second area that demands great care is depth of field, which is shallower at greater magnifications. Practically, this means that it is often difficult to keep even the important parts of a closeup image in sharp focus. A small aperture is often essential, even though this may weaken the image through diffraction. The depth of field can, in theory, be checked by stopping the lens down to its working aperture and then closely examining the view, but at considerable extensions there is usually too little light to be able to judge sharpness effec-

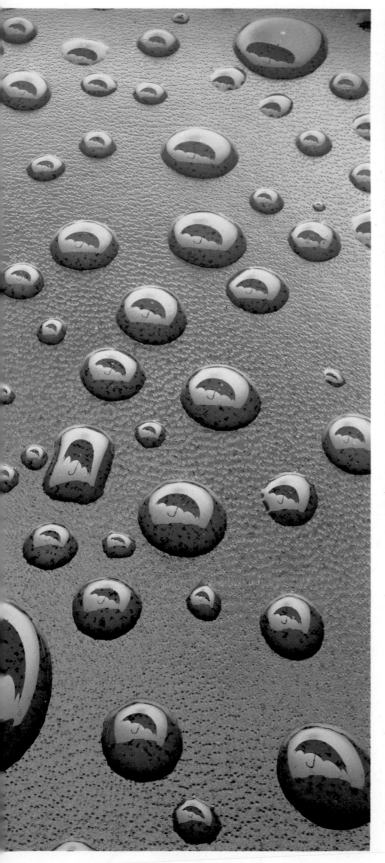

Three different approaches to closeup photography give an indication of the visual variety at these scales. The photograph of the tropical grasshopper *(far left)* was taken at night, using a macro lens set at its greatest magnification – 0.5 x. With subjects that are wary, and easily disturbed, it is not usually possible to take the time that most closeup photographs demand, and the most efficient technique on location is to standardize the position and setting of the lighting.

With flowers, on the other hand, provided that they can be sheltered from wind, it is normally possible, and often better, to use existing daylight, perhaps helped slightly with reflectors. More care can be taken with composition than with subjects that are likely to jump out of frame at any moment. These foxgloves *(above)* were photographed with a long-focus macro lens to flatten the perspective, at a small aperture to achieve reasonable depth of field.

In studio closeup photography, even more control is possible. In the main photograph *(left)*, the unfamiliar scale was used to illustrate a magazine article on rain – the raindrops themselves, reflecting an umbrella (actually, a card cut-out against a large studio light), are the subjects. By offering new visual opportunities, closeup photography lends itself to illustrative use.

tively. Depth of field tables are a more reliable, but painstaking, method. In order to make as much use as possible of what depth of field exists, closeup subjects often need to be positioned carefully. The swings or tilts of a good bellows can also be used to arrange the plane of sharp focus so that it coincides with the plane of the subject.

SUPPORTS

Although most cameras are designed for handheld use, a support such as a tripod has two important functions. One is to allow exposures at slow shutter speeds, which might be necessary because of dim light, slow film, a small lens aperture, or a combination of all these factors. The other is to permit careful composition, and to hold it while adjustments are made. Using a camera support has a radical effect on the way a photographer works, replacing freedom with precision. It encourages the photographer to plan and visualize a photograph before shooting it, and concentrates attention on the composition.

Supports vary in size and weight according to the format of camera and how portable they must be. Rigidity normally calls for bulk. In a large studio there are few restrictions on the size of tripod or camera stand – generally speaking, the larger the better. On location, however, a tripod has to be carried, and this means that some compromise must be made between giving support and being portable.

Tripod heads are often sold separately, but should be as sturdy as the tripods to which they are attached. The movements of pan-and-tilt heads are separated to allow adjustments in one direction at a time, while ball-and-socket heads give free movement in all directions and are quicker to use.

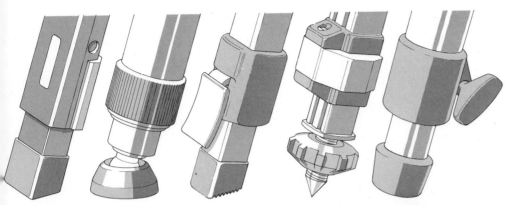

Left The rigidity of a tripod is strongly affected by the efficiency of the feet at gripping the floor or ground. For indoor use, rubber or plastic compound feet are usual, sometimes with ribbed "soles" to prevent slipping on a smooth floor. For outdoor use, where damage to the ground does not matter, a spike gives a very good lock.

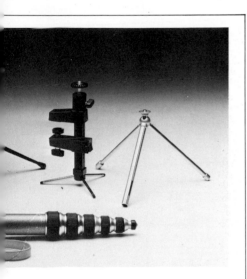

Left From a lightweight model that can be strapped to the side of a shoulder bag to a stand that is, by its size and bulk, virtually a studio fixture, camera supports are available in a wide range to suit different fields of photography.
The two supports at the left are studio models, intended for use on a level surface, and where portability is unnecessary. The large camera stand, with a counterbalanced arm and head on a massive column that is supported on a wheeled base, is, in many ways, the ideal studio support, being solid and with a wide range of adjustments. It is, however, heavy and costly. The second support is a large-scale tripod, its legs locked into a dolly, which adds to the stability and

allows rapid movement around the studio floor. The remaining tripods, in diminishing size, have essentially similar features – extendable, telescoping legs and a rising centre column. The third tripod from the right is fitted with a horizontal arm instead of a regular head: this is for photographs taken vertically downwards, such as copyshots, to avoid having tripod legs in the picture.

Inset This group of supports are all designed to be carried in a shoulder bag, or even in a pocket. The four pocket tripods can be used for low-level photography, or for regular work if a higher surface can be found. The monopod is intended as a steadying aid, and is useful for mobile work with long, heavy lenses.

Above The two most common designs of tripod head use, respectively, ball-and-socket and pan-and-tilt movement. Both are nearly always, as in this selection of heads from a major French manufacturer, locked by friction. Ball-and-socket heads allow rapid adjustment, but are relatively difficult to position with great accuracy. Pan-and-tilt heads separate the axes of movement, so that the direction of view can be altered more precisely.

CHAPTER 2

LIGHT AND FILM

Many substances react to light by changing chemically. Paintings and cloth fade, the effect of sunlight on chlorophyll makes plants grow and even our own skin darkens. In photography, the reacting chemical must be extremely sensitive, capable of responding in a fraction of a second, and to achieve this, most film emulsions rely on silver halides, which are a combination of silver and either bromine, chlorine or iodine. Other substances have been used in the past, and the high cost of silver means that films may change in the future, but silver halides have proved to be very convenient. Not only do they react to light, but they can be developed – that is to say, once exposed, the small changes can be exaggerated by adding other chemicals.

The principle of photographic film relies on the fact that the many small light-sensitive crystals in its coating react slightly to the light that falls on them; this reaction is then multiplied some thousand million times by development to form a visible image; in the crucial final stage, the image is made permanent by adding a chemical that prevents any further reaction.

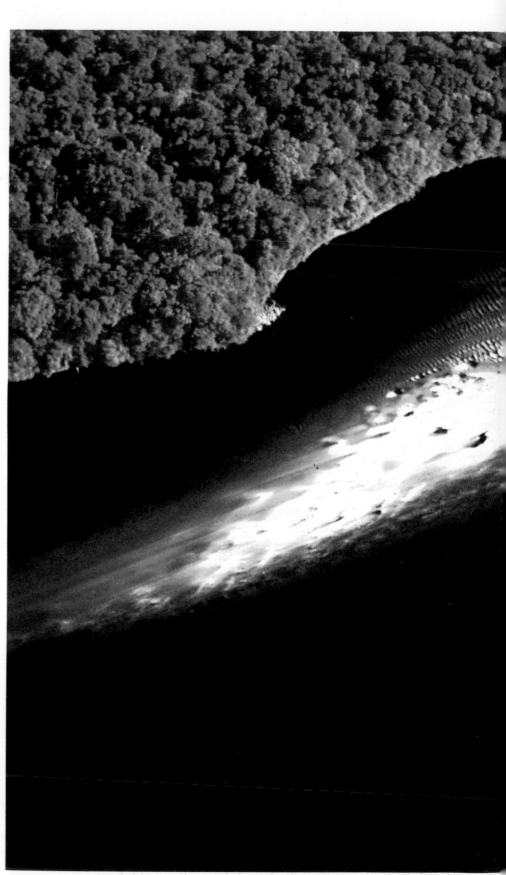

Above and right These two photographs, one a daguerreotype from about 1840 *(above)*, the other a modified-colour infrared aerial transparency, give some measure of the technical progress in recording photographic images that has taken place in slightly more than a century. The daguerreotype was the first practical photographic plate to see widespread use, but its images were monochromatic, difficult to view, could not be reproduced, and demanded exposure times too long for moving subjects. By contrast, colour photography now dominates the field, and by varying the dye sensitization of emulsions, it is possible to combine images visible to the eye with other regions of the spectrum that we cannot see.

Exactly how this process works depends on the way in which the light strikes the film. The camera lens organizes the light reflected from the subject into an image, but it is the quality of the light that sets the tone of the photograph. Light is as much a photographic material as film, and a successful image depends on selecting, using and controlling light with skill and knowledge. Studio lights depend on the photographer to position them; natural daylight is less tractable, but its variety can be exploited to a surprising degree. Both supply an ingredient that needs to be handled with care.

The earliest photograph, taken by Niépce in 1826, used a substance that hardened rather than darkened when exposed to light, a type of asphalt that was already used in engraving. Coated on a pewter plate, the asphalt was exposed in a camera to a view from Niépce's window. After about eight hours, the asphalt exposed to the bright parts of the scene was so hardened that it resisted the solvent which Niépce then poured over it; the unexposed, dark parts washed away.

Above left This 1848 calotype, taken by the inventor of the process, William Henry Fox Talbot, was printed from a paper negative. While its earlier rival, the daguerreotype, delivered only a single positive image, the calotype, being a negative process, made it possible to print a large number of identical copies; this ability to be reproduced has remained an essential feature of photography ever since.
Left The simplicity of such a straightforward subject as this sailing ship in harbour, photographed by Gustave le Gray in 1855, belies the great practical difficulties in location photography with wet collodion plates. Not the least of these was the long exposure time needed for an emulsion relatively insensitive by modern standards – something evident in this photograph by the apparent stillness of the water (over several seconds, small waves and ripples have coalesced into a mirror-like surface).

Within twelve years, Niépce's partner, Daguerre, had discovered a more sensitive photographic plate. Copper, already coated with silver, was sensitized by exposure to iodine vapour rising from heated iodine crystals. After the picture had been taken, the image, not yet visible, was developed by mercury vapour – a dangerous process with health hazards not fully appreciated at the time. The image was finally fixed with hyposulphite of soda, and the result was a finely detailed, delicate photograph. However, because of its mirror-like finish, it had to be viewed at a particular angle and, being a positive, could not be used to make a quantity of prints. Nevertheless, the exposure time had been reduced from eight hours to between 20 and 30 minutes, and although this was still too long for portraiture, which had to wait for later improvements, photography had become a practical possibility.

The daguerreotype was soon challenged by an alternative process, the calotype, that used

Right The use of celluloid instead of glass as a base for the light-sensitive emulsion, was another step in the direction of convenience, celluloid being lighter, less bulky and unbreakable. Celluloid, and its cellulose and polymer successors, became known simply as film. By 1914, when this photograph of Lady Hazel Lavery was taken by the portrait photographer Emil Hoppé (1878-1972), film sensitivity had been improved to the point when exposure times of only one or two seconds were possible using regular photoflood bulbs.

Left Dry glass plates, which could be stored before use, were so much easier to work with than wet collodion that location scenic photography, such as this view of the Columbia river in Oregon taken in 1867 by Carlton Watkins (1829-1916), ceased to be a major test of stamina and perseverance. Nevertheless, as contact printing remained the method of reproduction, the glass plates needed to be large (this one measured 22 x 18 inch (56 x 46cm)) and remained a considerable logistical problem.

paper instead of a metal plate and was closer to modern films in that it produced a negative image that could be used to make as many positive prints as the photographer wanted. The reproductive capacity made this process an important rival to the daguerreotype, despite the poorer quality of the image. The inventor was the Englishman William Henry Fox Talbot (1800-1877) who, starting, with a high quality writing paper, added coatings of silver nitrate and potassium iodide, followed by a solution of gallic acid and silver nitrate to sensitize the paper. Having made the exposure, the paper was developed in a second application of the gallic acid/silver nitrate solution. Once dry, the paper negative was ready for making contact prints.

The next important step in the progress of emulsions was the invention in 1851 of the collodion process by Frederick Scott Archer (1813-1857). Also known as the wet-plate process, the collodion process quickly replaced other systems because, despite the great inconvenience of preparing the plates, which had to be carried out on the spot just before taking the picture, it allowed exposures of as little as 10 seconds. To achieve this great sensitivity, the photographer had to pour collodion, a solution containing potassium iodide, onto a glass plate, tilt it in different directions until the coating was even, and then quickly dip the plate in a silver nitrate solution. Because the sensitivity was largely lost when the collodion dried, the plate had to be exposed wet, making life very difficult for the photographer on location.

By the 1870s, an emulsion made up of gelatin and silver bromide had been invented as a *dry* substitute for collodion, and soon plates were being mass-produced. Although glass, which is bulky and easily broken, has now been replaced by flexible film, black-and-white emulsion remains basically the same: the light-sensitive crystals, known as grains, are embedded in a layer of gelatin. Film was originally made of celluloid, but has since moved through nitro-cellulose to cellulose acetate to the immensely stable synthetic polymers of today. Whatever its composition, the use of film made it possible to roll up long strips of emulsion, the basis of motion picture film, 35mm film and rollfilm.

The precise sequence of events that follows the exposure of film to light is still not entirely understood. First, light releases photoelectrons and these combine with silver ions to produce silver atoms which form around small specks of impurity scattered throughout each silver halide crystal. At this stage, there is still no visible image on the film, and it takes a chemical developer to produce it. Development blackens the parts of the emulsion that were exposed to light, by reducing the grains of silver halide to metallic silver, which is dark.

Each grain is either developed – that is, blackened – or not; there are no halfway stages of grey. The final result, with a range of tones in the negative, is due to the number of developed grains in any small part of the film: if only a few have been developed, scattered among many developed ones, the tone will be a light grey, but if all have reacted, then the film will be black.

Colour film is a direct descendant of basic black-and-white emulsion. Colour is produced by combining three individual colours from different parts of the spectrum, using a principle which is similar to the way in which we see. Regular colour film uses three layers of basic emulsion, each one filtered so that it responds only to one colour – blue, green, or red. After exposure and development the three layers, whether viewed together as a transparency or projected together to make a print, give the impression of full colour. Development for colour is more involved than black-and-white processing, as the metallic silver, which is black, has to be replaced by coloured dyes. Very recently, the idea of creating a dye "cloud" where the silver grain was located has been used to make a new generation of black-and-white films which do not, at least in their developed form, contain any silver at all.

Right A modern range of professional general-purpose films covers formats from 35mm to 8 x 10 inch (20 x 24cm) sheet film, with different sensitivities to light and balanced for both daylight and photographic tungsten lamps; the end-product is either a transparency or print (the former for graphic reproduction, the latter for direct display). The ways in which these films respond to light can be further altered by placing filters over the lens. These can be used to alter colour balance or spectral response, to polarize the light, or to darken or tint a specific area of the picture.

EXPOSURE METERS

Exposure meters work by converting the responses of a light-sensitive cell into a reading that can be applied directly to the aperture setting of the lens or the speed of the shutter. Whatever the amount of light that falls on the cell, the reading will show how to record it on film as an average tone – a rudimentary but generally workable method of ensuring adequate exposure.

Most cameras now have their own light meter built into the body, capable of measuring the image seen through the viewfinder. In many situations, this provides very accurate readings, since the through-the-lens meter needs no adjustment to compensate for different focal lengths of lens, filters or extensions – it simply measures the light reaching the film. Some of the more advanced models actually take their readings from the film itself at the moment of exposure. Nevertheless, the basic problem remains that an exposure meter can only average the light falling on its cells, and does not discriminate between the importance of different parts of the image. To help correct this, many camera manufacturers bias the reading of through-the-lens meters according to the way that most people use cameras. The reading is usually weighted towards the centre of the view, where most photographers place the main subject of interest, and away from the upper third of the picture, which is frequently occupied by sky.

Handheld meters can be used to take the same type of reflected light readings – that is, measuring the light reflected from the subject – although typically the area from which the reading is taken is broader and less well-defined than the frame of the camera's viewfinder. Some models have attachments that limit the angle of acceptance to correspond to long-focus lenses. Unlike through-the-lens meters, handheld meters can also be used to take incident readings. Here, the meter is aimed at the light source, so that it measures the light falling on the scene and is uninfluenced by any tonal qualities of the subject. A translucent cover, usually in the shape of a dome, is fitted over the meter's cell for this type of reading. Handheld meters, although they take rather longer to use than their through-the-lens counterparts, are more versatile and allow thorough measurements in situations that are likely to pose difficulties, such as unevenly lit interiors.

The most precise readings of all can be made with a spot meter, which measures the reflected light from a precise 1° circle. Using a spot meter is similar in some respects to using a through-the-lens meter with a long-focus lens, but because the measurement is taken from such a small, clearly defined area, it is possible to build up an extremely accurate set of values for any scene. The most advanced spot meters use microprocessors to store and organize information from consecutive readings.

Below The most widely used of all light metering systems, through-the-lens (TTL) metering is virtually a standard fitting for SLR cameras. The principal meter displays, as seen through the viewfinder, are shown here *(left to right)*: matched needle display, where the exposure control is adjusted to align both pointers; centred needle display, in which the needle must be positioned between two indicators to give an average exposure; plus-minus light-emitting diode (LED) display, in which the upper dot, when lit, indicates over-exposure, the middle dot average exposure, and the lower dot under-exposure; LED scale display which shows the aperture setting needed for an average exposure; and liquid crystal display (LCD) which gives shutter speed and aperture information in digital form.

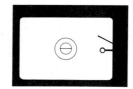

Right In the latest meter designs, traditional moving needle displays are being replaced by light-emitting diodes (used in the flash meter at left) and liquid crystals (in the spotmeter). Liquid crystals have the additional advantage that they can display digital information rapidly, and so can be used with microchips to perform sophisticated exposure calculations.

Above A spot meter, here an Asahi Pentax model, measures the amount of light reflected from a circle of 1° with great precision, and is the metering system of choice when the need for accuracy takes precedence over speed of operation. For more general hand held metering, the Gossen Lunasix, and similar competitive makes, fulfils most needs, and can make both reflected light and incident light readings, as well as being capable of accepting specialized attachments, such as flexible probes and a telephoto lens. The most traditional meter design is that of the Weston, which is relatively unsophisticated but rugged, and operated by self-powered selenium cells, which do not fade.

MEASURING LIGHT

Photography beginners often think that calculating the exposure is a difficult procedure, usually because most camera manufacturers make it seem more complicated than it should, to promote the sales of automatic models. While precise exposure measurement, particularly in unusual lighting conditions, does need care and some experience, the principles are actually quite simple. The sales pitch, however, for cameras that automatically adjust the shutter or aperture (or both) relies on getting across the idea that accurate exposure is rather mysterious.

To begin with, there is no such thing as one "correct" exposure for any given scene. Different exposures, short or long, produce different images, and the object of taking a reading is not to hunt for the perfect combination of shutter speed and aperture, but to produce a photograph that looks the way the photographer wants it to. In other words, the exposure depends not only on the subject of the photograph and the ability of the film to react to light, but also on the taste of the photographer.

In principle, the aim of calculating the exposure is to enable the range of brightness in the scene in front of the camera to be transferred onto film, either as faithfully as possible or according to the photographer's taste. Brightness (luminance, in technical terms) is an absolute quality, can be measured, and is not open to personal interpretation. For example, the

Below Even with an image that has very little contrast, there is no difficulty in calculating the exposure; the choice of setting can usually be based on personal preference. In this photograph, the exposure was deliberately reduced by one stop from the average meter reading, so as to intensify the colour saturation of the transparency. This approach is common among photographers whose work is usually reproduced photomechanically from transparencies, to ensure that the colours of the published image remain strong

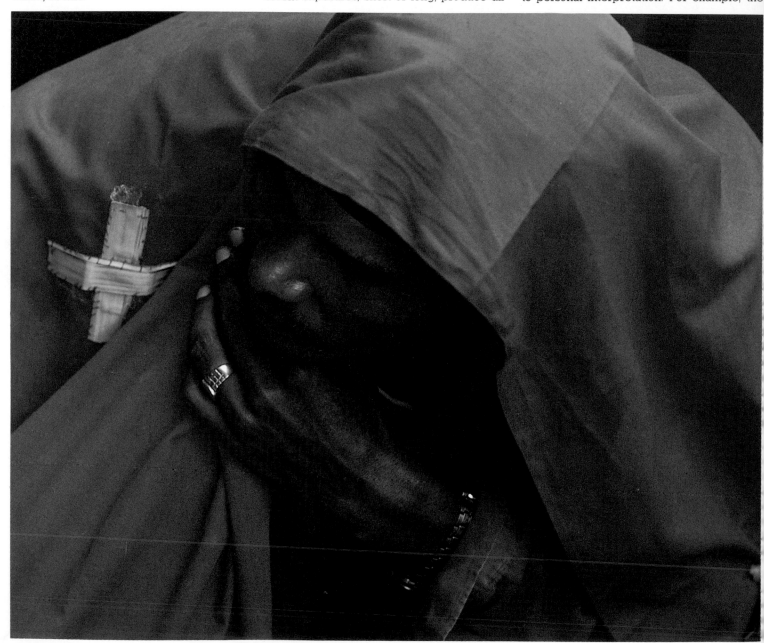

highlights in a well-lit landscape under a bright sun might be the brightest parts of a few clouds, and the darkest tones the shadows under trees and rocks. These two values set the limits for the brightness range; in such a setting the highlights might be as much as 500 times brighter than the deepest shadows. The human eye can adjust rapidly to all kinds of lighting conditions and can accommodate even this great a range without too much difficulty, but not so film. All regular emulsions are less capable than the eye's retina, and cannot record every tone faithfully in a scene like the one just described. In this lies the main exposure problem that most professionals face – film simply cannot cope with high contrast.

cloud highlights: EV14.5 1/60 sec f19

clear sky: EV14 1/30 sec f22

rock shadow: EV9.5 1/30 sec f45

sea: EV13 1/30 sec f16

crevice: EV9.5 1/30 sec f4.5

rock pavement: EV11.5 1/30 sec f9

Right In this scene the lighting conditions were fairly typical; both the general brightness and the level of contrast could have been recorded by any general-purpose film. The measurements in the main photograph are reflected light readings taken with a spotmeter and show, for a film speed of ASA 125, the exposure setting that would be needed to reproduce that particular part of the view as a mid-tone in the photograph. (EV stands for exposure value.) The contrast range, from EV9.5 to EV14.5, is only five stops, so that, on black-and-white film, any exposure between EV11 and EV13 could easily record every detail.

Right This view is an extreme example of the exposure problem that occurs when the contrast between highlight and shadow is very pronounced. The measurements, taken with a spot meter, show that while the darkest part of the interior registers only EV5 on an ASA 125 film, the sky outside is a bright EV15 – a contrast range of ten stops. Even black-and-white negative film has a useful range of only seven stops. In making the exposure, therefore, some detail had to be abandoned. The compromise made in this case was to lose the lightest tones of the sky, and all but a small part of the wooden window frame. The exposure was set at EV11 (½ sec, f32).

1 deepest shadow: EV5
  1/15 sec f1.4

2 sky: EV15 1/60 sec f22

3 hills: EV13.8 1/60 sec f14

4 water: EV14 1/60 sec f16

5 grass: EV11.5 1/60 f7

6 window frame: EV10.5
  1/60 sec f4.5

These considerations mean that using an exposure meter efficiently involves more than just averaging the brightness of the scene in front of the camera to find a middle value. It means checking first whether the film can meet the demands of the photograph. For example, the sunlit landscape mentioned earlier had a brightness range of 500 to one, which is nine stops. Most negative films have a useful range of only seven stops, and colour transparency film, even more widely used, covers only about five stops. As a result, there are many situations where both shadows and highlights cannot be preserved together.

A high contrast scene can be photographed using a middle-range, compromise exposure that would lose the darkest shadow detail and give some washed-out highlights, but would reproduce the middle tone normally. Alternatively, the exposure could be set so that the highlights still showed a hint of detail, but the penalty would then be featureless shadows. A third alternative would be to hold the detail in the shadows, but then the highlights would be grossly overexposed.

Photographers are frequently faced with these alternatives, and tastes vary. You might aim for a literal approach and try to represent the scene as faithfully as possible, or you might aim for a high contrast effect: some photographers come to prefer this approach, the English photographer Bill Brandt (b. 1905) being a notable example. Again, personal preference plays a large part in what is considered an acceptable *average* exposure – generally dark (low-key) or light (high-key).

The general procedure is first to evaluate the level and range of brightness in the scene, next compare this with the film, and finally, if the two are not similar, make the necessary compromise. This procedure, however, depends on having plenty of time to make the measurements, and also on having the ideal exposure meter for the situation. In reality, such a detailed approach may be impractical or unnecessary. If you are familiar with your materials and with the lighting situation, you can make an intuitive assessment; indeed, with photography that demands quick reactions, this is the *only* way to judge exposure. In any case, many subjects have such low contrast that an average reading will do.

Above To conceal the severity of the contrast, some printing controls were used for the main photograph opposite. The two photographs above were exposed for the brightest *(left)* and darkest *(right)* parts, to give some idea of the very different exposures that would be needed to show the interior and exterior elements of this scene. Neither photograph is satisfactory.

NATURAL LIGHT

Below **Below** By photographing in the direction of a low sun, contrast is dramatically increased, often giving good graphic possibilities. In this type of situation, there is usually a wider choice of exposure than with the frontal lighting in the photograph at right; by exposing for the highlights in the sky, the Parthenon of the Acropolis in Athens has been treated as a silhouette. Here, a hidden advantage of this darker exposure is that the scaffolding covering part of the building can no longer be seen.

Most photographs are taken by natural light, which has one source, the sun. Filtered, diffused or reflected by clouds, haze, the wall of a building or a window, sunlight gives an exceptional variety of lighting conditions, but it is often difficult to predict. The main control that a photographer has over sunlight is simply waiting, but it is important to know the best use to make of a particular condition and what to expect when the weather is changing, in order to treat sunlight as a true photographic ingredient.

Like all light sources, the sun has intensity, colour and direction. It is so distant that its intensity anywhere on earth, and at any time of the year, is more or less the same. Any differences in its strength come from other causes, such as weather conditions or its elevation above the horizon. With no more than a clear sky to block its rays, a high sun around midday is strong enough to need an exposure of about 1/250 second at f11 with ASA 125 film. (There are more precise ways of measuring the strength of sunlight, but they have little relevance to practical photography.)

The colour of sunlight is constant too, and appears to change only because of the atmosphere. Raw sunlight is white – in other words, it appears colourless to our eyes because we have evolved to see by it. The whiteness of sunlight can be measured as "colour temperature" on a scale that runs from deep red to intense blue. Basically, anything that is heated sufficiently begins to glow, and its colour depends on the temperature. The colour can also be affected by the object's chemical composition, but ignoring this, the precise shade of red, orange, yellow, white or blue (as the heat increases) can be pinpointed just by knowing the temperature. The sun at midday in middle latitudes has a colour temperature of 5400° measured on the Kelvin scale (similar to Celsius, but starting at absolute zero), and this is the accepted standard for white light.

Thirdly, the direction of the sun is, at least from our point of view, changing steadily all the time with the season and the time of day. At its highest, in the tropics, it can be directly overhead. Direction also depends on the relative positions of camera and subject.

The wide variety of natural light comes mainly from changes in the weather and atmosphere, which filter the sunlight in various ways. Even the clearest sky scatters some light, and the wavelengths that are affected the most are the short ones. Ultraviolet light is the first to be filtered, an important factor in photography as film is more sensitive to ultraviolet than the eye. At high altitudes – on mountains and from aircraft – colour photographs have a distinct blue cast, and haze is prominent in distant views. Even visible blue light is normally scattered by particles in the atmosphere (molecules, dust, water droplets), and it is for this reason that a clear sky appears blue. A low sun, on the other hand, appears reddish, as some of the blue

Below A setting sun almost directly behind the camera gives not only warmth to this scene in rural Thailand, but also saturated colours. Because the lighting is along the lens axis, there are no pronounced shadows; as a result, the tonal difference between the bright woodwork of the temple and the dark clouds behind is important in creating contrast.

Above With a subject that is already inherently warm in colour, such as these red sandstone formations in Arches National Park, Utah, a low sun enriches the colour. The contrast in this photograph has also been strengthened by positioning the camera so that the rocks are cross-lit, with deep shadows, and by using a polarizing filter to darken the blue sky.

Left Even between direct and indirect sunlight, such as on a day when scattered, moving clouds cast intermittent shadows, the quality of lighting changes significantly. Under cloud, sunlight is diffused, so that objects are lit evenly and do not have definite shadows. As a result, the image tends to be simpler than when the same scene is lit by a direct sun, which brings hard-edged shadows, a high contrast, and more variety of tone and colour. Compared next to each other, these two images of a water lily also show the lower – that is, warmer – colour temperature of direct sunlight.

Above Fog rolling off a dark lava escarpment dramatizes the already unusual rock formations. Under these conditions, timing is the essential ingredient, for the shifting clouds alternately hide and reveal different elements of the landscape, sometimes changing its appearance in a matter of seconds. In a situation such as this, it may be necessary to take several exposures. Although there was no guarantee that the fog would form in exactly the right way, the photograph shown here was the image the photographer intended, with the rock pillar given prominence by the layer of fog behind. An additional bonus was the scalloped formation of high clouds, which gave balance and interest to the top of the picture. (These were emphasized by printing-in during enlargement.)

wavelengths are held back by the scattering.

From clear sky to heavy cloud and fog, there is a full range of light diffusion. The more the light is diffused, the larger the light source, the lower the contrast and the dimmer the light. A thin haze of dust particles or pollution spreads the light very slightly, lightening shadows a little and softening their edges. A high layer of cloud does this even more, while a thick low cloud blanket from horizon to horizon diffuses the light so completely that there are no distinguishable shadows and it is impossible to tell the direction of the sun. The most diffuse of all natural light conditions is fog, which completely envelops its subjects.

As well as being diffused, sunlight is also reflected. The scattering that gives a blue sky is a form of reflection, and is immediately apparent in a photograph taken in the shade on a

clear sunny day – there is a pronounced blue cast on colour film. Clouds themselves are efficient reflectors, provided there is sufficient clear sky for the sun to shine through; with a large white cloud bank along one horizon, shadows are noticeably weaker. Bright surfaces on the ground also add to the illumination, and on snow or sand, an extra exposure of at least one stop may be needed.

No condition actually prevents photography, although really bad weather may make it uncomfortable. Each type of natural light has its good points and suits at least one kind of subject well. Even dull, overcast weather has a redeeming feature: with no highlights and no pronounced shadows, colours appear well-saturated. However, there are certain lighting conditions to which photographers have a particular attachment: allowing for differences in

Left Summer morning mist along the banks of a slow flowing river diffuses and softens the light to give pastel colours and a gentle tonal range. In contrast to the photograph opposite, the appeal of which lies in the impression of swirling and shifting fog, the evenly spread mist here envelops the subject and imparts a motionless quality. The pastoral subjects – a pollarded tree and wild turnip flowers – suit the quiet and delicate lighting conditions.

Right After sunset, the colour temperature rises dramatically, particularly if the sky is cloudless. With the sun below the horizon, all the lighting is indirect, reflected from atmospheric particles; as these scatter the short, blue wavelengths more than any other, a clear sky appears blue. Here, the white facade of a Connecticut Congregationalist church is a perfect neutral reflector for the blue twilight, and only the spire, catching a faint warmer glow from the west, gives a slightly different accent of colour. The eye tends to adjust to gradual changes in colour balance and so we remember scenes like this as more neutral in colour than they really are. To have corrected the blue cast with a colour balancing filter would have been to lose one of the important ingredients of this photograph.

Left and below
Photographing in the direction of twilight produces, to a greater or lesser extent, silhouetted images, as these two photographs show. One of the practical advantages of this is that such scenes usually benefit from less rather than more exposure, making hand held photography possible under low-light conditions. In making this kind of use of twilight, it is important to choose subjects with obvious, or interesting, outlines. Either the sky, which normally has a smoothly graduated tone when the sun is below the horizon, or its reflection in water, make a good background for silhouettes.

taste, subject matter and style, these have consistently given the opportunity for interesting images.

One of the most favoured is a low sun, either in the early morning or late afternoon. Its notable advantages are that it reveals texture in landscapes, efficiently lights tall objects such as trees and buildings, and is warm in colour. In addition, a fact that is not so often appreciated, low sun offers the greatest variety of lighting direction at a single time – backlighting for silhouettes, sidelighting for a pattern of shadows, and frontal lighting for rich colours are all possible. Although in most parts of the world a low sun can hardly be called a *reliable* light (clouds near the horizon commonly obscure it), it is usually interesting and efficient. Many photographers plan their shooting early or late to take advantage of it, and it is used frequently in professional location photography, where the subject has already been chosen, and the only major variable is the lighting.

A more unusual time of day is when the sun is below the horizon. Twilight, despite all the inconvenience of being short-lived and dark, offers some of the most interesting and graphic

Unpredictable light
Stormy weather conditions have the advantage of unpredictability, so that on the rare occasions when the sky clears, and the sun breaks through, the visual effect is often powerful. Such conditions can hardly ever be planned for, and usually call for opportunistic shooting, reacting quickly to the situation as it occurs. The short-lived rainbow *(above)* is a typical example – an unexpected break in a day-long rainstorm. Because the scene may last for only a few seconds, it is normally better to make the best composition from the existing camera position rather than risk losing the shot by searching for a different viewpoint.
In the case of the broken sunlight across the north walls of the Grand Canyon *(top)*, the vast scale of the view was an advantage: the sunlit patch took several minutes to move across the rim, and could be followed easily with a long focus lens. For the photograph of the Zapotec ruins at Monte Alban in Mexco *(right)*, the local weather conditions were such – a rapid early morning build-up of clouds over the mountain-rimmed basin – that there was a reasonable chance of this particular play of light occurring, it took, however, three days of waiting to capture it on film.

conditions for outdoor photography. For silhouettes it is practically unrivalled and this makes it useful for constructing abstract images. Because the light level is low, twilight can readily be combined with all kinds of artificial lighting – car headlamps, street lights, or lit interiors. In fact, to show the effect of nighttime in an outdoor scene, twilight is nearly always better than complete darkness, as it holds the outlines of buildings, trees and horizon. When there are no clouds, the sky close to the horizon is a broad, even tone, graduating smoothly to darkness above; with any subject that has a reflective surface – a lake, river or even a car – this is attractive, uncomplicated lighting.

The most unpredictable of all natural light – and so potentially the most exciting – is when the sun breaks briefly through clouds in a stormy sky. Its unexpectedness nearly always brings drama to a landscape, and the fact that the opportunity is a rare one gives a special and original quality to such photographs. The weather conditions in a storm are usually interesting in themselves, and the sudden appearance of the sun creates a strong contrast of colour and tone, and sometimes even a rainbow.

By contrast, the light from a large window that faces away from the sun is supremely consistent, at least for black-and-white photography. The balance of diffuse and directional qualities gives a broad light with soft-edged shadows, particularly effective for portraits. Many photographers, among them Irving Penn and Lord Snowdon, have used it extensively. It is the breadth of the window area that gives the special quality to what is often called northlight, and this is difficult to reproduce with artificial lighting. With colour film, however, this type of light has the disadvantage of giving a neutral balance only when the sky is cloudy; a blue sky gives a noticeable cast, and correcting it with filters is inconvenient.

Northlight gives such fine results because it is partly diffuse. The most strongly diffuse of all natural light – so strongly diffuse that it is shadowless – occurs in mist or fog conditions. The light is reflected from all sides and envelops the subject, but at the same time obscures the background. Mist can be strongly atmospheric and even mysterious. Depending on how dense the mist is, a subject in the foreground can be isolated and the scene simplified almost to the point of abstraction.

Above The two sisters in this portrait have been posed delicately and intriguingly: the younger seems wise and slightly forbidding, the elder protective yet more innocent. Their relationship is revealed by the northlighting which also accentuates their fine features. The outlines between the two girls are soft-edged, sometimes non-existent. The portrait was taken by Jean Harvey using a Nikon F2 with a 135mm lens.

Left *Quentin Crisp.* This portrait was captured ''almost by accident'' by Jean Harvey using a Nikon F2 with a 28 mm lens. Mr Crisp had been posing for photographs in his own flat, and relaxing for a moment he was caught on film in an ''unconsciously symbolic'' position. Under studio lights, in a studied pose, his sense of isolation and detachment would not have been natural. The mirror image accentuates his isolation: it is as if he does not exist in the ordinary world, almost as if he has been framed and discarded, an unimportant embellishment in his own room. More space is given in the picture to the bare wall and the surrounding squalor than to him. It is a poignant portrait, particularly revealing because it was unconsidered.

AVAILABLE LIGHT

Between natural daylight and the lamps and flash units designed especially for photography is a range of artificial lighting for which no regular films are balanced. Interiors, streets and public places are all lit with lamps that are rarely ideal for taking pictures, not least because they usually give a strong colour cast on colour film. Tungsten, fluorescent and vapour discharge lamps are the most common of these, and each emits light with a distinct colour – tones of orange, green, yellow or blue.

Mainly because our eyes adjust easily and naturally to a wide range of conditions, lighting that is quite different from sunlight can still

Above A rocket ride at Disneyworld in Florida acquires a surreal aspect from a time exposure of one second, which records the moving tungsten lights as circular streaks. Combining the last traces of deep blue twilight with the yellowish cast of the available tungsten illumination gives the image a strong colour contrast.

Right Without correcting the balance of colour temperature, regular daylight film was used for this Hong Kong night market scene lit by domestic tungsten lamps; the result is a distinct orange cast suffusing the baskets of seafood. Unless the purpose of the photograph is to document the colours of its subject accurately (as might be the case with a commercial still life), colour correction is essentially a subjective decision.

Left In a broad night view of a city, there is never one dominant source of artificial lighting, and the clarity of the image normally depends on the mosaic effect of large numbers of point sources of light. This photograph of Hong Kong and Kowloon from Victoria Peak contains every type of available lighting that photographers normally encounter – green fluorescent and mercury vapour lamps, yellow sodium vapour, yellow-orange tungsten from car lights and apartment windows, and even coloured fluorescent display lighting. Because no single source is more important than the others, problems of colour correction are irrelevant. By timing the shot so that a slight trace of residual daylight remains, extra definition is given to the buildings.

Right The blue-green appearance of these fluorescent-lit alcoves in the underground Salt Cathedral at Zipaquira, near Bogota, was only partly neutralized by using a mild red filter, so that some colour remained to offset the orange glow of a single tungsten lamp.
Below In this scene, lit principally by mercury vapour lamps, the subject – Jai-Alai players at the Miami Fronton – called for as much correction as possible (flesh tones rarely appear satisfactorily under coloured lighting). A cc40 red filter was used, and although this did not fully neutralize the blue-green cast, particularly as there was an admixture of yellowish tungsten lighting, the result is adequately balanced. Practically, when faced with awkward artificial lighting, it may be impossible accurately to determine the best filtration, so that either a range of filters must be used (if the subject is static and allows time for several exposures), or the photographer must trust to experience and hope that one filtration will be satisfactory.
Below right Most available light situations, particularly outdoors, are difficult to assess for correct exposure. This view of London's Tower Bridge is typical: the floodlit part of the bridge, and the moon, are the important elements in the photograph, yet they occupy only a small area of the picture; any averaging light meter would indicate gross over exposure. One answer is to use a spot meter. Another solution, used here, is to make a spot reading of the building with the camera's TTL meter before composing the shot.

Above In another example of how the pronounced colour cast of vapour discharge illumination can be used to advantage instead of being treated as a problem, the green fluorescent lamps lighting this South American village plaza were used for their colour contrast with the violet dawn sky. Opposed colours in an image introduce a visual balance.

Left The graphic interest of much modern urban architecture can often be enhanced by using available lighting at dusk, as the street and building lights frequently help to abstract the image. This is particularly true if moving lights are allowed to record as streaks, by mounting the camera on a tripod and using a time exposure.

Right Fireworks are an incandescent source of light, and although it is difficult to predict the results, displays can be photographed effectively with a time exposure. Because they burn as point sources of light, exposure is not critical: by leaving the camera shutter open, the burning showers create distinctive, though unpredictable, patterns – a form of streak photography. The most difficult problem is deciding where to aim the camera, setting it up on a tripod in advance. This photograph, taken with a long-focus lens so as to fill the frame with the display, was exposed for about five seconds at f5.6, using ASA 64 daylight film.

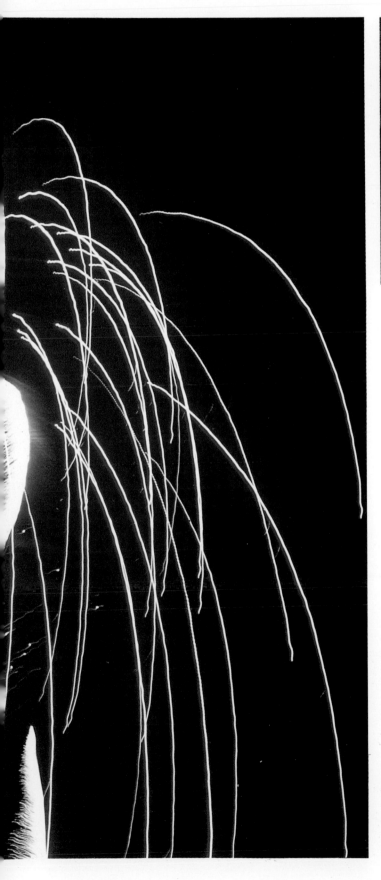

appear normal and "white". However, film does not adapt; it simply records light faithfully according to the way it is made, and on a colour film that is balanced for daylight, the illumination from a domestic tungsten lamp turns out orange. The lower the wattage or voltage, the lower the colour temperature, and so the redder tungsten light becomes.

More and more street lighting and lighting in public places is either fluorescent or vapour discharge, and these create difficulties that arise out of the differences between the way that we see colour and the way film records it. All vapour discharge lamps (and this includes fluorescent lights) emit light in a very narrow part of the spectrum. Sodium vapour lamps, which are often used for lighting streets and large buildings, are yellow, mercury vapour lamps blue-green, while fluorescent lamps are coated inside with a substance that makes them look white but generally records on film as green.

Because these lamps have what is called a discontinuous spectrum, it is not easy to correct the light with filters. For instance, as sodium vapour light entirely lacks blue, even a strong blue filter over the lens will not do much good. Fluorescent lighting can be filtered to give a close approximation to white, but as the exact colour cast varies between makes of lamp and even with age, this is difficult to do without first making a series of tests.

However, all this presupposes a need to correct coloured lighting and there are many situations where this is not necessary. Most cities at night have a mixture of many types of lighting; the variety of colours can add to photographic opportunities. Even one dominant colour can be turned into an advantage. As a general rule, coloured lighting is more likely to look odd in a photograph when it is the main light source, as in a room lit only by fluorescent lighting. When there is a mixture of light

Above The most basic source of artificial lighting is a naked flame – in this case an opium-smoker's lamp – but its special characteristics are not easy to record on film. The level of illumination is low, and when the flame appears in shot, the contrast is extremely high and makes flare likely. The ideal solution is a high-speed film, of at least ASA 400, and a lens with an aspherical front surface (this reduces flare).

sources, in a nighttime street scene, for example, and when none predominates, the effect does not seem unusual, even though it is not strictly "correct". One of the reasons why the different colours of available lighting can be easily accepted in photographs is simple familiarity – with the fast films on the market now, more available light photography is being published, most of it uncorrected for colour. As with so many other aspects of photography, we are to some extent conditioned by what we are used to seeing. A slight reddish tinge in an interior is almost expected, and even a moderate green cast from fluorescent lighting may pass unnoticed.

Often much more of a problem than colour is uneven illumination and overall low light levels. Generally, the larger the setting the more likely it is to contain pools of lighting with dark shadows in between. We may think a

room or a street is evenly lit, but this is often because our eyes can adjust rapidly to the differences. Correcting this problem becomes an exercise in calculating exposure under high contrast conditions, but often changing the viewpoint can help. Nevertheless, supplementary lighting, using photographic lights to fill in shadows and even out the contrast, is often needed.

Available lighting is usually dim, at least by the standards of daylight, and needs efficient camera handling and technique. For handheld photography, which is essential for candid work and reportage in general, fast films, fast lenses and careful timing are the normal solutions, together with some practice at holding a camera steady at slow shutter speeds. The other alternative is to mount the camera on a tripod and make a long time exposure. This usually incurs the problems of reciprocity

failure. Film is designed to work best over a narrow band of exposure times. Outside this range, reciprocity failure occurs, resulting in an underexposed image, altered contrast and, in colour film, a shift in the colour balance. The exposure must be increased above the assessed level to adjust.

Because of the fundamental differences between the way we see and the way film reacts, available light offers the photographer two basic choices: either to try and even out the differences and correct the photographic view to what the eye can see or simply to make creative use of the existing conditions. The first route means understanding the technical aspects of available lighting so that the right filters can be chosen and the right amount of fill-in lighting added, while the second route acknowledges the difficulties but puts them to work to make a strong image.

Above Neon display lighting is relatively straightforward to photograph: it illuminates nothing but itself, and so allows a wide range of acceptable exposure, and the coloured glass envelopes mask fluorescent lighting's inherently greenish cast. One precaution that must be taken is to keep the shutter speed at least as slow as 1/30 second to cover several cycles of the flickering neon tubes, or the display will appear unevenly lit. Few neon displays are so bright that a high shutter speed could be used. This sign in downtown Las Vegas was exposed at 1/8 second and f5.6, on ASA 64 daylight film.

Right A very long-focus lens (800mm on a 35mm camera) and a necessarily long exposure (one second) gives an impressionistic view of heavy freeway traffic in Caracas. The variety of available lighting found in cities makes it possible to avoid literal, predictable interpretations. By day, the same scene was much less interesting.

Left When the light sources in a photograph are mixed, then colour correction, if needed, is inevitably a compromise. In this interior view of an old Byzantine church in Athens, shafts of sunlight filtered through the cupola windows, while the lower part of the church was lit by tungsten lamps and candles. Some skylight illumination was added from behind the camera. Rather than try and correct fully for any one of these light sources, a compromise filtration of a pale blue 82A was used with daylight film. The low light levels called for a one-second exposure, which needed a tripod and additional filtration for reciprocity failure.

PHOTOGRAPHIC LIGHTING

A lthough daylight is by far the most common source of illumination used in photography, there are many occasions when it is insufficient or inadequate for the subject and type of photograph. The light level might be too low for the minimum shutter speed needed to freeze movement in a subject or for the aperture setting needed for a certain depth of field, or the subject may be too shadowed for a clear view. In this type of situation, some form of supplementary lighting is often needed. Then again, many photographers prefer to have as much control as possible over their photography, constructing the image to fit a preconceived idea. This is particularly true of still life and much of fashion and portrait photography, and calls for specially designed lighting equipment that can give precisely measured results.

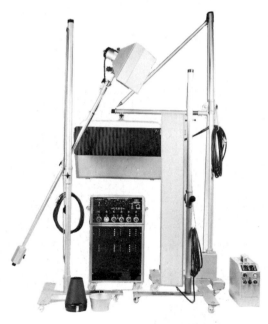

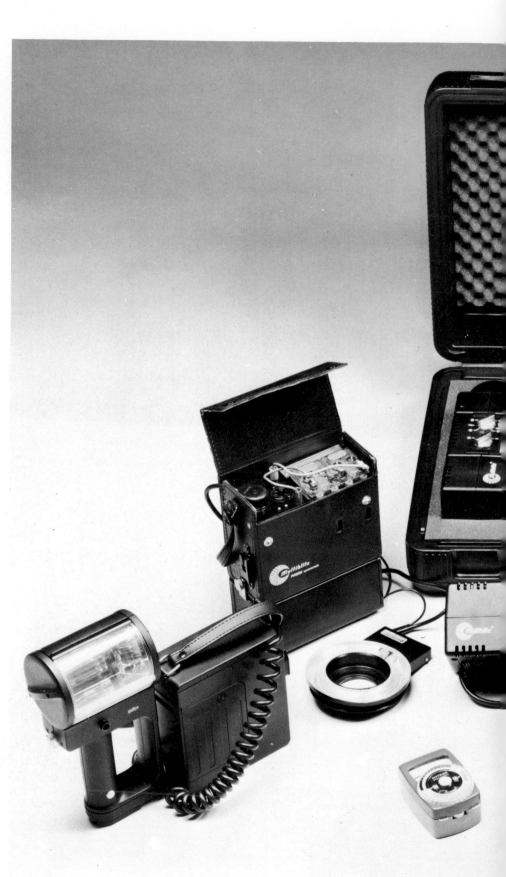

Above One of the most sophisticated and powerful ranges of electronic flash equipment is designed exclusively for studio use, and principally with large format cameras. The standard lens for an 8 x 10 inch (20 x 24 cm) view camera has a focal length of 300 mm or 360 mm, and consequently such shallow depth of field that aperture settings of as small as f64 are common in normal still life work; for this, the output of the 5000 Joule power unit shown in the centre of the picture is essential, particularly when the flash heads are diffused. The lighting heads shown here include a small square "window", a larger, cantilevered area light, and a trough-like head for illuminating backgrounds.

Left For work on location, flash units need, above all, to be portable. By far the most common are small, self-contained units that can be fitted onto the camera, or else to an adjoining bracket. Although the small size of the flash head, and the fact that they are intended to be used from the camera position, limit the style of lighting possible, such small units are extremely convenient. Most use replaceable or rechargeable dry cells, but many news photographers prefer separate wet-cell power packs, which are self-generating (two are shown at left). A more specialized design is the ringflash which, as its name suggests, contains a circular tube that surrounds the front of the lens to give axial, and therefore shadowless, lighting. For closeup work, particularly in enclosed spaces where an ordinary flash would throw deep shadows, the ringflash can be very useful. To achieve some of the control possible with studio lighting, some mains-powered units, such as the multiblitz heads in the case, are available as travelling kits, with various attachments to control diffusion. For all serious flash photography, a flashmeter (front row) is essential.

FLASH

Although tungsten lighting has been the mainstay of studio work throughout most of the history of photography and is irreplaceable for certain types of work, on most occasions and with most subjects, the advantage lies with electronic flash. Despite the high cost of the mains-powered units that are used in studios, flash freezes most movement, does not over-heat delicate subjects, and can be used irrespective of whether there is any other ambient lighting. The only real restriction on the speed is that the camera's shutter must be synchronized with the flash – focal plane shutters at up to 1/60 or 1/125 second, and between-the-lens shutters at any speed. This gives some choice as to whether or not to include other lighting – at a high speed and small aperture only the flash will register on the film, but slower speeds can be used to show more of the room lights and other continuous lighting.

The intensity of electronic flash depends on the ability of the unit's capacitors to store and release their charge. Portable flash units small enough to be mounted on the camera and large studio units with free-standing, separate power packs both work on the same principle – the electric discharge passes through a gas-filled transparent tube, and the longer its duration, the greater the output of light. Most flash tubes of the type used with large units are ring-shaped or, if they have to take a very powerful discharge, are in the shape of a coil. Linear tubes are also used for flash heads that have a large surface area; two or three of these, with the appropriate shape of head, can give a very even spread of light.

Even the slowest flash discharge from a large power pack is still faster than the top shutter speeds of most cameras, so that all normal movement can be frozen. Exposure is

Below Electronic flash units, even slow, powerful studio models, operate faster than the eye can react, making precise synchronization difficult in some situations. In the sequence of photographs below, of whisky being poured over ice in a glass, the exact image was unpredictable each time, so that the only practical solution was to make several exposures, and choose one after they had all been processed.

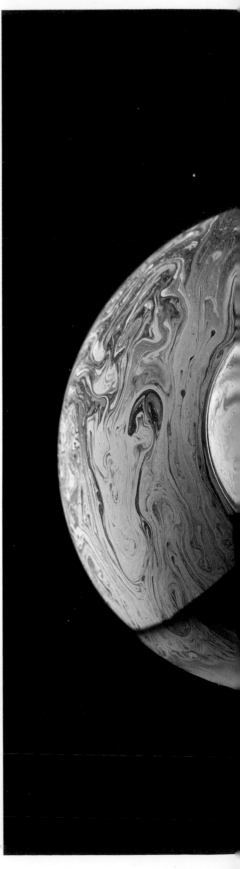

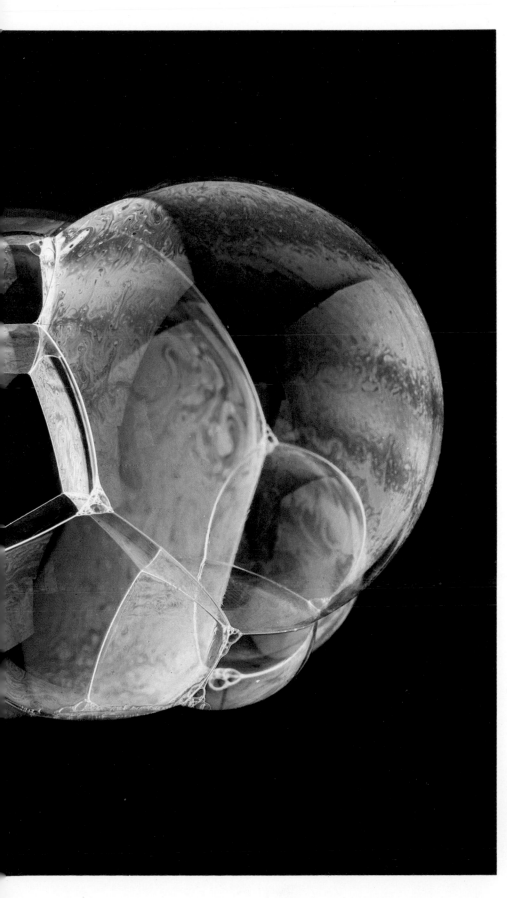

normally controlled by altering the power level on the flash unit or by adjusting the aperture of the lens. For more light than a unit can deliver, the studio must be darkened, the shutter left open, and the flash fired repeatedly; naturally, this only works with a motionless subject.

Because a flash discharge is so rapid, it produces much less heat than tungsten lighting. Not only is this easier on the subjects, but it makes it possible to enclose the flash tube in a variety of specially shaped heads. In particular, the kind of head known as an area light, which uses a sheet of opal perspex for diffusion, is only practical because flash tubes stay relatively cool.

To overcome the disadvantage of not being able to see the effect of the flash in advance, all studio flash units are equipped with a built-in modelling light – usually a tungsten lamp that is too weak to affect the actual exposure but sufficiently bright to give the photographer a preview. Units that use linear flash tubes usually have fluorescent strip lights for modelling lamps.

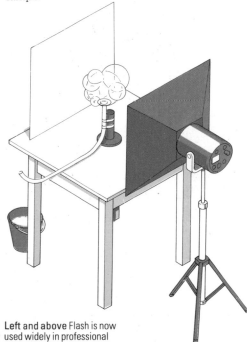

Left and above Flash is now used widely in professional studios for convenience as much as any other reason – its light output and colour balance is consistent and there are few problems of overheating. However, for subjects that involve movement, flash is virtually indispensable. This closeup photograph of soap bubbles, blown carefully up a narrow plastic tube, needed a rapid output of light to freeze the swirling patterns, sufficiently powerful to allow an aperture setting of f32 for adequate depth of field.

PORTABLE FLASH

Portable flash units, designed to be mounted on the camera or handheld, operate on essentially the same principle as full-sized studio units, but are used on different occasions. Being portable and mainly automated, they have the advantage of offering instant, uncomplicated lighting. By the same token, however, they are not capable of great subtlety, and the small size of the flash tube is frequently a problem: hard shadows and bright reflections do not suit many subjects. Units vary in power and size. The smallest are usually non-automatic and normally need to be used at full power; the largest consist of a separate power pack fitted with shoulder straps.

The principal use of portable flash is as fail-safe illumination – making an inadequately lit shot possible. In news photography and reportage work in general, the subject is often much more important than creative considerations and if a camera-mounted flash unit is the only way of capturing an image, then its aesthetic defects are secondary.

These units are also useful for fill-in lighting – relieving shadows in a high contrast scene. Backlit subjects, for example, always have high contrast, and if it is important to preserve shadow detail, some extra light will be needed. Fill-in flash works most realistically when used at a relatively weak setting, so that it does not compete for attention with the main source of light (usually the sun). A typical ratio of flash to daylight would be about one to three or one to four; how this is achieved depends on the particular unit. (With manually operated units, the setting can be reduced or the unit can be placed further from the subject, but with automatic units it may be necessary to cover the flash tube with neutral density filters or a folded handkerchief).

Portable flash units are designed essentially for convenience, and most have automatic circuitry, using a light-sensitive cell that can react so quickly to the light that is reflected back from the subject, that the flash discharge is cut off as soon as a predetermined level of brightness is reached. Once the lens aperture and flash controls have been set, the unit produces consistent results. The most advanced flash units link their circuitry to that of the camera's electric shutter and viewfinder display.

Although all these units are intended to be used close to the camera, there are two problems associated with this position. The first is that light falls off *away* from the camera, so that the correct level of brightness is only possible at a certain distance; anything closer will be overexposed, while backgrounds at any real distance are invariably dark. The second is that this type of flat lighting does not suit very many subjects, and can produce an odd-looking bright red reflection from the eyes of anyone looking straight at the camera (caused by light reflecting from the retina). More often than not,

these effects are a nuisance, although there are occasions when the rapid fall-off can be used to isolate a subject. Holding the flash head on an extension lead away from the camera is one simple way of varying the lighting; if there is a large light-toned surface nearby, such as a white ceiling or wall, this can be used as a reflector to soften the light, by aiming the flash in that direction rather than straight at the subject.

Below When the light levels are low and the subject is moving too fast for a time exposure, flash is essential, and small camera-mounted units make handheld shooting easy. Nevertheless, the quality of light from a small electronic flash is often less than satisfactory – shadows are harsh, and because the intensity of the light falls off in the direction that the camera is pointing, backgrounds are usually severely underlit. One solution, used here by photographer Ian Berry, on an assignment covering Rio de Janeiro's Carnaval, is to combine the flash with a slow shutter speed so that the ambient lighting is also included.

TUNGSTEN LIGHTING

The simplest and least expensive type of lighting designed specifically for photography is the tungsten lamp. Tungsten lamps are similar to domestic light bulbs, but for more light and a higher colour temperature they are uprated, generally to between 500 watts and 1000 watts for still photography. Because electronic flash has gradually replaced tungsten lighting in many areas of still photography, the greatest variety of tungsten equipment is now produced by and used in the motion picture industry.

The standard lamp is the photoflood, which is simply a large, powerful version of a domestic bulb. Other varieties are reflector bulbs, which are partly silvered inside to increase their efficiency, and clear high-intensity lamps, for use inside reflectors and other housings. The tungsten filament gradually vapourizes with time and a black deposit forms inside the glass, lowering the colour temperature and making it slightly warmer in appearance. To avoid this problem, the most efficient tungsten lamps contain halogen gas: in these tungsten-halogen lamps the filament burns at a very high temperature, and the vapourized product is redeposited on the filament rather than on the glass, so there is no blackening with age.

Type B film is specifically balanced for most tungsten lamps, which have a colour temperature of 3200K. A few lamps are slightly less yellow, at 3400K, and are designed to be used with the less common Type A films. For daylight photography, tungsten lamps are normally covered with sheets of blue acetate.

Tungsten lamps can be fitted to a variety of housings to shape and direct the light, but because the lamp gets hot quickly there are restrictions on the design of lighting heads. The simplest reflector is a silvered metal bowl – shallow for a broader spread of light, deeply recessed for a more concentrated beam. Some of the more elaborate housings, which are perfectly suitable for still work, employ adjustable lenses for precise control.

The problem with tungsten lights is that they are both hot and weak. Because they have a high wattage, the heat is intense, which not only makes them uncomfortable for close work or in studio conditions but also means that they cannot be used with subjects that are likely to wilt, melt or suffer heat damage – for example, flowers and icecream suffer under tungsten lighting. In addition, there are some situations where the light intensity is just not high enough, particularly when both high shutter speeds and great depth of field are needed. In a studio fashion shot, for instance, the swirl of a dress would need a shutter speed in the order of 1/500 second to appear sharp; to achieve this effect, a whole battery of high-intensity lamps would have to be used with a fine-grained emulsion. In closeup work with a view camera, where depth of field is of critical importance, apertures of f45 or f64 are not uncommon – here, a tungsten lamp would demand an impractically long exposure.

Tungsten has no rival, however, for photographing large interiors, particularly where it is important to retain the appearance of a room's existing lighting. Its intensity can be carefully adjusted to balance with incidental lighting such as table lamps. Electronic flash, although powerful over short distances, is at a disadvantage in large spaces, as the only way of increasing its output is to fire it a number of times; this often takes longer than a time exposure under tungsten's continuous light, and this practice can damage the flash heads.

Tungsten also excels when the image needs to be blurred deliberately. Sometimes the most effective way of conveying a sense of action is to use a slow shutter speed, so that a moving object gives a streaked image. For this type of photograph continuous lighting is essential.

Right and far right These two historical set-piece interiors, one an American nineteenth century general store, the other an engineering workshop of the same period, were both entirely lit by tungsten lighting, for full control. Even the daylight is simulated, being diffused through translucent plastic screens taped to the outside of the windows. Strong diffusion reduces the light output, and this, combined with the f45 apertures necessary for depth of field with the 4 x 5 inch (9 x 12 cm) view camera used for some shots, called for exposure times of around 60 seconds.

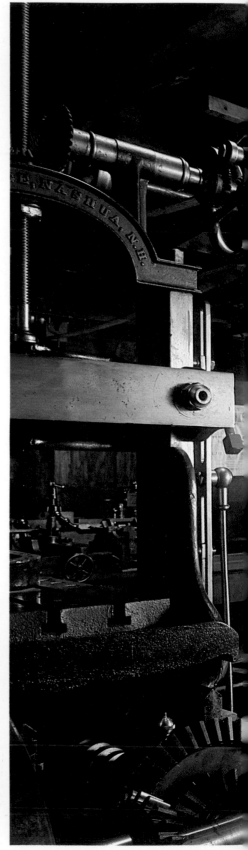

USING LIGHT IN THE STUDIO

A studio has one outstanding advantage: it enables the photographer to exercise control over almost every aspect of the image. On location, photography is largely at the mercy of existing conditions, in particular of the level of light. In an interior setting, however, lighting can be tailored precisely to the needs of the subject and the style of the photograph.

Controlling the quality of lighting is one of the most important elements in studio photography, and depends principally on the direction of the lights and to what degree they are diffused or concentrated. When the subject has a shiny surface, such as glass or polished metal, the shape of the light source also becomes important because its reflection will appear in the photograph.

Each subject and setting demands its own specially designed lighting setup to enhance certain features and suppress others. This is one of the delights of studio work – being able to transform the image by means of lighting, improvising for each new situation. Neverthe-less, while rigid lighting formulae are not compatible with interesting studio photography, there are a few general principles which apply to most subjects. A single light, for instance, is simpler and less obtrusive than several together, and although more effort is required to light all the important parts of the subject with an acceptable range of contrast, there are many situations, especially in still life photography, where the natural, uncomplicated effects gained by this method are very satisfying.

The direction of the light source is another important consideration. Front lighting, with the lamp close to the camera, throws few shadows and therefore produces a flat effect, but gives good colour saturation and shows the maximum amount of detail. With overhead lighting, more or less at right-angles to the camera's line of view, the contrast range is greater and highlights are picked out more effectively; this looks natural because we are used to seeing most things lit from above. However, overhead lighting gives heavy

Below and bottom In this set of commercial shots the camera and lighting equipment remains basically the same. The ways in which these are used, make a radical difference to the styles of lighting, although only one light source is used in each case. The standard still life lighting arrangement, an area light suspended directly over the subject, itself placed on a white sheet, gives a tonal distribution that is generally pleasing and suits a whole range of subjects. This setup graduates the tone of the background, giving a sense of depth and a contrast with the highlights on the top surface of the subject – here the rim of the lens.

Above and right Probably the most efficient way of illuminating glass objects is from behind, with an area light. This heightens contrast in the structure of the glass itself, so giving substance to a transparent subject. A careful arrangement of black cards is necessary, to prevent flare degrading the image, and to give dark edges to the outline of decanter, stopper and glass.

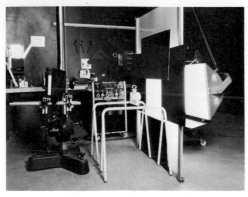

Above and left Objects that have reflective surfaces, such as this bottle-opener, pose a special problem in lighting – because they reflect even the photographic lamps, they can appear as a confusing mixture of highlights and irregular shadows. The most common solution is to use a very large area light – sufficiently large that its reflection covers practically all of the subject. Here, a trace frame (covered with translucent tracing paper) has been suspended below the main light. Added interest has been given by placing the bottle-opener on another reflective surface – dark plastic. The curved surfaces of this subject unavoidably reflect the darkened parts of the studio, but this is no real disadvantage as it helps to define the shape.

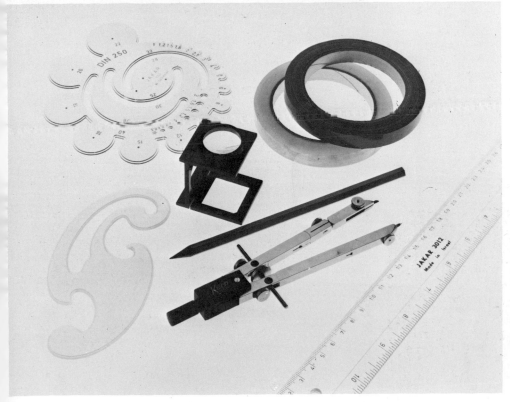

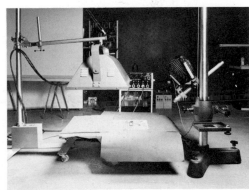

Above and left In this arrangement of drawing instruments, both solid and transparent subjects are combined, and for clarity, two lighting techniques are used: backlighting, in the form of an area light underneath the subject, for the French curves and lens of the lupe, and toplighting, for the remaining objects. Some care is needed in situations like this, in balancing the output of the two lights – here, the backlighting has been given prominence.

shadows beneath tall objects; for full-length portraits, and subjects with similar proportions such as bottles, a more effective lighting direction is from one side. To preserve detail in the shadows, a reflector – a sheet of white card, polystyrene or crumpled silver foil – is nearly always needed. With the light slightly behind the subject but angled more towards the camera, there are more reflections and better representation of texture, but at the expense of detail and colour. Total backlighting, with the light directly behind the subject, gives either a silhouette if the light source is large, or a thin halo if the light is a hidden point source.

Apart from adjusting the position of a light, quality can be manipulated to a fine degree by diffusion. Most of the heads and lighting attachments are designed to spread light, increasing its area and so softening shadows. For the majority of subjects a diffused light source is the

most appealing. Each method of diffusion offers a subtle variation on the theme – a white translucent umbrella gives a broad, simple diffusion, but with no control over the spill of light onto the immediate surroundings; a boxed area light, on the other hand, is more precise and so better suited to intricate still life photography. Area lights, because they use a diffusing sheet of plastic to give a regular, even-toned shape, are also useful if the subject itself is reflective.

In the end, however, the right lighting for a studio photograph can only be decided on the merits of each situation and to a great extent depends on the photographer's preferences. Photography is a highly fashionable medium, in few respects more so than in lighting trends. An approach that seems elegant at the time may come to seem clichéd or unimaginative through sheer over-use, so that photographers begin to cast around for fresher alternatives.

Below While simplicity is a good general principle in lighting straightforward subjects, when subjects are placed in a simulated setting, the scale and complexity of the image is usually increased, and more lights are often necessary. These antique clocks were given a period setting, and while one heavily diffused light source was adequate for the principal subjects, the windows behind required additional lighting, also diffused. The level of the window lighting was set as high as possible so as to give an impression of daylight.

Left For this portrait, the setting was not a studio but an ordinary domestic interior. However, with such a formal, direct treatment (a 4 x 5 inch/9 x 12 cm view camera was used), the lighting needed to be planned in as rigorous a fashion as if it were in a studio. A broadly diffused light, made of large sheets of translucent plastic, provided the main illumination from the left, while a spot reflected from the ceiling augmented the effect of the wall lamp. Some light was additionally spilled onto the papers on the floor. Often, in situations such as this, a studio must be virtually assembled on location.

Left This photograph of a rare golden cowrie shell, is intentionally uncomplicated in effect, but demanded a painstaking lighting procedure. The surface is highly reflective and curved, but the immediately obvious alternatives of either highly diffused lighting from all directions or a commercial dulling spray were rejected because they would alter the textural qualities of the shell's surface too much. Instead, a sheet of tracing paper was taped above the shell in the same curved shape, and lit from above. The result is even lighting without losing the polished appearance.

Above The green onyx egg, being translucent, lent itself to an unusual lighting technique. Placed on a sheet of opalescent plastic, a single light was arranged underneath, and masked down with a small circular hole cut into a sheet of black card. The effect is to concentrate light inside the egg, so that it appears to glow.

BLACK-AND-WHITE FILM

In most black-and-white films, the printed image is made up of small grains of metallic silver, each too small to see with the naked eye. The impression of graininess in a photograph comes from clumps of these grains, which are distributed throughout the emulsion. The silver halide crystals in a unprocessed film are either converted into black silver during development or not – there are no halfway stages of grey. The tones in the image depend on the size of the developed grains and on how closely they are packed. If in one part of the negative only a small proportion of the crystals have developed, then the result will be a very pale tone, which will later print almost black. If, however, an area has been strongly exposed to light, most of the crystals will be developed into silver grains, and will be so dense that on the print they will register hardly any tone at all.

This "all-or-nothing" principle of development means that film manufacturers can produce emulsions with different sensitivities to light. A large crystal of silver halide will, given the same exposure to light and the same development, darken more than a small crystal, so that an emulsion containing large crystals will respond more readily to light – in other words, it will be "faster". It will also have a coarser texture, particularly in parts of the picture that have an average tone and no detail. This is the inevitable price that has to be paid for the benefits of a highly sensitive film that can be used in low light. There is, in fact, a simple relationship between the speed of a film and the clarity of its image: high resolution needs small grains, which make a film slow, while a high speed needs large grains, which tend to break up the image. An added consideration is that, in a fine-grained emulsion, most of the crystals tend to develop all together when exposed to the same level of illumination, and this gives a fairly high contrast – far more so than the jumbled sizes of crystal in a high-speed film.

For ordinary black-and-white film, the choice is between speed and graininess. Most film manufacturers have standard ranges – commonly slow, fine-grained emulsions at around ASA 25, medium speed, moderately grained emulsions at around ASA 125, and fast, grainy emulsions with ratings of about ASA 400. Some very fast films are also available, rated at ASA 1000 or more. These speed ratings are an attempt to make standard comparisons between films from different manufacturers.

Right These four exposures were made on slow, medium, fast and extremely fast film. At a moderate enlargement from the 35mm negatives, the differences in graininess are apparent but not particularly important; more noticeable is the greater contrast of the slow emulsion, when compared with the faster. However, when a small section of the image is greatly enlarged, graininess noticeably affects the image in the films. The fine edge is lost in the ASA 400 emulsion, while the grain structure overwhelms detail in the ASA 1000 film.

Kodak Panatomic ASA 32

Kodak Tri X ASA 400

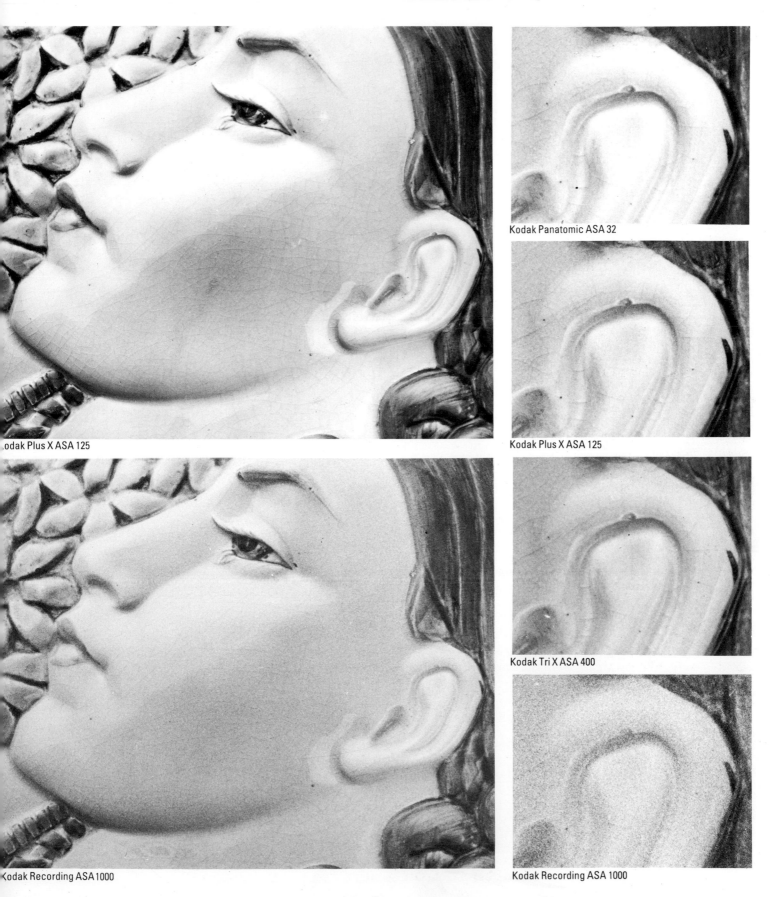

odak Plus X ASA 125

Kodak Panatomic ASA 32

Kodak Plus X ASA 125

Kodak Tri X ASA 400

Kodak Recording ASA 1000

Kodak Recording ASA 1000

Because most photography is basically concerned with presenting a view similar to the way that we see, the majority of films are manufactured to respond to the same wavelengths as the human eye. This involves, even with a standard black-and-white emulsion, incorporating dyes to make up for the different reactions of light-sensitive salts.

However, for some special uses, there are films available that respond in unusual ways to light, and even to invisible radiation. For graphic arts use, there are emulsions known as orthochromatic which are sensitive only to blue light, not red; they can be used in the darkroom under red safelighting. Other films, known as line or lith emulsions, have such a high contrast that they produce images composed of just two tones: black and white, with no intermediate greys. Their primary use is in copying flat artwork, but they also have interesting pictorial possibilities. These films are usually orthochromatic as well, so that they can be developed by inspection under a safelight.

One specialized variety of line film – Agfacontour – uses quite sophisticated photographic chemistry to give an image that records only the lines separating different tones. Intended for darkroom use rather than direct

Right Black-and-white infrared emulsion, available as Kodak's High Speed Infra-Red Film, is sensitized so that it responds to invisible infrared radiation in addition to normal "white" light. Many subjects do not reflect in the infrared as they do in visible light, so that the photographic effects are difficult to predict. Unusual filters over the lens, such as the visually opaque Wratten 87, allow only the infrared radiation to reach the film, and give the most characteristic results, which include a high contrast in outdoor scenes, and virtual elimination of haze. (The molecules and dust particles in the air that are responsible for this are too small to scatter the short infrared waves.) Many objects reflect infrared radiation from slightly below their surface, and a mild diffusion of some details is common, as in this photograph.
One disadvantage of High Speed Infra-Red Film is pronounced graininess, which allows only moderate enlargement, and for subjects where it is important to hold detail, such as architecture, the 4 x 5 inch (9 x 12 cm) film size is preferable to a 35 mm roll. Infrared film can be used for spectacular pictorial effects, such as rendering vegetation almost white, or it can be used, as here – to give a subtle difference to the normal tonal values of a scene.

exposure in the camera, it can produce complex graphic images.

Infrared films, made by Kodak, have a spectral sensitivity that extends beyond the deepest red that the human eye can see. By recording these invisible wavelengths, infrared film can, with appropriate filters to block ordinary "white" light, produce very unusual images of conventional scenes. Some objects reflect the infrared radiation from the sun quite differently from the way they reflect visible wavelengths – green vegetation, for example, is highly reflective and so appears very bright on the film.

Black and white film	Speed (ASA)	Sensitivity	35 mm	Roll	Sheet	Comments
Normal contrast						
Adox KB17	40	O	●			100 ft (30 m) rolls
Ilford Pan F	50	P	●			
Kodak Panatomic X	32	P	●	●		
Adox KB21	100	P	●			100 ft (30 m) rolls
Agfapan 100	100	P	●	●	●	
Ilford FP4	125	P	●	●	●	
Kodak Plus X	125	P	●	●	●	
Agfapan 400	400	P	●	●	●	
Ilford HP5	400	P	●	●	●	
Ilford XP1	variable	P	●			Final image in dye
Kodak Tri X	400	P	●	●		
Kodak Recording 2475	1000	P	●			
Kodak Royal X Pan	1250	P		●		
Kodak Prof Copy	25	O			●	Available USA only
Kodak Gravure Pos	20	O			●	
Agfapan Vario-XL Prof	variable	P	●			Final image in dye
High contrast						
Kodalith type 3	12	O	●		●	35 mm in bulk rolls
Kodalith Pan	40	P			●	
Specials						
Agfacontour		O			●	Special effects
Agfa Dia-direct	100	P	●			Reversal slide film

O = Orthochromatic   P = Panchromatic

DYE-IMAGE

While the conventional black-and-white process, with a silver image as the end-product, has remained unchallenged for decades, a different technology has been developed recently. In certain situations the results of this process are superior. Using some of the principles of colour film manufacture, a new type of black-and-white emulsion produces an image that contains no silver, has very fine grain that actually becomes *less* noticeable with increased exposure, and also has an exceptional latitude.

These dye-image films – Ilford's XP-1 and Agfa's Vario-XL – form their latent images in the conventional way, with silver halide crystals, but they are then processed in a way that replaces each developed silver grain with a dye cloud. Special processing chemicals are available for these films, but they can be developed almost as well in the standard C-41 colour negative process.

By replacing the traditional metallic silver grains with dyes, these films, although nominally rated at ASA 400, have the finely textured image of much slower conventional films, and so in many respects combine the best of both worlds – fine grain and high speed. For detailed subjects this lack of graininess is an immediately obvious advantage, although over broad areas of average tone, such as an overcast sky, the slightly mottled, unstructured texture may not appeal to photographers who like to see sharply defined grain.

Unlike conventional black-and-white films, the fine grain of dye-image emulsions actually become finer in denser areas of the negative. This unusual effect can be put to definite use by deliberately overexposing the film in order to achieve an extremely fine-grained image.

However, probably the greatest benefit of dye-image films is their latitude, which is so great that images overexposed or underexposed by as much as two f-stops will still give good prints, without any adjustment to the development. Although this latitude is a means of insuring against exposure mistakes, it has two positive uses: it makes it possible to rate the film at different ASA speeds in the middle of a roll, and it provides a wide range of tones. Both advantages cannot be exploited at the same time – the choice is between either convenience or quality.

With two f-stops' latitude in either direction, dye-image films can, in effect, be rated anywhere between ASA 100 and ASA 1600. This means that, having shot several frames normally at ASA 400, a photographer can then work on a still life set where the finest grain is essential; on the same film the end of the roll can then be used for low-light photography.

Another way of treating the great exposure latitude is to use it for extended tonal range: at a normal ASA 400 exposure, dye-image films will record more detail in both highlights and shadow areas than regular emulsion. This removes the need to alter development in order to adjust contrast, and can reduce the amount of shading and printing-in when making an enlargement.

When compared directly with conventional black-and-white films, these dye-image emulsions show greater sharpness (for their speed) and a greater tonal range – both major advantages. Pushing development to increase contrast, however, does not work as well as it does with a silver-image film, so that in low-light or with low-contrast subjects, conventional emulsions are more satisfactory.

Right These simulated negatives, taken on Ilford XP-1 400, have been enlarged 10,000 times to show the difference between dye-image and silver halide processing, and give some idea of the reasons for the graininess to be seen in some ordinary enlargements *(left)*. The dye clouds *(right)* are, by contrast, semi-transparent. The dye-image process is used for both scientific and artistic purposes. For example, an eye surgeon can more easily determine the need for a certain operation without the graininess in a photograph, which could be confused with the structure of the eye. Similarly, the process is used to discover faults or cracks in the legs of oil rigs. Photographs taken at a distance can also be enlarged without the usual, coarse result.

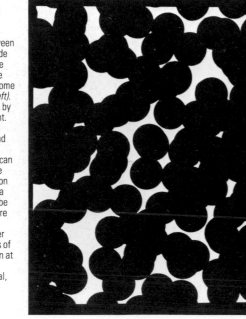

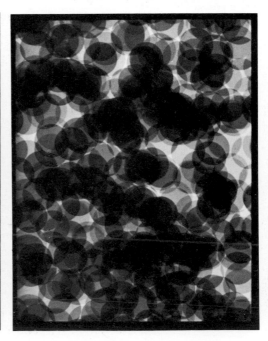

Left The practical differences in the quality of image between the new film and regular black-and-white emulsions are noticeable here. From the same camera position, the lid of a silver box was photographed on Ilford XP-1 *(left)* and Kodak Tri-X *(right),* each used and processed as ASA 400 film. As claimed, the Ilford dye-image film is better able to handle the high contrast of the polished bas relief. The background area, carefully chosen to reveal differences in graininess, shows that the Tri-X has a more defined grain structure than the XP-1, but this is only evident at a considerable enlargement. For most photographers, the wide latitude of dye-image film is probably its most useful quality.

RECORDING COLORS

Early black-and-white film was virtually insensitive to red light, and even modern emulsions respond to colors differently from the way we actually see them. Film overreacts to the shorter wavelengths – blue, violet, and ultraviolet – and responds poorly to the longer wavelengths, such as red. In black-and-white photographs, where colors are represented by different tones, blue skies can appear too pale (because the negative is dense and allows little of the light through to the print) and reds often appear almost black, so that a ruddy complexion or reddish makeup can produce an unpleasantly high contrast.

The tonal reproduction of colors can be altered quite drastically by using strongly colored filters in front of the lens. Using a filter of the same color produces a lighter image, while a filter of a complementary color gives a darker appearance on the print. To darken a blue sky, for example, a filter that blocks blue light must be used: yellow is effective, but orange and red even more so.

The effects of using filters can be quite strong, although this depends largely on how pure the original colors are. In nature, colors are often degraded – vegetation, for instance, is rarely an intense green, and so reacts poorly to filtration and is further weakened by haze.

Judicious selection of filters also makes it possible to adjust the tonal separation in a photograph. Two colors that are distinct from each other in real life can turn out the same shade of grey in a black-and-white print; by using a filter that matches one of the colors, the two can be separated.

no filter

Wratten 16 orange

Wratten 47 blue

Above There are two reasons for altering the tones in which colors are recorded in a black-and-white image: to differentiate between colors that might otherwise appear to merge with one another, and to match our perception of the lightness and darkness of certain hues. To emphasize the differences, well-saturated colors – red, orange, yellow, green and blue – were chosen for this sequence of photographs. With most subjects, however, particularly landscapes, colors are frequently impure, so that filters have a less obvious effect than shown here.

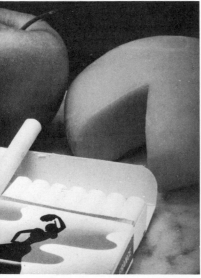

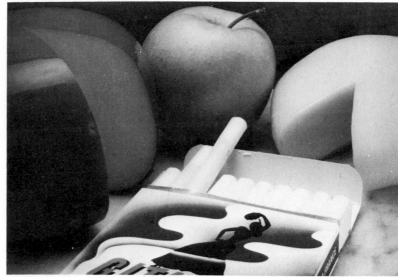

Wratten 8 yellow

Wratten 25 red

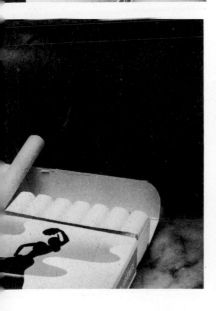

Wratten 58 green

Left With no filter, regular black-and-white panchromatic film renders most colors as we would expect to see them, except for red and blue: the emulsion is over-sensitive to blue, which consequently appears very pale, and under-sensitive to red, which here seems too dark.
A yellow filter goes some way to restoring the tonal values of the packet of cigarettes and the large Dutch cheese. It also lightens the smaller yellow cheese: that is a normal characteristic of all filters – they pass light of their own color quite freely, but partly block other wavelengths. An orange filter has a more pronounced blocking effect on the blue design of the cigarette packet, making it appear stronger. A red filter does the same, and also darkens the green apple, but lightens the skin of the red cheese in a very pronounced way.
By contrast, a blue filter has, in many ways, the opposite effect of the red – the same cheese appears almost black, while even the yellow cheese is much darker, and the blue design on the packet virtually disappears.
Finally, the green filter lightens the tone of the apple – its own color – but also darkens the red cheese.

DEVELOPING

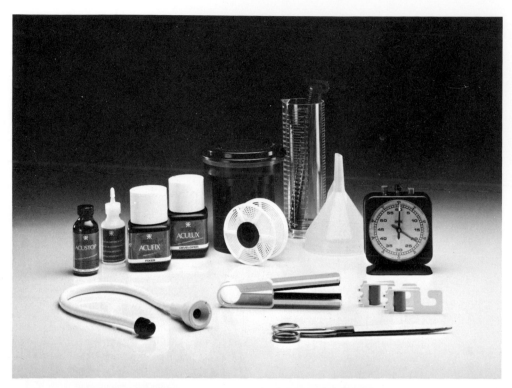

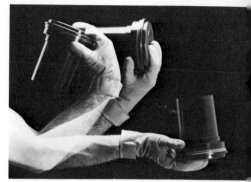

Left The basic materials and equipment for processing black-and-white film are few and inexpensive. Developer and fixer are the principal chemicals; stop bath and wetting agent are useful additions. A graduate and funnel are used for measuring out and diluting the chemicals, and a thermometer for monitoring the developer temperature. Developing tanks are available in plastic, with reels that are threaded from the outer edge inwards, and stainless steel, with reels threaded from the core outwards. Scissors are needed to cut the film before loading in the tank. The most convenient design of timer is that which can be preset for each stage, and has a clearly visible face. A filtered rubber hose is used for the washing stage, clips for hanging the film to dry, and squeegee tongs for wiping the film dry of water droplets.

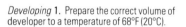
Developing **1**. Prepare the correct volume of developer to a temperature of 68°F (20°C).

2. Pour the developer into the tank, already loaded with film, and set the timer. Remove air bubbles with a sharp knock.

3. To maintain the developer at the correct temperature, immerse in a 68°F (20°C) water bath, except when agitating.

4. Just before the end of the development time, empty the tank, discarding the developer if it is a one-shot solution, or returning it to its container if reusable.

Film developers work by reducing the silver halide crystals in the emulsion to metallic silver, which remains as a visible and dark deposit. Although many chemicals can do this, the ones that are useful in photography start work first on those halides that have been exposed to light, and act in proportion to the amount of light that has fallen on the film. In this way, the image is developed. To prevent the developer acting on unexposed areas of the emulsion, and so causing fogging, other chemicals are added to the solution.

By far the most popular developer is a combination of metol and hydroquinone, known generically as M-Q and produced by many different manufacturers. Kodak's D-70 is a widely used example of this formula. The metol is soft-working and gives good detail, while the hydroquinone gives great density; the combination is a good versatile developer with fine-grained results.

In fact, developer chemistry has improved so much that fine grain is now standard. Graininess is, in any case, determined more by the emulsion itself than by the developer, and modern specialized developers are designed for more specific qualities, such as high acutance, high energy and high contrast.

High acutance developers are designed to provide greater sharpness in a negative, and they do this by working more actively in areas of fine detail than in broad, heavily exposed parts of the emulsion. They also tend to form thin, sharp edges of silver around areas of different densities, which adds to the overall impression of clarity. Tetenal Neofin and Paterson Acutol are both acutance developers, and even some standard developers, such as Kodak DK-50 and Agfa Rodinal, improve acutance when strongly diluted.

High energy developers are so vigorous that they develop shadow detail strongly and have the same effect as increasing the speed of the film. These can be useful for low-light photography, but disadvantages include a tendency to fog, high contrast and pronounced grain. Paterson Acuspeed is an example.

Finally, line film is used for the highest

contrast. This is developed in a formula that produces an image with virtually no intermediate tones - simply dense black silver or clear film.

Because of slight variations in the formula between makes of the same type, the choice of film and developer can create subtle differences in the image. Most photographers experiment until they find a combination that satisfies them, and then stick to it. One influence on the decision is the form in which the chemicals are sold. Powder is often cheaper and easier to store, while liquid is more conve-

nient to make up. For continuous daily use or long runs, a developer that can be replenished is economical, but for occasional use, a "one-shot" developer, which is discarded after one process, is probably better.

The action of the developer depends on how concentrated the solution is, how long the film is left in it, and its temperature. Within certain limits, these can be varied to raise or lower the film speed and to change the contrast. (The more development, the more contrast and vice versa.) Obviously, with so many variables, including the differences between films and developers, there is no single method of altering contrast. One important consideration is graininess – the more the development, the coarser the grain, so that extending development to increase the speed of a slow, fine-grained film is a waste of effort. The instructions packed with film and developer are the best guide, at least as a starting point.

To stop the action of the developer, the film is either rinsed in water, or in a stop bath of dilute acetic acid. The acid neutralizes the developer more rapidly and effectively than water is able to do. The purpose of this rinse is to prevent developer being carried over into the fixer, where it could cause stains. Some stop baths

contain an indicator dye which changes colour to show when they are exhausted.

After the rinse, the developed film must be fixed, to prevent further darkening. To do this, the remaining, unexposed silver halides must be dissolved. How long the negative lasts depends on the thoroughness of the fixing. One chemical – hypo – is used universally for fixing. It works best at a concentration of about 20% to 40% (stronger solutions penetrate the emulsion less easily). Some fixers contain alum to harden the emulsion and so make it resistant to scratches; others contain ammonium chloride to speed up the action.

Finally, the film must be washed to remove all traces of the fixer, which would otherwise make the image fade in time. The temperature of the water is not particularly important, but the time and flow are. Generally, at least an hour's washing is needed for fine grain film, slightly less for a coarser grained emulsion. The film is then hung to dry, in a dust-free atmosphere, and ideally in a gentle flow of warm air. Drops of water must be removed with a rubber squeegee or sponge, otherwise drying marks will mar the emulsion. A few drops of wetting agent in the final wash help to avoid this marking.

left To make sure that the action of the chemicals is carried out evenly across the film, the loaded tank must be agitated by inverting it. Follow the film manufacturer's recommendations for frequency of agitation: too much will give more development than planned and may cause surge marks, while too little will give uneven development.

. Pour indicator stop bath into the tank to halt all development, and agitate as before.

6. After about 30 seconds, return the stop bath to its container, checking its colour to see if it is yet exhausted.

7. Pour in fixer, setting the time as recommended by the manufacturer. Agitate as before.

8. After fixing, the film may be removed briefly for inspection in full light. All further stages can be carried out without the tank's lid.

. Using a filtered hose, wash the film in the tank. Insert the end of the hose deep into the cover of the reel, and use only a mild flow of water.

10. After washing, add a few drops of wetting agent to avoid later drying marks.

11. Attach one clip to the end of the film, and draw out from the reel.

12. When hanging the film to dry, draw a squeegee lightly along its length, to remove drops of water.

INTENSIFYING AND REDUCING

Even after development, the structure of a negative image can be altered in several ways, using chemicals. Intensification increases the density of the negative by adding silver or some other metal to the existing silver deposits. Reduction converts some of the silver image into a compound that can then be dissolved away.

The basic function of both intensifiers and reducers is to convert poorly exposed or developed negatives into ones that can be printed, and they are nearly always used as corrective measures. However, they do have additional effects, and can also be used to alter the grain structure and contrast. There is some risk in treating original negatives with chemicals; it may be safer to apply the reducer or intensifier to the print instead, or to make a copy negative and work on that.

There are many chemicals that will do the job, with varying effects. All tend to soften the gelatin. To counteract this effect, it is usual to soak the negative in a hardening bath first. Intensification and reduction invariably exaggerate grain; this is usually a disadvantage, particularly if the negative is to be enlarged substantially, but is occasionally sought after.

The most commonly used type of intensifier acts proportionally, adding density according to the original distribution of tones. In other words, the effect is the same as increased development. Chromium, silver and mercury intensifiers are all common, although chromium is especially popular because it gives relatively little increase in graininess. Mercury intensifier exaggerates grain more than most, and needs to be handled with great care, as it is very poisonous. A relatively new intensifier uses quinone and thiosulphate to give very strong density on modern high-speed films.

Above and right The thin, underexposed negative (*above*) was intensified chemically in a proprietary solution for the result (*right*). The procedure was straightforward: the negative was soaked in water for about 10 minutes, then transferred to a dish containing the intensifier and agitated gently. The degree of intensification is proportional to the length of time the negative remains in the solution, but in most cases, between one and three minutes will increase the contrast by two or three times. When the desired amount of intensification was reached, the negative was washed for 20 minutes, and dried. One of the noticeable side-effects of intensification is the increase in graininess, which can add character of a sort to some images, but for highly detailed, textural views, is usually a disadvantage.

Altering film development
One of the basic problems of exposure is that the degree of contrast allowed by a film does not always fit the brightness range in the subject. In this situation it is useful to alter the contrast of a film by changing its development.
Under-development lowers contrast and so extends the tonal range *(1)*. Over-development increases contrast, compressing the tonal range *(2)*. Therefore, with a high contrast subject, where bright highlights and dense shadows cannot both be recorded on a normally processed negative, under-developing the film (by shortening the time or diluting the chemicals) will help. To compensate, the exposure will have had to have been increased.
On the other hand, if the subject is flat, increasing the development (by extending the time, raising the temperature or increasing the concentration of developer) will make the image more lively. In this case, the exposure must have been reduced. For this type of contrast control, adjustments in the order of a half or one f-stop are normally made. This control is easier with sheet film than with rollfilm, as single images can be given individual processing.

Some intensifiers, such as copper chloride, add to the dense areas of the negative in greater proportion than they do to the thin areas, and so can be used to increase contrast. Others, like chromium if it is only partly bleached or redeveloped, add more in proportion to the negative's light areas.

The most widely used type of reducer dissolves silver equally from all areas of the negative – that is, not in proportion to the original deposits – and so increases contrast. This is often used to clear up fog. Ferricyanide reducers, such as Farmer's Reducer, are the most common.

Other reducers, such as permanganate/persulphate and Farmer's, when used in two solutions (ferricyanide bath first, followed by hypo), act in proportion to the original image and can therefore be used to correct the high contrast that overdevelopment can cause. Some reducers even work super-proportionally, leaving greater density in the heavy areas of the negative than in the lighter; ammonium persulphate does this, and gives a strong reduction in contrast.

Above and left The overexposed negative (*left*) was given chemical reduction to make printing practical (*above*). As with intensification, the procedure began with a soak in water for 10 minutes; the negative was then agitated gently in a dish of Farmer's Reducer for several seconds. Less time is needed than for intensification, and the negative must be carefully watched to avoid dissolving too much of the silver image. After the reducing solution, the negative was washed for 20 minutes, and dried.

MAKING A COPY NEGATIVE

For darkroom processes that involve contact printing, such as the platinum process, using printing-out paper and those where extremely accurate register is essential, a large negative has to be used, preferably about 8 x 10 inch (20 x 24cm). 35mm and 2¼ x 2¼ inch (6 x 6cm) film is too small to allow really detailed manipulation, and the standard procedure in professional labs is to make an enlarged duplicate negative. This also has other advantages. The large image area makes retouching possible, and sometimes the tonal gradation can be improved by giving more or less light to different parts of the image while making the duplicate. Finally, valuable negatives are often duplicated for safety, and it is no more trouble to make an enlarged duplicate than one that is simply the same size.

Using a direct-reversal film such as Kodak Professional Direct Duplicating Film, the procedure is as simple as the production of an ordinary black-and-white print. Processed in a standard developer, this film produces in one step a negative from a negative. Unlike most printing papers and negative films, a shorter exposure gives a dense image, while increasing the exposure produces a weaker negative. Since exposure varies with enlarger equipment, a series of tests with a standard negative helps to establish a basic level. The sensitivity of the film is roughly similar to that of many printing papers.

For accurate assessment, the copy negative should be compared with its original on a light box. As with most duplicating procedures, there is usually a tendency for the copy to have higher contrast than the original. This is an automatic advantage if the original is flat, but with a negative which already has high contrast, precautions need to be taken: shadow areas can be given less exposure by shading them from the enlarger's light, dense highlights can be given additional exposure, and the development time can be shortened.

The final result is a print-sized negative that is robust, easy to handle, and can be used for a large number of special processes. By altering the density and the contrast of the duplicate negative, it can be tailored to suit different techniques.

Above With the 50mm enlarger lens stopped down to f11 for maximum sharpness, this 35mm negative was exposed for 30 seconds and the 8 x 10 inch (20 x 24 cm) copy negative (*right*) developed for two minutes in Kodak D-163.

1

2

3

Basic procedure **1.** Place the original negative in the enlarger's carrier, in exactly the same way as for printing. **2.** Using a regular printing easel, focus and frame the image.

3. Using a weak red safelight (the duplicating film is sensitive only to blue light), expose the film. A test strip may be necessary to calculate the exact exposure time and aperture setting.

Here, the shadow areas are shaded to hold detail. Develop for about 2 to 2½ minutes in a dish. (The actual time will depend on the developer and on the level of contrast desired.) Rinse in water for 30 seconds. Fix for 5 to 10 minutes, agitating frequently. Wash for 20 to 30 minutes in running water. After a weak bath of wetting agent, hang to dry.

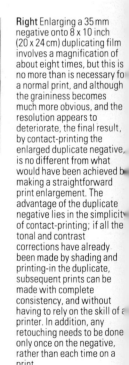

Right Enlarging a 35mm negative onto 8 x 10 inch (20 x 24 cm) duplicating film involves a magnification of about eight times, but this is no more than is necessary for a normal print, and although the graininess becomes much more obvious, and the resolution appears to deteriorate, the final result, by contact-printing the enlarged duplicate negative, is no different from what would have been achieved by making a straightforward print enlargement. The advantage of the duplicate negative lies in the simplicity of contact-printing; if all the tonal and contrast corrections have already been made by shading and printing-in the duplicate, subsequent prints can be made with complete consistency, and without having to rely on the skill of a printer. In addition, any retouching needs to be done only once on the negative, rather than each time on a print.

COLOR FILM

Color photography is made possible by the fact that a full color spectrum can' be created by combining just three colors. These three basic colors are known as primaries, and to be effective they must be spaced equally along the visible spectrum. Color film, therefore, contains three layers of silver bromide, each sensitive to a different primary color: blue, green and red. Normal silver bromide is, in any case, very sensitive to blue, so it is principally the other two layers that must be sensitized with appropriate dyes, one to green and the other to red. These three layers do not divide up the spectrum neatly but overlap intentionally, which helps to reproduce mixed colors. The colors of the actual dyes are those that are complementary to the primaries: yellow, magenta and cyan absorb, respectively, blue, green and red.

Our eyes are capable of adjusting to considerable differences in color temperature, and we tend to overlook the orange cast of tungsten lighting or the blueness of shaded areas under a clear sky. Color film, however, must be balanced (that is, sensitized during manufacture) for one particular color temperature. Daylight color films are therefore designed to give accurate color reproduction under midday sunlight – 5500K – while nearly all of those designed for use under tungsten lighting are balanced for 3200K. Either type of color film – daylight- or tungsten-balanced – can be used with lighting of a different color temperature by using an appropriate color balancing filter over the camera lens.

Reversal film (slide film) produces transparencies with positive images which are viewed directly on a light box, in a magnifying viewer, or with a slide projector. They are also preferred in graphic reproduction – for books and magazines. Negative film is designed for color prints. Transparencies can also be used to make prints, either directly or by means of an intermediate negative; conversely, color negatives can be copied to produce transparencies.

Modern color films use variations of what is known as dye-coupling development. The image is exposed onto silver bromide and developed into silver, in the same way as black-and-white film, but during development dye-couplers are attracted to the silver image in the three layers. These produce the color; the silver is then removed. In the final image each silver grain is replaced by a dye "cloud" so that, effectively, color films do show graininess even though the silver grains are no longer present. The high resolution that comes with fine grain can only be achieved at the expense of a slow speed rating, while a fast film is necessarily grainy.

There are two main types of color film. Nonsubstantive films, such as Kodachrome, contain no color materials themselves; these have to be added during complex processing by the manufacturer. The advantage is a thin film and high resolution, which is the basis of Kodachrome's great popularity among professional photographers, even though it is a film designed for amateur use. Other films, which make up the majority of those on the market, contain the color couplers in the layers; as a result, development is relatively simple and can be undertaken by users.

One unavoidable fact, which luckily only causes problems occasionally, is that the three-color process is not accurate. Despite the overlap between the three dyes, there are many subtle hues that cannot be reproduced. This difficulty arises when certain flowers are photographed, or when color film is being duplicated. However, this basic deficiency is not as serious as it sounds because pure colors are not common in nature. Color film is designed just to give a pleasing sensation of color, which it does in most cases perfectly well.

Manufacturing film
Kodak produces over 650 different types of film, but is particularly well-known for its color film. These photographs illustrate some of the stages in film manufacture.
1. First, the film base or support is made. Dry cellulose acetate is dissolved in solvents to produce a clear liquid called "dope". The dope is piped to giant roll coating wheels which revolve slowly, spreading the dope in a thin coating. The solvents in the dope are then driven off by hot air, leaving a solid sheet of strong, clear plastic.
2. The base leaves the wheel, is dried for a further hour and is then wound into large rolls.

1

2

3

4

3. The next stage is the preparation of emulsion. Gelatin is mixed with inorganic halide and silver nitrate. Silver nitrate crystals, extremely light-sensitive, form, suspended in the gelatin. This operation, and subsequent stages, takes place in darkness. Each emulsion is adjusted according to the type of film being made. In the case of color film, chemicals are added to make the emulsion more sensitive to the light of different colors. Thin coatings of the emulsion are then applied to the film base. These coatings must be of uniform thickness and great precision is required to achieve accuracy to one-millionth of an inch.
4. The film is cut to size, wound on spools or in magazines, or packed flat. Finally, the film is inspected, placed in cartons and transferred to special storerooms.

PROCESSING

Because the original silver image in colour films must be replaced with colour dyes, there are more processing stages than with black-and-white film. Also, the addition of colour as another variable makes the conditions under which the film is processed more critical – there are fewer tolerances in temperature, timing and composition of the chemicals, and the set procedures must be followed with greater accuracy.

Colour developers are not interchangeable in the same way as black-and-white developers are, and the chemistry must match the emulsion. Kodak's E-6 process is the most widely used among reversal films; some other manufacturers, such as Fuji, produce film that can be developed on it.

Transparencies need reversal processing. This means that development takes place in two stages: the first produces a negative silver image in the same way that normal black-and-white film is developed. At this point, the negative image is in stable silver, while the parts of the film that have no image still contain unexposed silver halides. The whole film is then exposed – to light, or by chemical means – so that the still-sensitive silver halides can produce a positive image. They do this under the action of a second (colour) developer. At this stage, the film contains a black silver negative image and a positive image made up of both silver and coloured dyes. All that remains is to bleach away the silver to leave a positive colour image. Taking into account fixing and other intermediate baths, a typical reversal process, such as E-6, has nine steps.

Colour negatives use a more direct process, with one developer that produces a negative image in silver and dye. Bleaching then removes the silver. Kodak's C-41 process is the most widely used. Because the dyes used in colour film – in particular the magenta and cyan – are far from perfect, colour negatives also contain an orange mask to ease printing.

As with black-and-white emulsions, increasing the development raises contrast, while reducing it lowers contrast, and this can be used to control image values, but only to a limited extent. The three layers do not respond identically to the altered development, so that some shift in colour cast occurs; this varies between makes of film. Nevertheless, in certain areas of still life photography, for example, it is common practice to push colour transparency film by one-third or half an f-stop in order to increase the contrast slightly and so clean up highlights.

1. With all the chemicals assembled, and at the recommended temperature, pour the colour developer into the developing tank, and start the timer. Agitate as necessary.

2. Just before the end of the development time, start to pour the developer back into its container, so as to finish draining the tank on time. Add the next solution and reset the timer.

3. Add the fixer in the same way, and wash with a hose and water filter. All steps following the bleach can be carried out with the tank lid removed.

4. Some processes require the film to be soaked finally in stabilizer. After this bath, dry the film by hanging in an atmosphere free of dust.

5. Reversal processing chemistry varies _____, but the most widely used is _____ ere. Start by pouring _____ k. Start the timer.

6. Follow the recommendations for agitation. Empty the tank so as to finish at the end of the seven-minute development time.

7. Wash for two minutes with a hose and filter, or else simply add water, agitate and drain, twice.

8. Drain the water, then add the reversal solution for two minutes. Re-check the temperature of the colour developer, which will be added next.

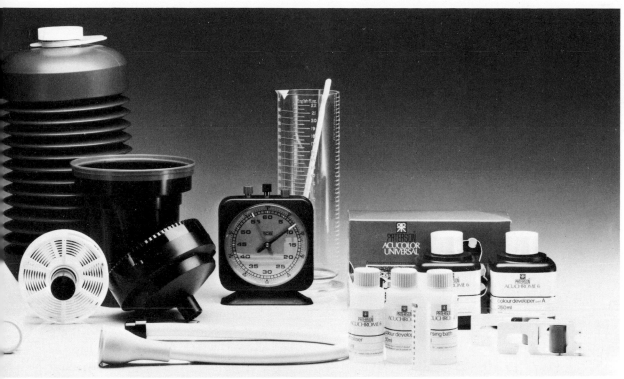

Above Equipment shown here is *(left to right)*: squeegee tongs, funnel, collapsible chemical container, film reel, developing tank, rubber hose, timer, graduate and thermometer, processing kit and drying clips. Commercial processing kits are available for small quantities of film, which suits most amateur use, although most professional photographers use custom labs to develop their film, for time and convenience. Most processing kits provide concentrated solutions, which are then made up into stock solutions.

Colour film processing is straightforward but requires stringent control of timing and temperature and, of course, absolute cleanliness. Because the chemical solutions are expensive, and more are used than in black-and-white processing, they should be stored efficiently, in such a way that they are not liable to oxidization. One of the best designs of container is collapsible, so that the volume can be adjusted, and no air need remain inside. Once the stock chemicals have been made up from the kit, label each container. Although it is not strictly

necessary to use a separate graduate for each solution, if fewer containers are used they must be cleaned thoroughly after each use, to prevent contaminating other chemicals.
To maintain the several chemicals at the correct temperature – 100°F (37.8°C) for the commonest processes, E-6 reversal and C-41 negative – the simplest and least expensive method is to stand the solutions in a large bowl of heated water; the first developer can be heated to the exact temperature, while the water surrounding the other chemicals can be two or

three degrees warmer, to allow for cooling during the process. An accurate thermometer is essential. First developer temperature is the most critical, and needs to be accurate to within 1°F (½°C). Colour developer has rather more latitude, and the other solutions much more. A purpose-built thermo-statically controlled solution bath is expensive but ensures accuracy.
As there are several timed stages, it is better to have a timer that can be preset each time, rather than rely on memory. It also helps to keep a list of all the things

prominently displayed. For washing, use a hose and filter, and for drying use a squeegee to remove water droplets from the film.

After returning the reversal solution to its container, add the colour developer, making sure that the temperature is correct. After six minutes, replace with stop bath.

10. Return the stop bath to its container after two minutes. Add bleach for seven minutes, and then fix for four minutes.

11. Wash for six minutes and then soak in stabilizer for one minute. Remove the film to dry.

12. Dry by hanging in a dust-free atmosphere. Replace the stabilizer in its container.

COLOR FILM BRANDS

Whereas different brands of black-and-white film do not vary a great deal within any particular range of speed, the extra dimension of color makes it possible to distinguish between color transparency films from different manufacturers. Color films can be judged on color fidelity, speed and graininess, sharpness and color saturation. Manufacturers can also vary the dyes and their sensitivity to perform at their best under certain specific conditions. For instance, one manufacturer may aim for a rich blue to enhance the appearance of holiday snapshots. Another may try to reproduce flesh colors as accurately as possible. Yet another may produce a film that gives adequate results over a range of color temperatures rather than accurate results under just one type of illumination.

Because color film can only ever produce an acceptable impression of color rather than a precise reproduction, any overall judgement is essentially subjective. Most photographers choose one or two color emulsions for the majority of their work; in this way, they become familiar with their characteristics under a wide range of conditions.

Above and left The differences between color emulsions can be clearly seen, when the photographs are sufficiently enlarged. A small section of the Kodachrome 25 transparency *(above)* remains extremely sharp, with virtually no graininess; in fact, at 100 lines per millimeter, this film has one of the highest resolving powers. In addition, colors are well-saturated, and the reds and yellow are particularly vivid. By contrast, the Ektachrome 400 transparency *(left)* suffers for its extra speed by being relatively flat, with poorer color saturation, and a grain structure that is more noticeable even at a lesser magnification: it resolves only 63 lines per millimeter. In addition, it is slightly blue overall – a feature that help it record tungsten-lit nighttime scenes more accurately, but may be a disadvantage in balanced lighting.

Kodachrome 25

Kodachrome 64

Ektachrome 64

Ektachrome 200

Ektachrome 400

Left When judged side by side, a single scene photographed on different makes of color film shows up differences that would normally go unnoticed. At the same time, however, none of these differences is outstanding, and for general photography, any of the films used here, with the single exception of the infrared emulsion, would be satisfactory. Most photographers tend to be partisan about their preferred choice of color film, but as this series shows, there are more similarities than differences. The films chosen for this test are all reversal (color negatives have to be printed, and this introduces so many variables that individual film qualities are masked), and represent the brands most commonly available.

The two Kodachrome emulsions differ in principle from the others in that the color dyes are added during processing. This confers the advantage of very little graininess, a quality that accounts for their widespread professional use, despite being marketed by Kodak as amateur films. Apart from this, the major scale of difference for all the films is in sensitivity to light. As with black-and-white emulsions, film speed is achieved only at the expense of graininess, while good resolution of fine detail is possible only with a slow film. As a result, most color film manufacturers produce a range that covers slow, high resolution films (ASA 50 to ASA 100), and fast, grainy films (around ASA 400). In addition, Kodak produce Kodachrome 25, which allows great enlargements with little break-up of the image. Within these broad groupings, some makes are better than others at resolving detail. Color fidelity also varies; inevitably so, because the limitations of the three dyes used in these films prevents absolute accuracy, so that most films are designed to reproduce *certain* colors well. Ektachrome infrared is an unusual emulsion, sensitive to both normal "white" light and invisible infrared radiation. Because many objects reflect infrared radiation in different proportions to the way they reflect light, the results are difficult to predict. Being over-sensitive to blue, it should be used with a yellow filter.

Agfa CT18

Agfa CT21

Fujichrome 100

Fujichrome 400

3M 400

Ektachrome Infrared with 12 yellow filter

INSTANT FILM

Instant film has revolutionized many fields of photography, and will continue to do so as its processes are improved and extended to different products. Although it is most popular for family snapshots, it also has a wealth of more serious uses. Photomechanical reproduction is possible directly from instant prints (although not quite as easily as from transparencies, for which most separation-making is geared). Instant prints can also be used by professional photographers as an important intermediate stage to test composition and lighting.

The different types of instant films, virtually all of which are manufactured by Polaroid, have special image qualities. This impression is the result of very high resolution and average acutance. (Being contact-printed, the images are particularly sharp.) In other words, fine details are recorded particularly well, although the edges between different tones are not as crisp as in many regular prints made from conventional negatives. The almost imperceptible haze over a very precise image is a quality often admired in Polaroid prints.

While Polaroid materials give a higher contrast than their conventional equivalents, the tone separation within their narrow range is particularly good, and it is extremely difficult to reproduce the print quality of a Polaroid original by enlarging a normal negative taken of the same scene. Although the narrow contrast range is obviously a disadvantage in many situations, it can be used to bring life to subjects photographed under very flat lighting. Type 51, which gives exceptionally high contrast prints, is ideal for dull weather photography or for copying faded originals.

The most important advantage of instant films is, however, their immediacy. Reproduction quality prints can be made with virtually no delay, so that it is possible to assess results on the spot and, if necessary, correct them. Although conventional processes have accustomed photographers to working with a significant gap between picture-taking and picture development, the various Polaroid products offer the obvious benefits of being able to create an immediate image.

Most black-and-white Polaroid materials work by means of a disposable negative, a self-contained pod of chemicals and a receiving paper that becomes the print. After exposure, a conventional silver image develops on the negative when the chemicals in the pod are squeezed over it by rollers. The unexposed silver halide is then dissolved by a fixing agent, and migrates to the paper opposite, where it develops into a metallic silver positive image. The film is then opened by peeling, and the print separated from the remainder. Types 55 and 665 (the differences are those of format) deliver, in addition to a print, a useable negative with extremely high resolution; when exposed outdoors, this can be stored in a special bucket containing sodium sulphite, which preserves it until it can be hung to dry.

Polacolor, which is used in the same way as the peel-apart black-and-white materials, also has a negative which is discarded after development. This negative, like conventional colour materials, is made up of three layers, each sensitive to a different colour. However, each layer is actually in two parts: a silver halide emulsion and a dye developer. The chemical pod, when squeezed, releases an alkali solution which activates the dye developer; the dyes then pass through to the receiving paper which forms the print.

The more recent SX-70 process uses many of the same principles, but both emulsions and

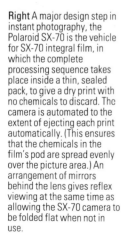

Right A major design step in instant photography, the Polaroid SX-70 is the vehicle for SX-70 integral film, in which the complete processing sequence takes place inside a thin, sealed pack, to give a dry print with no chemicals to discard. The camera is automated to the extent of ejecting each print automatically. (This ensures that the chemicals in the film's pod are spread evenly over the picture area.) An arrangement of mirrors behind the lens gives reflex viewing at the same time as allowing the SX-70 camera to be folded flat when not in use.

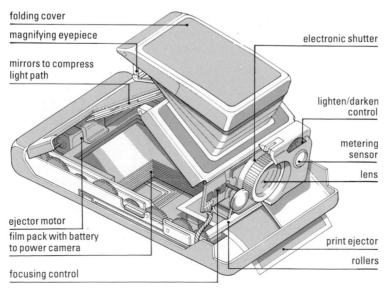

folding cover
magnifying eyepiece
mirrors to compress light path
electronic shutter
lighten/darken control
metering sensor
lens
ejector motor
film pack with battery to power camera
focusing control
print ejector
rollers

Left With this range of
cameras and camera
attachments, instant
photography can be practised
at both amateur and
professional levels, from fully
automated snapshots to 8 x
10 inch (20 x 24cm) prints
made with a regular studio
view camera. The Polaroid
600 SE is built in the style of
a rollfilm press camera for
quick, uncomplicated use,
but accepts 5 different
instant films. The 640 model
camera is simple,
inexpensive, and takes a new
ASA 600 print film for basic
amateur photography. The
two versions of the SX-70
camera differ in that the
Sonar One-step focuses
automatically on the subject
by means of a reflected sonar
beam.
The three holders at the front
of the group are for use with
standard cameras as an
alternative to normal film;
the 545 takes individual
sheets of 4 x 5 inch (10 x
13cm) film, the other two
take film packs for use on
Hasselblad cameras.
At the rear of the picture is
the equipment needed to
produce colour 8 x 10 inch
(20 x 24cm) prints with a
large studio view camera: a
film holder, and a
motor-driven film processor
that spreads the chemicals
over the film more evenly
than would be possible by
hand.
Apart from the 640 and SX-70
cameras, which use a single
type of film, the equipment
shown here makes it possible
to use a range of instant film
types.

Type 52 Polapan

Type 59 Polacolor ER

Type 58 Polacolor

Type 57

Type 55 negative

Type 51

Types of Polaroid film
Above Several Polaroid emulsions are available in sheet and pack form, with characteristics that differ in film speed, contrast, and even the wavelengths to which they are sensitive. Type 52 is one of the most popular 4 x 5 inch (9 x 12 cm) sheet films, having a relatively high film speed of ASA 400, but giving high resolution prints that are well-graded across the contrast range of about six stops. (All instant films have rather high contrast when compared with regular emulsions, and generally look best when used for low-contrast scenes.) Type 57, and its rollfilm equivalents types 87 and 107, have such a high film speed – ASA 3000 – that they can be used in dim light with a reasonably fast shutter or small aperture. By comparison with type 52, the contrast is higher, and the image grainier. Type 55, and the rollfilm pack Type 665, produce both a print, which is similar in some respects to the image quality of type 52, and a negative, which can later be used to make regular prints. The film speed is ASA 50, but as a properly exposed print accompanies a slightly thin negative, ASA 25 is a better rating for negatives. Type 51 is a specialized emulsion, giving prints that have very high contrast and are very blue-sensitive – in this example, the blue ink is so overexposed that it is virtually invisible in the print. Its film speed is ASA 320 in daylight, but in tungsten ASA 125.

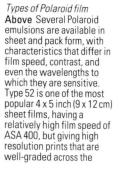

Right The dyes used in Polacolor prints are well saturated and very resistant to fading, making them useful as final images – for display or even for photomechanical reproduction – rather than just as tests. Polaroid 59 is the newer, improved version, having richer colors and cleaner whites than the earlier Type 58. The color saturation of these prints can be enhanced by prolonging development, although this tends to introduce a slight bluish cast, which needs the correction of red and yellow filters.

Type 55 print

chemicals are contained between two thick outer layers, and nothing is discarded. The chemical pod, which is squeezed through the layers of emulsion, contains both dyes and the dense white pigment titanium dioxide. This pigment eventually becomes the background to the developed dye image. To ensure an even spread of chemicals across the picture area, SX-70 film is designed to be used in special cameras, which roll out the prints by means of an electric motor. Polacolor 600 and Kodak Instant Picture Print Film must also be used in special cameras with automatic ejection. The metallized dyes used in Polacolor and SX-70 are very stable, and resist fading better than conventional colour materials.

Although processing is automatic, considerable control over image values is possible with many types of instant film. While some films are designed only for use in special cameras, many can be exposed and processed in backs that attach to view cameras and some rollfilm models. Special instant film cameras, being tailored mainly for the amateur market, are generally fully automatic, but a Polaroid back on a regular camera allows all the normal controls – aperture, shutter speed, movements, multiple exposure – to be exercised. With automatic models, exposure can be altered to a small extent by means of a simple darken/lighten control (this generally allows up to one f-stop overexposure or underexposure), but for more adjustment than this can offer, a neutral density filter can be used. Placed over the lens, it reduces exposure, but over the sensor it increases the amount of light reaching the film. A ND 0.30 filter has a value of one f-stop, a ND 0.60 filter two stops.

Integral films such as SX-70 develop automatically for a standard time, and so allow little interference. With some other Polaroid films, however, altering the development time can

Above The coating applied to black-and-white Polaroid prints removes the last traces of reagent. By delaying coating; the reagent is allowed to continue working on the light areas of the print. This can be useful in brightening white backgrounds: compare this Type 52 print treated in this way with the one on the previous page.

Above Automatic instant film cameras, such as this SX-70, have a simple lighten/darken control, with a range of approximately two f-stops.

Above To alter the exposure beyond the range of the lighten/darken control, a neutral density filter can be used, either over the sensor, as shown here, to increase exposure, or over the lens, to decrease exposure.

Above Type 55 negatives need to be cleared in a solution of sodium thiosulphate before being allowed to dry. On location, plastic bucket, available from Polaroid, can be used to store up to eight negatives in this solution.

Instant film types	Format	Print size	Speed ASA
Colour print			
Type 809 Polacolor ER	Sheet	8⁷⁄₁₆ x 10⁷⁄₈in (22 x 27cm)	80
Type 808 Polacolor	Sheet	8⁷⁄₁₆ x 10⁷⁄₈in (22 x 27cm)	80
Type 59 Polacolor ER	Sheet	4 x 5in (10.5 x 13cm)	80
Type 558 Polacolor	Pack	4 x 5in (10.5 x 13cm)	80
Type 58 Polacolor	Sheet	4 x 5in (10.5 x 13cm)	80
Type 108 Polacolor	Pack	3¼ x 4¼in (8.3 x 10.8cm)	80
Type 668 Polacolor	Pack	3¼ x 4¼in (8.3 x 10.8cm)	80
Type 88 Polacolor	Pack	3¼ x 3⅜in (8.3 x 8.6cm)	80
SX-70	Pack	3½ x 4¼in (8.7 x 10.5cm)	N.a.
Polaroid 600	Pack	3½ x 4¼in (8.7 x 10.5cm)	N.a.
Black-and-white high-speed print			
Type 57	Sheet	4 x 5in (10.5 x 13cm)	3000

Instant film types	Format	Print size	Speed ASA
Type 667	Pack	3¼ x 4¼in (8.3 x 10.8cm)	3000
Type 87	Pack	3¼ x 3⅜in (8.3 x 8.6cm)	3000
Positive and negative			
Type 55	Sheet	4 x 5in (10.5 x 13cm)	50
Type 665	Pack	3¼ x 4¼in (8.3 x 10.8cm)	75
Fine grain print			
Type 552 Polapan	Pack	4 x 5in (10.5 x 13cm)	400
Type 52 Polapan	Sheet	4 x 5in (10.5 x 13cm)	400
High contrast print			
Type 51	Sheet	4 x 5in (10.5 x 13cm)	125 Tungsten
			320 Daylight

affect the image. With all the black-and-white films except the positive/negative types (55 and 665), extended development darkens shadow areas and short development lightens them. With the appropriate exposure, this can be used to alter contrast, as the lighter-toned areas of the print are unaffected: to raise contrast, the exposure is increased by about half an f-stop and the print developed for at least twice the recommended time. For less contrast, the exposure is reduced and the print is developed for the minimum recommended time, although in this case there is some risk of streaking or mottling because of insufficient development. With Polacolor, reducing development is not satisfactory, but extending it produces more saturated colours and deepens blacks. At the same time, the print tends to acquire a bluish cast, which can be corrected by using weak yellow and red filters during exposure.

Another useful way of clearing up highlights in a black-and-white Polaroid is to delay applying the coating that protects the surface of the print. Apart from its protective value, this coating also removes the last traces of reagent, which would otherwise continue to work on the image. If the print is left uncoated for several minutes, the highlight areas will become lighter, and the contrast increased (middle and dark tones are unaffected).

Finally, with any camera that allows multiple exposure, the contrast of a Polaroid print can be reduced by pre-exposing the film. This means, in effect, fogging the whole area of the emulsion very slightly, to lighten the shadow areas. To do this, the camera is aimed, out of focus, at any light, even-toned subject, such as the sky, a white wall, or a sheet of paper, and an exposure is made that is about three stops *less* than the meter reading. The film is then ready to use: the lighter tones of the image are not

Above Polaroid produce a wide range of products, for use both in special cameras, such as the SX 70, and in film backs that can be attached to regular cameras. Most of these are for professional and scientific use. Kodak produce only one film, for the amateur market.

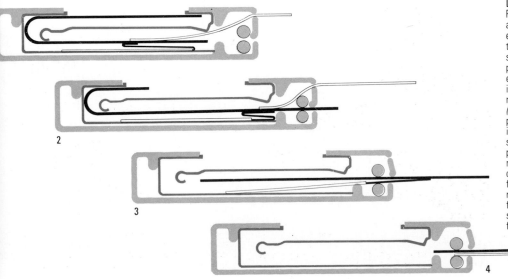

Left For rapid shooting, Polaroid film packs are available for some emulsions. Inside each pack, the several negatives are stacked separately from the printing paper *(1)*. After exposure, a small white tab is pulled to draw the negative round to the back of the pack *(2)* to face a sheet of printing paper. Then a larger black tab is pulled, to draw the sandwiched negative and paper out through a pair of rollers *(3)* which break a chemical pod. Once removed from the film pack *(4)* the negative can be separated from the paper after some seconds to reveal a fully formed image.

Right This photo, taken by Paul Joyce using a Polasonic 1 SX-70 with a new Supercolor Time-zero SX-70 instant film, demonstrates the use of instant photos as an art-form. The camera has automatic focusing and exposure settings; the photographer had only to fix on the flash bar – but the resulting colours are startlin and the detail is clear. The most interesting aspect is th picture within the picture, a result of the spontaneous development of the first. The outcome of a delay in development might have been simply a picture of tomatoes.

Above Sometimes, the special properties of Polaroid films can be made use of in ways not originally intended by the manufacturer. In Polaroid SX-70 prints, used to produce the Peter Gabriel record cover at left, the package of chemicals squeezed over the picture area from the pod underneath takes more than an hour to dry thoroughly, and for the first several minutes is quite soft. After the exposure has been made and the image has started to form, the picture can be distorted by applying pressure to the front – or better still, the back – of the mutilated sandwich of dyes, white titanium dioxide, and other constituents. Well-planned creative use was made of this technique by burnishing the Polaroid portrait of singer Peter Gabriel, to make his face look like it was melting.

affected, but the shadow areas are opened up.

In all controlled conditions, such as a studio, and whenever the technical requirements leave some doubt as to the final appearance of a shot, Polaroid film is widely used as a means of assessing exposure, color balance, composition and other elements of the image. Improvements can then be made on the spot, and the client can be shown how the image will work. This is particularly valuable when a view camera is used, as the inverted image on a ground glass screen is often difficult to take in at a glance.

On other occasions, Polaroids are useful when the subject is moving so fast and unpredictably that it is impossible to predict the final image. For instance, if the photographer is

trying to take a picture of an egg breaking as falls onto a hard surface, even with some mean of synchronizing the egg and the camera shutter, there is no way of telling exactly ho the image will be until the film has been de veloped. With conventional film the delay ma be impractically long.

Another use of instant film, particularly i photojournalism, is as a means of winning coop eration from potential subjects. People wh might be shy or uncooperative in normal ci cumstances often respond very well to an offe of an instant portrait. Rather than promise send prints back later, an immediate photo graph is a good method of generating goodwi which in many assignments is an essentia commodity.

CHAPTER 3

THE DARKROOM

The collodion wet-plate process of the 1850s and 1860s meant that photographers had to prepare their emulsions immediately before taking a picture; if not, the collodion would dry in about 20 minutes and lose its sensitivity to light. The darkroom was an integral part of early photography; for outdoor work it was often in the form of a portable dark tent. Photographers such as Roger Fenton (1819-1869), the first secretary of The Photographic Society, London and best known for his coverage of the Crimean War, even went so far as to travel from one location to another with a darkened van. For every shot, he had to clean a large glass plate, coat it with collodion, soak it in a silver nitrate solution to make it sensitive to light, then lower it into a holder. After making the exposure, the plate had then to be processed in the darkened van as soon as possible.

Although these early darkrooms were essential for preparing and handling plates, printing used such slow materials that until the 1870s it could be done in sunlight, in contact with the negative. Under typical conditions, a contact print took about 20 minutes in direct sunlight. Only the development of the faster silver bromide papers made enlarging practical.

The development of the enlarger meant that the original negative no longer had to be the same size as the final print. This allowed a choice in both the size of film and the size of reproduction; most importantly, it enabled cameras to be miniaturized. The enlarger also created the need for the present style of darkroom. The silver bromide emulsions that were sensitive enough to respond to a projected image could become fogged easily by light leaking through cracks in doors and windows.

The first enlargers used daylight as a light source, but later this was replaced by gaslight, allowing more freedom in positioning the enlarger. Eventually, electric light bulbs became the standard source of illumination; apart from providing greater consistency than a flame, electric light made it possible to use enlargers vertically, a more convenient arrangement which allowed the paper to be laid flat.

In principle, very little has changed in darkrooms since the introduction of the enlarger. Black-and-white papers remain insensitive to red light – as were all photographic emulsions

originally, films included – which means they can be handled under a red safelight instead of in complete darkness. Progress in other areas of darkroom technology has been mainly in the form of improvements rather than radical alterations. Speed and ease of processes, and better image quality have been the major results of these changes. The growing popularity of colour printing has brought improvements in the accuracy of equipment to meet the more critical processing demands, and has encouraged manufacturers to find ways of sealing

more and more of the darkroom processes in light-tight containers, so that much of the work can now be carried out in normal light. The sophistication and extent of darkroom equipment depends partly on the type of printing undertaken, and partly on the value that a photographer places on convenience. For basic black-and-white printing, very little is needed beyond the enlarger itself, but care and time must make up for the lack of automation. Colour printing and special effects introduce more critical dimensions, and increase

Right This picture of Roger Fenton's second photographic van was taken at Pont-y-Pont, Lledr in North Wales. After his voyage to the Crimea, he travelled around Britain taking a large number of landscape and architectural pictures.

he need for the type of expensive equipment that can maintain accuracy of timing, temperature, filtration and other factors.

The enlarger is the central piece of equipment and most important purchase for any darkroom. It has to be able to deliver a consistent quality and quantity of light through an optical system that is capable of resolving the detail present in the negative, and it must be able to enlarge this image within a certain range. It must also be constructed and mounted sturdily enough to resist vibrations that could cause loss of sharpness in exposure times that commonly vary from about five to 30 seconds. The majority of enlargers are designed for 35mm negatives, reflecting the relative popularity of film and camera formats. Enlargers capable of projecting large sheet formats are disproportionately expensive and built mainly to professional standards; these larger models can often be mounted on a wall in order to save space, or are free-standing.

Enlarger accessories include an easel, or printing frame, which should have adjustable

Above In 1854 the British government commissioned Roger Fenton to photograph the Crimean War. The wet collodion process he was using in the later 1850s necessitated his travelling in a horsedrawn van with an assistant, as the photograph shows, because he was not only carrying domestic essentials such as books, dishes and glassware, but also heavy photographic equipment, which included his range of cameras, a tripod, chemicals and grooved boxes for hundreds of glass plates. He described the vehicle as "the foundation of all my labours". He returned to London with 300 negatives of well-composed views of the campaign; these were to comprise the first comprehensive documentation of war. 49 silver prints are now in the Royal Photographic Society's historical collection. There were, however, no action scenes, which were beyond the capabilities of the process and probably the durability of the van.

Below Darkrooms differ too much for any one to be considered typical, but this specimen layout contains most of the features needed for film processing and printmaking, in color and black-and-white, by a single photographer working in 35mm or rollfilm format. The dry stages, where original negatives are handled and enlarged, are well separated from the wet processes, to avoid contamination, and by arranging all the equipment on waist-high benches around the room, everything is easily accessible. The more ordered the layout, the less problem there is in locating materials and equipment when working in darkness.

masks so that prints of different sizes can be held securely and flat; a timer that can be preset, preferably connected to the lamp switch in the enlarger head; a focus magnifier; a contact printing frame; and a safelight. For color enlarging, either an additional head is needed if the enlarger is adaptable, or a separate color enlarger must be provided; a color analyzer simplifies the filter calculations needed for accurate color balance, and a voltage stabilizer ensures consistent color temperature and light output from the lamp.

Darkrooms are normally divided into two sections, both in function and layout. Enlarging is the first, "dry" stage; processing is the second. Chemical contamination of negatives

and other materials used in the dry section can be avoided by keeping the enlarging and the processing functions separated in different areas of the room. For black-and-white printing, three chemical trays and a wash tray are sufficient, with running water, a thermometer, and some means of maintaining the temperature of the developer at around 60°F (20°C). An electrically heated tray is needed if the room is normally cold. Tongs protect skin from contact with chemicals and reduce cross-contamination between solutions. Special film washers are more efficient and mean that less water is used. Prints can be dried in racks, between blotters, suspended from clips on a line, or in an electrically heated drier.

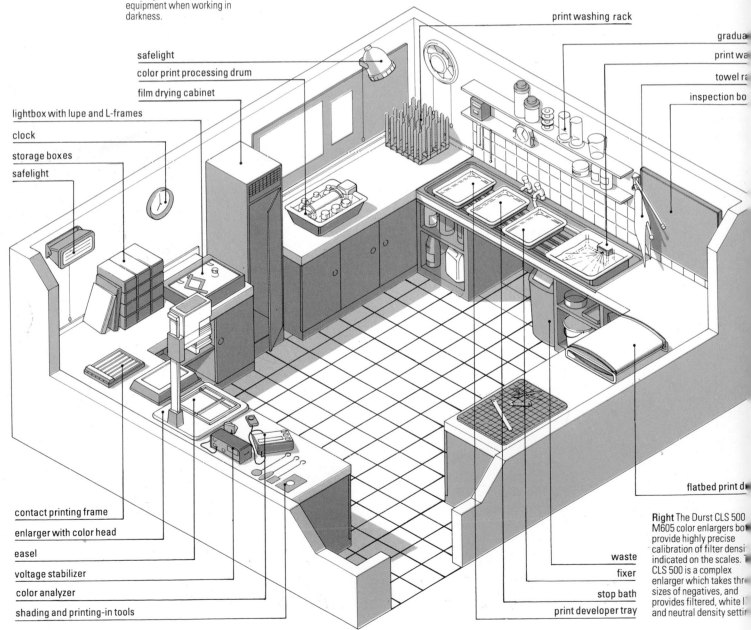

safelight
color print processing drum
film drying cabinet
lightbox with lupe and L-frames
clock
storage boxes
safelight

print washing rack
gradua
print wa
towel ra
inspection bo

contact printing frame
enlarger with color head
easel
voltage stabilizer
color analyzer
shading and printing-in tools

flatbed print d

waste
fixer
stop bath
print developer tray

Right The Durst CLS 500
M605 color enlargers bo
provide highly precise
calibration of filter densi
indicated on the scales. T
CLS 500 is a complex
enlarger which takes thr
sizes of negatives, and
provides filtered, white l
and neutral density settir

BLACK-AND-WHITE PAPERS

Choosing the printing paper for a negative depends on the characteristics of the negative, the tastes of the photographer and the eventual use to which the print will be put. Like film, printing paper consists of an emulsion attached to a base. Different types of emulsion and bases are available. Also like film, the choice of developer affects the final image.

The two standard chemical components of printing paper are silver chloride and silver bromide. Silver chloride gives strong, warm blacks with a fine grain, but is very slow; silver bromide is fast enough for practical enlarging but gives colder and slightly weaker blacks. Most modern papers have a silver bromide emulsion, but some, known as chlorobromide papers, use both chemicals to achieve a warm-toned image. The warm-to-cold colour differences between makes of paper that use varying proportions of silver bromide and silver chloride can also be modified by the choice of developer.

Ideally a printing paper should have a long tonal range, with brilliant highlights, dense blacks, and good separation between tones. Most makes of paper are fairly similar, but with top quality papers intended for display, such as Ilford Galerie, some manufacturers go to great lengths to extend performance at either end of the tonal scale and the cost is accordingly higher. For various reasons, it is difficult to assign speeds to paper in the same way as film, but in practice this is no real problem, as an initial test strip is easy to make.

The most important variable is contrast. Most makes of paper are available in a number of grades, which extend from 0 to 5, from soft to hard. These contrast grades are not strictly comparable between different makes, but in most cases grade 2 is considered "normal". A normal negative, therefore, which is usually judged to be one that has a scale of about 20 to one (the ratio of densest highlight to weakest shadow), should print well on a sheet of grade 2 paper. A high contrast negative will give a more normal-looking print on grades 1 or 0, while a flat negative is usually better printed on grades 3, 4, or in extreme cases, 5. After a little practice, it becomes easy to judge by eye the grade that a particular negative will need.

grade 0

grade 2

grade 4

Right Unlike most film, black-and-white printing paper has very little latitude, and is intended to be developed through to the full recommended time – between 90 seconds and two minutes. Because there is insufficient latitude to compensate for differences in contrast between negatives, most printing papers are available in different grades. In these photographs, a single negative, itself adequately exposed and with an average contrast range, has been printed on six different paper grades – from 0, which is very flat and intended for negatives with high contrast, to 5, which is extremely hard and is for use with soft negatives. To make comparisons easy, the exposures were adjusted to give the same tone for the area of wall directly over the lefthand doorway. The softest grades reveal the greatest amount of detail but the image extends to neither black nor white, while the hardest grades make full use of the *paper's* tonal range, but give a harsh image that has no detail at either end of the scale. The contrast of different makes of paper varies, but is generally similar. Multigrade paper produces the same effect on a single paper by means of blue and yellow filters.

grade 1

grade 3

grade 5

An alternative to a set of graded papers is variable-contrast paper, containing soft to hard contrast in one emulsion. This is made by mixing two emulsions, one of a high contrast that is sensitive only to blue light, and the other of low contrast, sensitive to green light. This paper gives normal, grade 2 contrast when exposed to white light from the enlarger head, but with a blue filter only the high contrast part of the emulsion is used, and with a yellow filter (more efficient than green for this purpose) only the low contrast part reacts. So, with a graded set of filters, the contrast can be finely tuned with a single type of paper.

The paper base of the print also affects the image. The thickest – doubleweight – holds its shape well and is good for display prints, parti-cularly large ones. Singleweight paper is cheaper and also less prone to cockling at the edges when dried, but creases easily. Traditional print paper is made from pure fiber, and although fixing, washing and drying are time-consuming, its surface qualities mean that it is generally preferred for exhibition work rather than the newer resin-coated papers. Resin-coated papers have a medium weight fiber base treated with synthetic resins; the fiber is effectively sealed, so that the emulsion washes clean in only a few minutes, and drying is rapid. However, the plastic finish can craze, resists some retouching methods, and is not particularly popular for display among traditionalists.

Print surfaces vary from glossy to matt; although a matt print is easy to view because it does not catch distracting reflections, a glossy finish actually gives denser blacks because the smooth surface scatters less light. For this reason, glossy prints are usually preferred for graphic reproduction in books, magazines and newspapers. Fiber-based glossy papers need to be glazed for the smoothest finish, and this involves heat-drying the print face down on a polished metal plate; glossy resin-coated papers, however, produce virtually the same effect with no special procedures. For display prints, many photographers prefer the semi-gloss finish that comes from drying fiber-based glossy paper normally.

In addition to regular papers, there are others with bases toned in different colors. Some also have distinct textures.

elow Here a single
egative has been printed
nto the average grade of a
election of commercially
vailable papers.
Tinted linen base
Kentmere textured matt
White linen
Fiber-based glossy
glazed
Resin-coated glossy
Ilford Galerie
Chlorobromide fiber-based
att
Fiber-based glossy
nglazed
Chlorobromide fiber-based
ossy unglazed
. Resin-coated semi-matt

7

8

Printing-out paper produces an image without the action of a developer – simply by slow contact printing in sunlight. In addition to being extremely easy to use, printing-out paper has extremely fine grain and gives excellent separation of tones. Its principal disadvantage is that the image fades with time to an overall dark tone. Fixing arrests this fading, but at the cost of turning the image pale orange-brown. The solution is to bathe the print first in a gold toning solution; this gives a purple-brown tone and a permanent image.

Printing-out paper
Using the duplicating technique, make a print-sized negative. The negative should have a high contrast to compensate for the flattening effect that the printing-out paper will have on the image.
1. In subdued tungsten light, place the paper and negative in a contact printing frame.
2. Place the frame in direct sunlight for the fastest results – printing will take longer on a cloudy day.
3. When the paper shows a deep purple-brown through the weakest shadow areas of the negative, the print is ready. This may take two to four minutes. The image should be denser than finally desired.
Wash in running water for about 15 minutes to remove unexposed silver salts. This will weaken the image and make it appear reddish.
Place in the gold toning bath for 15 to 20 minutes, agitating gently. The image will gain density again, and turn purple-brown.
Wash in running water for 20 minutes. Fix for five to 10 minutes. After washing thoroughly, hang to dry. (The emulsion is too delicate for a flatbed or rotary dryer.)

BASIC PRINTING

Making a print is basically a matter of following a set procedure. Provided the negative has been properly exposed, has an average overall density, a normal range of contrast, and carries an image that was photographed as intended, then there is no need for any special or corrective techniques.

Absolute cleanliness is essential to avoid the contamination of chemicals and to prevent small blemishes which are exaggerated by enlargement. A further precaution is to make a definite separation in the darkroom between the dry part of the process (from selecting the negative to exposing the paper) and the wet part (from development onwards).

Having selected the picture intended for enlargement, and decided on the print size and cropping, the only variable in straightforward printing should be the exposure, which can be altered by varying the lens aperture of the

1. Select which image you wish to print from the contact sheet.

2. Check that the enlarger lens and condensers are correct for the format of negative. With the empty carrier in the enlarger head, adjust the lamp until the picture area is evenly illuminated, with no darkening at the corners.

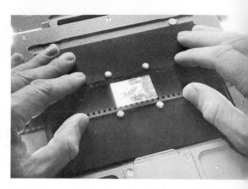

3. Place the negative in the carrier with the emulsion side facing down. Using a lightbox makes alignment easier.

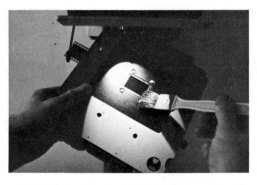

4. With the enlarger lamp switched on and the room lights off, hold the carrier at an angle under the lens to check for dirt on the negative. Remove dust with an antistatic brush.

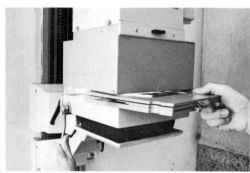

5. Place the carrier in the enlarger head.

6. Adjust the easel to the size of print required.

7. With a sheet of white paper in the easel to aid focusing, raise or lower the enlarger head and adjust the lens focus until the image is properly framed and sharp.

8. If the negative is difficult to focus normally, use a grain-focusing magnifier, and adjust the focus until the grain is as sharp as possible.

9. Choose part of the negative that includes the most important tones and place a ruler as a guide for positioning the test strips.

nlarger and the time. Most enlarging lenses, ke camera lenses, give their best resolution hen closed down to about two or three f-stops elow their widest, and for most negatives nlarged onto 8 x 10 inch (20 x 24cm) paper this a normal setting; the exposure can then be aried by altering the time. However, with a ense negative, or a considerable enlarge- ent (both reduce the amount of light reaching e paper), the exposure times may become

Basic printing Photographic printers inevitably develop their own methods of working in the darkroom, according to the type of negatives they work with, their equipment, and their own personal tastes. For such an elementary procedure as printing a simple negative, there is a surprising amount of

idiosyncrasy. The sequence shown here, while thorough, may not suit every darkroom worker, and is a guide rather than a set of rules. It will, however, ensure consistency, which is the quality that all successful basic printing procedures have in common.
For the sake of simplicity, this sequence assumes 35 mm as

the negative format, and the use of an unglazed fibre-based paper. Large format negatives need less enlargement to produce the same size of print, and so require either shorter exposure times or a smaller aperture. Large *thin* negatives, however, are more likely to buckle under the heat of the enlarger lamp

and may need the precautions of a preheated enlarger, small aperture setting (for greater depth of field), or a glass carrier. Resin-coated paper needs shorter processing times, as it comes to full development more rapidly and does not absorb chemicals so thoroughly. Also, it should be air-dried rather than heated.

. Under safelight illumination (from now until the strips are ixed), cut a sheet of normal grade paper into strips.

11. Set the lens aperture – with a normal negative the setting should be about two f-stops less than maximum for the best resolution.

12. Expose the test strips one by one in an identical position alongside the ruler. Expose one for the estimated correct exposure, another for half of that, and the third for double.

. Develop the test strips for between 90 seconds and two nutes (depending on the paper and developer being used) at °F (20°C), agitating continuously.

14. Drain and rinse in the stop bath for about 15 seconds.

15. Fix for the recommended time (this varies according to the type of paper; resin-coated papers need less time than fibre papers). Switch on the room lights and examine the strips. The illumination must be bright enough to distinguish all the tones. Note the best exposure. If all the strips appear flat, select a harder grade of paper for the print.

. Under safelight illumination, place a full sheet of paper in e easel, having adjusted the exposure time and aperture etting. Expose and then process the sheet in the same way as e test strips. When placing the paper in the developer, slide it quickly and smoothly, rocking the tray gently. Wash for the commended time.

17. Dry by hanging from clips, in a drying tray, between blotters, or in a flatbed or rotary dryer. Prints may have a slightly different appearance when dry than when wet.

inconveniently long, increasing the risk of the negative shifting slightly because of the heat. Or, with a thin negative or very small degree of enlargement, the time may be reduced to just one or two seconds, making consistent timing difficult. In either case, the aperture would need to be used for control.

Aside from these variations, absolute regularity is essential. Printing papers are intended to be fully developed, which takes between 90 seconds and two minutes at 68°F (20°C) in the recommended strength of developer. Short development renders the darkest areas of the print grey rather than black, and can also cause unevenness in the shadow areas. Extended development, although increasing contrast slightly up to a point, eventually causes fogging, whereby highlights acquire a light grey veil. Although there are certain occasions when altered development may be desirable, for a straight-forward print, development-by-inspection is poor technique. Under red safelighting it is not possible to judge the subtleties of tone, and non-standard development makes it difficult to judge the effects of exposure variation.

Below If, as in this example, the same subject has been photographed at different exposures, then the critical choice of negative should be made by examining the strips of negatives rather than the contact sheet. Contact printing is only a guide to the general features of the image, and will not show the density or tonal range accurately. Look for a negative that contains detail at both ends of the scale – highlights and shadow. In this case, of the four negatives shown below, the last is the best.

Left and far left As was apparent from even the contact sheet, the success of this print would depend on being able to reproduce very slight differences in tone, and over a full range. This would make accurate exposure in the enlarger important. The most critical areas of the picture were judged to be the lighter tones of the marble, and in the negative these contain very subtle differences. Overexposure would, at all costs, have to be avoided, as this would block the highlights and give empty areas lacking in any texture. The test strips were aligned to cover these lighter areas and, in addition, as full a tonal range as possible. The exposures of the three test strips shown on the opposite page were, from left to right, 5, 10 and 20 seconds. From these, the best exposure was judged to be 8 seconds, and this was used for final print.

PRINTING CONTROLS

Every stage in the photographic process alters the image in some way, and a thoroughly realistic photograph – one that reproduces every tone and detail exactly as it was in the original scene – is virtually impossible. By far the most common departure from reality is an increase in contrast, for no regular emulsion can accommodate the range of contrast that the human eye can. This is one of the basic problems of exposure measurement.

Typically, a negative will record less detail in the lightest and darkest areas of a scene than is actually visible. This difficulty is then usually exaggerated in the print, which is even less able than the negative to hold a long tonal range. Frequently, the details that can just be seen in the shadows and highlights of a negative will not print without special help.

Using a variety of paper grades is the standard way of handling this problem, but this is by no means a universal solution. For instance, if the difficulty in a particular negative occurs only in the highlights, most of the picture area will print perfectly well on a normal grade of

paper. In this case, a softer paper grade would certainly hold the highlight details, but the other tones in the print would not be so well separated – it would appear flatter in the important areas, and seem less lively overall.

Printing controls provide the answer to situations like this, and are widely used as a means of refining the image. In essence, they involve varying the amount of light that reaches the printing paper: holding back light from certain parts of the picture to keep them lighter is known as shading, exposing other areas to more light in order to darken them is called printing-in. With a high contrast negative, the shadows, which are thinner, can be shaded, and the highlights, which are denser, can be printed-in; the effect, even with a normal grade of paper, will be to print a fuller range of tones.

Different tools are needed, depending on the types of control needed. For shading, dodgers are normally used – shaped pieces of black card attached to thin rods or wires. The more nearly they match the shape of the area to be shaded, the better. To merge the outline of

Below For the reasons described on the opposite page, this negative has a very high contrast range overall, but lacks contrast in the important dark areas of the ceiling and columns. In the printing, therefore, the arched ceiling and upper columns need to be held back, as does the part of the floor in the shadow of the altar. The tonal imbalance in

the ceiling also needs slight correction. The very dense windows above the altar must then be printed-in, the precise amount of extra exposure being limited by the fogging threshold of the paper (too much light from the enlarger turns highlights an "empty" grey).

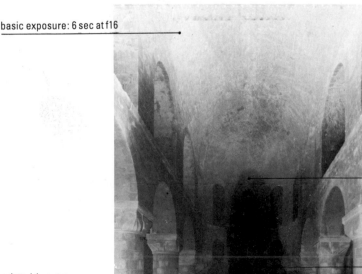

basic exposure: 6 sec at f16

shaded to give 3 sec at f16

printed-in extra
4 sec at f16

printed-in extra
9 sec at f16

Above Two straightforward prints, without any shading or printing-in, were made specifically to show the problem that a printer would face with this negative. Neither would be seriously considered for a final print. The upper print was timed only for the shadow areas of the ceiling, while the lower was exposed to give simply an acceptable result for the window area. Both disregard the remaining parts of the image. In a case such as this, the printing controls must bridge the gap between the two versions, compensating in a single print, for both highlights and shadows.

Left Like many architectural
interiors of the period, St
John's chapel in the heart of
the Tower of London was
designed to function and be
seen by natural light. The
most impressive effect is in
the early morning, for the
altar faces east and the
sunlight streams down the
aisle. Under artificial
lighting, the power and
proportions of this fine
example of Norman
architecture would have
been lost, and the
photograph was taken
without any additional
illumination. The penalty of
choosing this approach was a
difficult negative – difficult
not only because the contrast
range is high, but also
because all the important
tonal detail is concentrated
in the shadow areas.
Therefore, while the contrast
of the negative as a whole
needs to be reduced, the
local contrast, in the shadow
areas, needs to be enhanced.
As a soft grade of paper
would be quite inappropriate,
extensive printing controls
are the only answer, using a
hard (grade 4) paper.

the shaded area with the rest of the picture, the dodger is held several inches above the print and moved continuously during the exposure. A clenched fist can be used for a larger area, and a finger for areas close to the edge of the print. Alternatively, a large sheet of glass can be held above the print, with a shape either cut from black paper stuck on top, or painted on with photo-opaque.

For printing-in, a sheet of opaque paper or card is normally used, with a hole cut out of it. As it is often difficult to position this precisely during the exposure, particularly if the negative is dense, some printers use a card that is black underneath (to prevent light from reflecting back onto the print), but white on top – the image is then projected on the surface of the shading card. A completely exposed sheet of printing paper can also be used, or even partially cupped hands. For strong printing-in, a small, shaded flashlight can be shone on parts of the print from a short distance away.

The sequence of printing should be planned, sometimes with the aid of a small sketch if the exposures are liable to be complex. The simplest type of printing involves only one exposure (a basic time for most of the print with one area shaded for part of it), but some negatives may need several separate exposures, particularly if there are a number of different areas to be printed-in. Trial-and-error is often the only way.

Printing controls can be used to extract the maximum amount of information from the negative, but they can also be an integral part of the entire picture-making process – building an image in the darkroom whose tonal range may bear little resemblance to the original negative. Shading and printing-in can be used to obscure some elements, reveal others, and even to isolate a subject almost totally. Perhaps the real value of printing controls is that they demand a careful study of the negative and the image.

Below and right For this Scottish landscape, printing controls were used, not so much to compensate for a technical deficiency in the negative, as to produce an image that goes beyond a strictly realistic interpretation. By giving most of the sky area ten times the exposure needed for the hills, printing controls were used to bring as much drama to the scene as possible. (A straight print from the same negative is shown below.)
The only tools used were the printer's own hands, shaped to fit the contour of the hills. Rather than print in the clouds as unremitting gloom, the small area framed by the distant valley was held back, to give the impression of a shifting, unpredictable storm. The cloud cap at the left of the picture was also judged worth emphasizing, and kept light. Minor adjustments to the water and left foreground, made to balance the image, completed the special printing.

COMPOSITE PRINTING

In composite printing, two or more negatives are exposed separately onto a single sheet of paper. The value of this technique is that it provides the opportunity to juxtapose quite different images in a relatively simple way. The separate images may be photographed with the deliberate intention of combining them in one print, but there are also surprisingly good opportunities to be found from searching through existing files of stock negatives. Photographs of no special interest in themselves may, when brought together, produce a lively image.

Technically, the key to composite printing is masking – leaving a dense area in one negative for the image from the second negative. How this is done depends very much on the negatives themselves. The simplest case is where one negative has a large dense area, such as a sky, and the other negative is a silhouette – no extra masks would need to be constructed, as the dense parts of each negative automatically complement each other.

Otherwise, masks need to be applied or made. One method is to block out unwanted parts of the negatives with masking tape or photo-opaque, and provided that detailed work on a small negative is not needed, this method is straightforward. For more complicated outlines, an accurate mask can be made by exposing a negative to line film, either by contact printing or, in order to allow finer retouching, by enlarging. Alternatively, a hand-traced mask can be made by cutting around the outline of the image projected onto a sheet of black paper, or by painting around the outline of the image projected onto a sheet of glass, using photo-opaque. The more complex the preparations, the more reliable the final stages of the printing are likely to be.

A relatively simple method is to choose the negatives to match without a great deal of masking. To register the images exactly, their outlines are traced onto a sheet of paper taped to the easel. With five separate exposures, however, each must be tested and then timed accurately, so that the densities will match in the final print. For all composite printing, development must be strictly by time, and not by inspection.

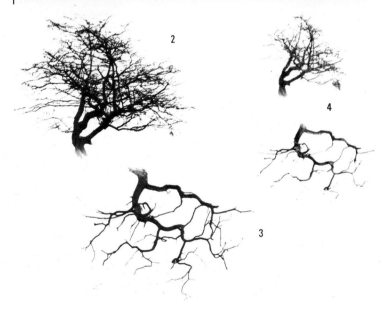

Right For this surrealistic image, three separate negatives were used, two of them printed twice – a total of five individual exposures for one print. The basic landscape negative was chosen for its featureless upper half, which could be easily masked for subsequent printing of the trees. To make each floating tree realistic, roots were added by printing a portion of a negative of bare branches. The second, smaller tree was included to give depth to the scene; by shortening the exposure, the image is weaker, so that an impression of distance is given by aerial perspective. Positioning the trees over the sea was not critical, but merging tree trunks with roots called for careful registration. This, together with the need for the tones of each negative to balance, made it a sensible precaution to prepare several prints at the same time.
1. With the enlarger lens set at f11, the seascape was exposed for 30 seconds, with the bright area in the centre of the picture printed in for an additional 20 seconds. The sky was masked in the negative carrier.
2. The second negative was masked with photo-opaque and exposed for 7 seconds at f11. The base of the trunk was shaded to fade off gradually.
3. For the roots, a negative of some branches was used – upside down. It was exposed masked and shaded in exactly the same way as the second negative, so as to blend with it.
4. For the smaller tree, the process was repeated, but at a smaller aperture, so as to give a fainter image.

Composite printing
1. First select the background negative. Stock photographs are a good source of material. A dense area on the negative (that is, a clear area on the print) simplifies the process.

2. For this composite print, the second element chosen was a floating tree. Two negatives were specifically shot, each a silhouette. With red masking tape and liquid photo-opaque, mask out the unwanted parts of the image.

3. Tape a sheet of white paper on the easel. This will serve as a registration guide. Place the background negative in the enlarger and adjust the focus. Trace the outline of its key elements on the paper.

4. After testing to find the correct time and aperture setting, expose several sheets of paper identically, being careful to fit each one into exactly the same place in the easel.

5. Store the exposed sheets of paper in a light-tight box.

6. Replace the first negative with the second.

7. Position the image of the second negative according to the outline already sketched on the easel. Mark it in the same way.

8. Expose the second negative onto each of the papers already exposed. Repeat the process for any subsequent negatives. After processing the prints, retouch as necessary.

RETOUCHING BLACK-AND-WHITE PRINTS

Even taking the greatest care in printing, minor blemishes are difficult to avoid. The most common are specks of dust and minute hairs, either attracted to the negative by static electricity or, more dangerously, embedded in the gelatin; they appear white on the print. Pinholes and scratches appear black, while other marks, such as fingerprints and stains, are generally darker than the image.

Basic retouching – known in its simplest form as spotting – is an essential print-finishing skill that is relatively easy to master. At a more advanced level, retouching can be used for gross manipulation of the image, and the reason that this is usually done on the print rather than on the negative is that mistakes are not irreversible, as they may be with an original negative, and the larger image size makes the retouching less noticeable.

Much cosmetic retouching can be avoided by taking certain precautions, particularly at the processing stage. Careful inspection of the emulsion surface when it is hung up to dry may reveal small particles stuck to the soft gelatin – these should be removed by further washing. Drying should take place in a dust-free atmosphere. The interior of the enlarger should be cleaned out with compressed air occasionally, although not immediately before printing, as this will stir up dust. When printing, the negative should be treated with an antistatic gun.

A set of fine sable watercolour brushes needed for spotting. Because the work is invariably delicate and detailed, only the best quality brushes will do – the shape of a wetted brush determines the accuracy of the spotting. Retouching colours are normally sold in pairs, one blue-black, the other brown-black – so that the precise colour of the print can be matched. Either dyes or pigments can be used.

For dark blemishes, knifing is the normal technique. An extremely sharp blade is essential, and the skill lies in shaving so delicately that only the very top layer of emulsion is removed. Knifing down to the paper base makes subsequent spotting almost impossible – the colour will soak into the damaged surface and spread.

Retouching should always follow chemical treatment, such as bleaching or toning. Knifing should precede spotting. If the retouching has been extensive, the variation in surface texture may spoil the appearance of the print, particularly when it is viewed by reflected light. One solution is to spray the entire print with varnish. This has the added advantage of protecting those areas that have been retouched with water-soluble pigments, which might otherwise be smudged by later handling. To build up a smooth surface, spray several light coatings, allowing a few minutes for drying in between each.

Using a retouching brush
1. First mix different tones of retouching colour, and test the proportions on a spare print to match the colour of the print.

2. Dilute the colour with water.

3. Wet the retouching brush in clean water, and drain the excess against the lip of the jar.

4. Draw the brush back against your hand, twirling it gently, to draw the hairs to a point.

5. Pick up some colour, rotating the brush so that the colour is evenly distributed.

8. Wash the brush thoroughly, down to the base of the hairs, and store upright to dry.

Retouching
1. First work on the print's dark blemishes, such as negative scratches. Shave the print gently with a rounded scalpel blade. Check by viewing the print by reflected light.

2. Shave the area until it is a little lighter than the surrounding image, but do not scrape the emulsion right down to the paper base.

3. Wipe away the shavings.

4. Retouch with a brush and dye.

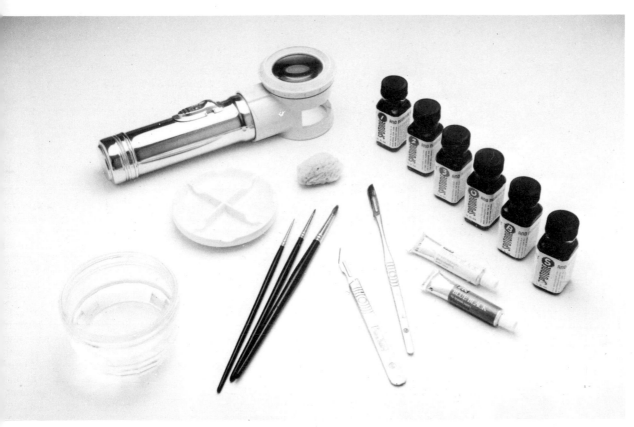

Above Most black-and-white retouching can be done with the small selection of tools and materials shown here. Dark areas can be removed with a scalpel; a rounded blade being used for shaving, a pointed blade for picking off details. Retouching colours are available in different hues, so that the exact colour of the print can be matched; pigment, in the two tubes, gives dense coverage but is less permanent than dyes, in the row of bottles. A jar for water and segmented palette for mixing are used with a set of sable brushes, and the print surface can be wetted with a small sponge. The magnifying glass shown here is particularly suitable for fine retouching, having a battery-powered light, and a gap for inserting a knife or brush.

. Test against a thumbnail. The rush should be just moist enough o apply the colour easily – too little iquid will cause unevenness in the potting, while too much will form mall pools on the print

7 Retouch

. Pinholes can be removed in one stroke with the tip of a pointed lade.

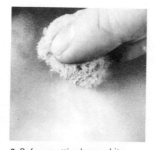

6. Before spotting large white blemishes, moisten the surface with a sponge dipped in water, to open up the emulsion. Warm hardened prints with a heater.

7. Begin spotting by applying a weak dye with the tip of a small brush.

8. Build up to the required tone with several weak applications rather than attempt to match the density with one dab.

9. Continue adding dye until the blemish is no longer noticeable.

AIRBRUSHING

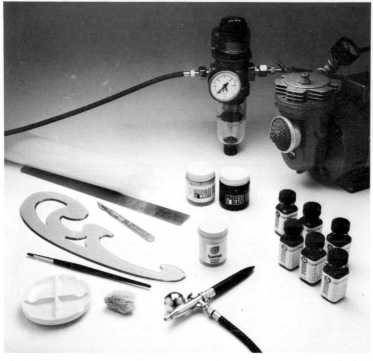

Right Although small cans of compressed air are suitable for occasional use, serious airbrushing needs a compressor, and a water trap (which collects condensation in a small plastic bowl and prevents droplets reaching the airbrush). Either dyes can be used in the airbrush, or pigment, if diluted to the consistency of milk. These should be mixed beforehand in a palette. To mask off areas that are not to be sprayed, adhesive masking film (cut with a scalpel, and rule or French curves) or liquid mask can be used. After use, the airbrush should be cleaned with a brush and sponge.

The airbrush is the ideal retouching instrument for photography and in fact was first developed for this use. Although it is an expensive piece of equipment and demands considerable skill, it is perfect for producing smoothly graduated tones over large areas – and in a manner that matches photograhic reproduction. With care, even the texture of the airbrushing, which consists of fine particles of the pigment or dye, can be made to match the graininess of the print.

The airbrush works by regulating the flow of compressed air fed into it by a flexible pipe, so that the colour in a small reservoir is blown out in a fine, controllable spray. Downward pressure on the control button increases the air flow, pulling back releases dye or pigment from the open reservoir inside the top of the airbrush.

The two most widely used air supplies are aerosol cans and electric compressors. Aerosols are convenient and small, do not involve any capital expenditure, and produce a steady supply at a high pressure: on the debit side they are expensive for large amounts of retouching, and may run out at an inconvenient moment. Electric compressors are invariably used for professional work, and although ex

Preparing masks
1. Peel masking film from its backing.

2. Lay the adhesive film over the dry-mounted print. It may not be necessary to cover the complete print, but always mask the borders.

3. With a scalpel, cut away the film over the area to be sprayed, being careful not to cut through to the print.

4. Peel away the unwanted film.

Using the airbrush
1. If using pigment, add water until the liquid has the consistency of milk. Liquid dyes need no dilution.

2. With a brush, or alternatively a dropper, fill the reservoir of the airbrush.

3. Press the button down to start the airflow.

4. Pull the button back to increase the flow of colour. Never pull the button back before pressing, as this will cause splattering.

ensive to buy, cost hardly anything to run. To void water building up in the hose (sooner or ater it will spurt out through the nozzle, possbly spoiling the retouching), a condensation rap is usually fitted between the compressor nd the airbrush.

To ensure an even tonal gradation, an airbrush is best used in relatively broad strokes. A mask is nearly always essential to define the area being retouched. Masking film is good for any edges that can be cut easily with a scalpel although cutting into the print is a danger), while masking fluid, which is painted on, but can be peeled off when dry without affecting he surface of the print underneath, is probably more convenient for intricate outlines. For making soft edges, a mask can be cut from paper or card, and held just above the surface.

Although not permanent without a coat of varnish, pigment, particularly process white and process black, is relatively easy to use: it rarely forms pools on the surface of the print, and can be used to build up solid layers over he image. Dyes blend in better but more easily form droplets if sprayed on one area too long. Constant movement of the airbrush is important.

Left and below The graduated tones that an airbrush is so efficient at producing, blend in particularly well with photographic images. Here, a plain image of a ceramic jug on a featureless white background has been treated in two ways to add depth and setting. For the graduated background, only a loose, handheld card mask was used, to prevent colour spattering the lower part of the picture. For the table-like surface, a hard mask was cut from masking film.

Alternatively, paint on masking fluid over he area to be protected.

6. After spraying, peel away the film. Make sure your hands are clean.

Test the flow on a spare print.

6. For smooth tones, hold the airbrush at a slight downward angle and sweep across the masked print in broad strokes, continuing beyond the edges of the mask. The distance of the airbrush from the print determines how broad the spray will be.

PLATINUM PRINTING

In most respects, the developments in dark-room technology have been undisputed improvements, as might be expected. In a few instances, however, processes and materials that had fine qualities were abandoned, usually for reasons of cost. Although platinum printing has seen only sporadic use since the turn of the century, it still remains one of the best print-making techniques in black-and-white photography. It is capable of intense blacks, an extremely long tonal range, allows manipulation of contrast and colour by altering the proportions of chemicals, and is permanent – a set of qualities with which even the most fastidious printer would be happy. The one disadvantage that prevents commercial applications is the high cost of platinum. Nevertheless, for fine

gallery prints the platinum process is still used.

Because no commercial emulsions are available, the paper must be sensitized by the photographer. For this, the best quality 100% rag paper is necessary – the type of paper used for watercolour painting. This is coated with a solution containing potassium chloroplatinite and ferric oxalate, and allowed to dry. The solution is not very sensitive to light and none of the work has to be carried out in a darkroom; subdued artificial light is quite satisfactory. This, however, creates a problem: the low sensitivity makes the platinum process unsuitable for enlarging, so that a full-sized negative is needed for contact printing. Original negatives taken with an 8 x 10 inch (20 x 24cm) view camera are ideal, or enlarged copy negatives.

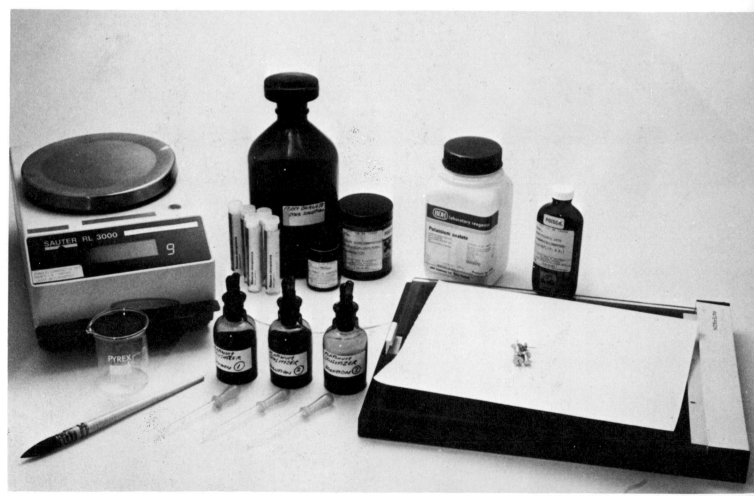

Above The chemicals needed for platinum printing are ferric oxalate and potassium chloroplatinite for the emulsion (the potassium chloroplatinite is the costly item), potassium oxalate for development, and dilute hydrochloric acid for the

clearing bath. As platinum printing is not a regularly used process, some of the stock solutions must be prepared from basic chemicals; this is particularly important for the ferric oxalate, which must be completely free of ferrous

salts. Making up the chemicals is, however, fairly straightforward, and calls for an accurate balance, a graduate, flask, stirring rod, funnel and filter papers. Wherever water is called for, the distilled variety should be used.

To make the developer Dissolve one part of potassium oxalate in 48 parts of hot distilled water (120°F/49°C). This developer will keep indefinitely, Use at 28°F (20°C).
To make the clearing solution Make up a solution of one

part of hydrochloric acid in 6 parts of distilled water. Add the water to the acid, not the acid to the water. Hydrochloric acid is extremely corrosive, and protective gloves should be worn when handling it.

o make the sensitizer solution

tock solution 1	Quantity	Method
istilled water xalic acid erric oxalate	1 oz (29.5 cc) 8 grains (0.5 gm) 120 grains (7.8 gm)	To help the chemicals dissolve, heat the solution to 120°F (49°C). If the ferric oxalate is in solution rather than dry, there is no need to add water.

tock solution 2	Quantity	Method
istilled water xalic acid erric oxalate otassium chlorate	1 oz (29.5 cc) 8 grains (0.5 gm) 120 grains (7.8 gm) 2 grains (0.13 gm)	The same remarks given for stock solution 1 apply.

tock solution 3	Quantity	Method
istilled water otassium hloroplatinite	1⅛ oz (34.5 cc) 108 grains (7.0 gm)	This also should be heated, to help the chloroplatinite dissolve.

Stock solutions (in drops)					
	Very soft	Soft	Average	High contrast	Low contrast
1.	22	18	14	10	—
2.	—	4	8	12	22
3.	24	24	24	24	24

All these solutions will keep indefinitely if stored in amber glass bottles.
By combining these three solutions in varying proportions, it is possible to adjust the contrast of the print from very soft to very hard.

latinum printing
. Measure out drops from the three stock olutions of the sensitizer. The proportions of ach depend on the contrast needed in the rint. About 50 drops will cover a 8 x 10 inch ²0 x 24 cm) print. Only make up the solution mmediately before use.

2. Pin high quality handmade watercolour paper to a board, and coat evenly and quickly with the sensitizer solution, using a camelhair brush. The pins prevent excessive wrinkling. Work quickly before the solution dries. If hairs come off the brush, leave them until the paper is completely dry, when they can be removed easily.

3. Leave the paper in the dark for about 10 minutes, and then dry it thoroughly over a heater or hot-plate until it turns yellow-orange and crackles slightly when flexed. Be careful not to singe the paper.

4. Place the paper in a contact-printing frame with a full-sized negative. (Use the copy negative technique if necessary.) For a clean white border to the image area, a mask can be cut from opaque cardboard and taped to the negative.

. Expose either to sunlight or an ultraviolet mp. The actual time should be worked out by esting with small strips of sensitized paper, ut it will normally be between 20 and 30 inutes. The progress of the printing can be hecked by carefully lifting one corner of the aper – a faint yellow-and-grey image ppears.

6. Develop the print fully in the potassium oxalate solution at about 68°F (20°C). Most of the development happens in a few seconds, but continues for up to about two minutes. It is impossible to over-develop. Agitate during development.

7. Having replaced the developer back in its bottle, rinse the paper in three successive baths of 1:60 dilute hydrochloric acid to remove iron salts, for five minutes each. The first two baths will turn cloudy, and should be discarded, but the third bath can be used once more on a later print.

8. Wash for 30 minutes, and then dry by hanging. The print can later be flattened in a dry-mounting press or with an iron.

Exposure, either to direct sunlight or to an ultraviolet lamp (the latter gives more consistent and controllable results), generally takes about 20 to 30 minutes, and the print is developed in a solution of potassium oxalate. There is no danger of over-development, and when the image has reached its full density, it needs no fixing. Instead, three weak baths of dilute hydrochloric acid clear away remaining iron salts, and the print is washed and dried. The final image is matt, so that there are no reflections to interfere with viewing. The tonal range can be extended and the blacks deepened by resensitizing the paper, contact-printing a second time with the same negative, and repeating the entire process; the previously developed platinum image remains unaffected, but the second printing adds density. Because the contrast can be altered by varying the composition of the sensitizer solution, the second printing gives considerable control over the image – a high contrast solution, for example, would simply strengthen the shadow areas without affecting the rest of the image, while a soft solution would strengthen highlight detail more.

Below Although the extent of its effect is largely lost when reproduced in a book, platinum printing has the ability to handle a very wide tonal range without losing all shadow detail. As a result, it can be successful for high-contrast images. By recoating the paper and making a second printing, extra density is added to the shadow areas and can contribute to an impression of tonal richness.

Below For this photograph of duck-shooting in the Norfolk Broads, *Gunner working up to fowl*, taken in 1886 by the British photographer Peter Henry Emerson (1856-1936), the platinum print was an ideal vehicle, having a long tonal range and the density that this delicately-lit morning landscape needs. The platinum print, for all the care and craftmanship it calls for, is essentially a realistic method of photographic reproduction: by being able to show detail throughout a print, from the shadow areas to the highlights, it encourages literal rather than graphic or manipulated representations of scenes.

TONING

Toning has had a varied history, ranging from complete neglect to indiscriminate and unsubtle use. Some of the finest and most delicate examples were produced in the late nineteenth century, when toning was used as a deliberate attempt to increase the range of expression of monochrome photography. At that time the absence of colour in photography was generally considered more a nuisance than an aesthetic refinement, as it often is today. Many photographers of the period become highly skilled at matching the tone to the subject, and at creating subtle variations within a single print.

Colour printing removed this basic need for toning, and a further argument against its use, at least for many professionals, was the growing use of photography for graphic reproduction. Toning is only really useful for display prints; even the four-colour reproduction used on these pages cannot fully capture its subtleties. As a result of these developments, toning has acquired a pictorialist reputation, and more often than not it is criticized for that.

Toning baths work by changing the silver image to silver sulphide, by substituting another metal for the silver, or by using colour developer and a chosen colour coupler to replace the silver. The last method, which is comparatively recent, follows the principles of basic colour chemistry and produces an intense hue; the effect is generally quite strident, and very different in character from the traditional processes.

The most common toner is sulphur toner, which uses the bleach-and-redevelop method to produce a sepia finish. The finer the grain of the print, the warmer the final tone will be, so that for the richest results, a blue-black silver bromide print is best. A bleach bath converts the black metallic silver into a silver salt, which a second bath of sodium sulphide then changes into brown silver sulphide.

Variations in the sepia tone are possible, and sepia toning can be used in conjunction with other toning baths, such as gold toning. It is also common as a first stage in hand-colouring and, as bonus, makes the image permanent.

Toning The following steps describe the basic method for toning.
1. Make a dense print, with details in the light tones clearly visible. Toning will lighten the result.
2. After washing (if the print is dry to begin with, soak it again thoroughly to soften the emulsion), immerse in the bleach bath, agitating for two to three minutes until the image has faded to a pale yellow. The shadow areas will be the last to bleach.
3. Wash until all traces of yellow disappear from both the paper and the water.
4. Place the print in the toning bath. The brown tone will develop in a few seconds. For a richer appearance, the print should be given an additional toning bath for about three minutes *before* the bleach.
5. Wash until the pungent smell of hydrogen sulphide disappears.
6. Dry the print.

These illustrations show the same print at various stages of the toning process.
1. Original black-and-white silver bromide print.
2. Bleached print.
3. Toned print.
4. Toned print after an additional toning bath before bleaching.

1

2

3

NO 6925

GOLD TONING

The most useful and versatile metal toners use gold chloride. There are various formulae, but all of these toners have the effect of plating the silver image with gold; being impervious to change, gold gives permanence to any print. This archival treatment is a basic use, but gold toning can also produce a variety of tones. Depending on the formula, the type of paper, and the duration of the bath, gold toning can create a final tone of blue, blue-black, purple-brown, or a range of reds.

The range of colours shown in these examples were produced with Tetenal Gold Toner, one of the few prepackaged solutions commercially available. In each case, the prints were developed, fixed and thoroughly washed before the treatment. Bathing a bromide print directly in the toner for 20 minutes gives a blue-black image, but if a similar print is first sepia-toned, the gold toner produces a brownish tone. On chlorobromide paper, the same treatment gives an orange-brown result.

The effects of gold chloride solution are progressive and depend on how long the print remains in the bath. The print will turn purple-brown after only a few minutes; prolonging the treatment up to 20 minutes gives a strong red. Toning by inspection makes it possible to select the exact colour of the final print. A final wash in water completes the treatment.

1

2

Gold toning The aesthetic value of gold toning is very much a matter of personal taste, although the subtleties of its effect can only be appreciated properly when viewing a photographic print, rather than a reproduction in a book or magazine: this technique is most relevant for display prints. Toning tends to suit historical subjects and is often used in advertising and other commercial applications to give a period atmosphere. Another advantage of the technique is that if it is well-executed, the range of

tones in a print will be affected differently, giving an appearance of depth. This effect is particularly useful for subjects such as the example shown here, where the room is large and richly decorated. The photograph shows the Painted Hall in Greenwich Hospital, a masterpiece of trompe l'oeil decoration – even the fluting on the columns is painted.

These examples show the same print at various stages of gold toning.
1. Original black-and-white silver bromide print.

2. Print gold-toned for 20 minutes.
3. Print toned first in a sulphide bath and then in gold for seven minutes.
4. Print toned in sulphide/gold for 20 minutes.
5. Chlorobromide paper gold-toned for seven minutes.

COLOUR PRINTING

Processing colour film is more complex and demands more accuracy than regular black-and-white development. Similarly, producing a colour print is more involved than the enlarging techniques already described. Fortunately, the fact that colour prints are so popular among amateur photographers (most professionals use transparencies because they are useful for graphic reproduction) has stimulated manufacturers to simplify the processes, so that colour printing is not especially difficult, given the right additional equipment.

On the dry side of the darkroom, the main concern is to achieve colour fidelity; to do this, the projected image must be filtered in some way, and the light from the enlarger head must be kept constant. A colour enlarger has a different head from a black-and-white enlarger – the head gives diffuse illumination in order to mix the filter colours thoroughly and keep contrast low, and has three filters – yellow, magenta and cyan – which can be mixed in various proportions to suit a particular negative and batch of paper. Dyed filters are relatively inexpensive, but fade with use; dichroic filters are more costly but are virtually permanent. For measuring the colour balance precisely, a colour analyzer reduces the amount of testing needed to find the right combination of these filters. As even small fluctuations in voltage (which are common) alter the colour

Right The table shows filter factors from which you can calculate your new exposure to allow for filter changes. Divide the original time by the factor(s) for the filter(s) you have removed. Multiply the result by the factor(s) for each filter you have added and round off your result to the nearest second.

Filter	Factor	Filter	Factor	Filter	Factor
05 Yellow	1.1	05 Magenta	1.2	05 Cyan	1.1
10 Yellow	1.1	10 Magenta	1.3	10 Cyan	1.2
20 Yellow	1.1	20 Magenta	1.5	20 Cyan	1.3
30 Yellow	1.1	30 Magenta	1.7	30 Cyan	1.4
40 Yellow	1.1	40 Magenta	1.9	40 Cyan	1.5
50 Yellow	1.1	50 Magenta	2.1	50 Cyan	1.6

Filter	Factor	Filter	Factor	Filter	Factor
05 Red	1.2	05 Green	1.1	05 Blue	1.1
10 Red	1.3	10 Green	1.2	10 Blue	1.3
20 Red	1.5	20 Green	1.3	20 Blue	1.6
30 Red	1.7	30 Green	1.4	30 Blue	2.0
40 Red	1.9	40 Green	1.5	40 Blue	2.4
50 Red	2.2	50 Green	1.7	50 Blue	2.9

red bias

green bias

correctly balanced

10 blue   20 blue

10 green

20 green

Colour printing While a colour transparency is, from the user's point of view, a direct means of producing a photograph, a colour negative introduces a second step – printing. Although this gives more opportunity for exercising control over the final image, it also introduces more variables. For basic, unmanipulated printing, a prerequisite is to be able to achieve a realistic colour balance, and this nearly always requires a filtration test, even if a colour analyzer is used to recommend the basic filters that are needed. With experience, a printer can judge accurately from a single test what filtration to use for the final print. Otherwise, two or three may be necessary. To make it easier to judge filtration, and to avoid a complicated series of tests, one very useful method is to choose one negative for a complete range of tests with all possible filters, and to use the assembled prints, as

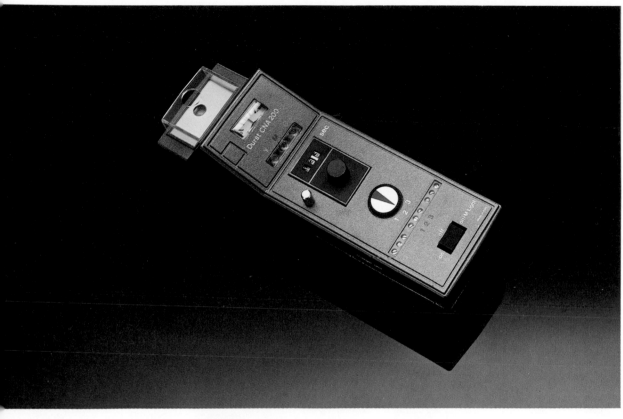

Left By reducing the amount of guesswork needed in judging the filters that will be needed for printing a colour negative or transparency, a colour analyzer saves time and, in the long run, expense (colour chemicals and paper are costly).

0 red	20 red	10 yellow	20 yellow	10 magenta	20 magenta	10 cyan	20 cyan

hown above, for comparison with subsequent prints from ther negatives. Here, a ingle negative has been rinted with two strengths of ach of the six colour filters. *inned to the darkroom wall, series of prints like this nakes a useful reference for ssessing colour casts in any ther photographs.

In choosing a test negative, look for an image that contains either a neutral colour or one that is easily recognizable, such as flesh tones; it is also useful if the negative contains several basic colours.
In the tests above, a colour negative was used; as a result, the filter in each case

produces an *opposite* colour cast (for example, a green filter enhances red). When printed directly from a transparency, filters produce a bias in their own colour.

Below The most convenient method of processing single prints is in a processing drum: as colour development must take place in complete darkness, there is no advantage in tray processing, which also wastes chemicals. As an alternative to monitoring the temperature by eye, a thermostatically controlled bath ensures a high degree of accuracy.

Right *Colour processing* The essential steps in colour enlargement are, in practice, little different from those in black-and-white printing, despite the complication of measuring the correct colour balance. The subsequent processing, however, differs in two ways. First, the procedure has more stages and is more exacting; secondly, most colour papers are nowadays processed in an elongated drum.

1. Having loaded the paper into the drum in darkness, add warm water to bring the drum to the correct temperature. This should take about one minute.

2. Pour the water into a container for later use, and add the developer, which has already been warmed to the correct temperature.

3. Start the timer and begin rolling the drum steadily, either by hand or on a motorized cradle. Continue rolling for the full development time.

4. Discard the developer, beginning a few seconds before the end of development. If the kit includes a stop bath, add this, roll as recommended, and empty.

5. Pour in the bleach/fix, start the timer, and roll for the recommended time. Discard the bleach/fix and fill the drum with the warm water used at the beginning of the process.

6. Remove the lid, and carefully pull out the paper by its edge. Wash the print in an open dish as you would a black-and-white print. Clean all equipment thoroughly without delay.

7. After washing, gently sponge off excess water.

8. Hang the print to dry in a dust-free room. A portable hairdryer, used at low heat, will accelerate drying

temperature of a lamp, a voltage stabilizer is an important addition.

On the wet side of the darkroom, temperature and time control must be particularly stringent. To make the maximum use of the expensive colour chemicals, a horizontal print-processing drum is a simple but valuable piece of equipment; it has the further advantage of allowing the processing to be carried out in full light. The correct temperature can be maintained by keeping the chemicals in a bath of preheated water, or by using a special electric heater. For consistent agitation, a motor-driven cradle can be used to roll the drum back and forth.

There are two basic methods of colour printing: from negatives or from transparencies.

Negative printing gives better quality and more control; direct transparency printing makes it easy to assess the results and is simpler than making an intermediate negative.

In either case, while a contact print will give some clue to the filtration needed for each original, one of the most widely used techniques in colour printing is to make a sequence of prints from one standard negative or transparency, with different filters. When this is displayed in the viewing area of the darkroom, it makes it easier to judge colour bias and identify the filters needed to correct it. It is unlikely that the first test print will be correctly balanced for colour. Two or three tests will probably be needed, unless a colour analyzer is used.

Printing controls can be used as they are with black-and-white printing: with colour negative enlargement the techniques are exactly the same, but with transparency enlargement the procedures are reversed (that is, shading darkens, printing-in lightens). Colours can also be controlled in selected areas of the picture, by shading with coloured filters. When enlarging a colour negative, a local colour cast in the test print (such as blue shadows) can be removed by holding a filter of the same colour over the area. To achieve the same effect when enlarging directly from a transparency, use a filter of the *complementary* colour (for instance, a yellow filter to reduce blue).

HAND-COLOURING

Below Hand-tinting with
watercolours was a popular
and common practice in the
early days of photography,
and used by both amateurs
and professionals to make
prints look more realistic.

Colouring monochrome prints was once a widely used technique. Before colour photography became practical, hand tinting offered one way of attempting realism, but it is now used mainly for aesthetic qualities. A delicacy of tone and fine control over colour values sets hand-coloured prints apart from conventional colour prints.

Today the techniques used in hand-colouring are influenced by the purposes for which it is used. Occasionally, there may be a need to produce a realistic appearance (if the only available photograph is monochrome but the image has to appear in colour), but for the most part hand-colouring does not compete directly with colour photography. Authenticity is rarely necessary or desirable, and it is more usual to approach hand-colouring with some emphasis on illustrative style. Most retouchers who specialize in hand-colouring have their own preferences.

Water-based dyes are the most widely used – being water-based, they do not obscure the underlying photographic image, and as dyes they penetrate the emulsion and can be tinted over without running. Subtle colouring is nearly always more effective than strong tints. Either pastel dyes are used, or regular dyes are heavily diluted. For full control, the normal practice is to build up to the desired colour by applying several weak tints. In the darkest areas of the print, these tints can become lost in the existing photographic image; for this reason, it is easier to work with a print that is light and has already been toned. Resin-coated papers are not normally suitable.

It is important to avoid showing brushstrokes so that the colouring will blend in with the basic image. To this end, a plain wash of water is laid over the area that is about to be coloured before adding the dye. The wash then helps the dye to blend into the emulsion smoothly.

Hand colouring
1. Weakly printed black-and-white print. Because the black silver would mask the colouring of darker tones, this print is not suitable for tinting.

2. Sepia-toned print. Toning reduces the image, so that some of the lighter tones diappear. Use a second copy of the original for reference when colouring the highlights. Sepia toning establishes a warm base, but other toners can be used if a different colour bias is wanted.

3. Airbrushed background. To create a large graduated area, airbrushing is easier than applying a wash, but the dye does not penetrate the emulsion as thoroughly as it would if applied with a brush. Because the brown tone already provides one colour element, blue was sprayed at the top, and a very light violet close to the bottom – the result is a background that is graduated in colour as well as in density, giving the figure of the doll more prominence.

Left The finished print. As a general rule, restrained colouring is more realistic. Here only pastel dyes were used, and were applied in several weak layers. To achieve the overall depth necessary to make the colouring appear realistic, apply colours selectively, favouring the darker areas, and lay slightly different hues next to each other. Here, for instance, three separate but close colours were used on the sash, and the gold chain was tinted with pastel yellow and pastel red, applied separately.

LINE CONVERSIONS

Line film is an extremely high contrast emulsion that can be used in a number of interesting ways to alter the image of an existing negative or transparency. Whereas most black-and-white emulsions are designed to have as long a tonal range as possible, line film, when used with the appropriate developer, can simplify a continuous-tone image into just two components – black and white. In other words, depending on the exposure, a particular tone will either appear as a very dense black, or it will not be recorded at all. As these films are orthochromatic (sensitive to blue light only), they can be handled in red light, which is very convenient.

One direct use of line film, when it can be exposed in the camera, is in copying prints or artwork that have no continuous tone: for instance, type, woodcuts or engravings. Because of the film's high contrast, the tone of the original paper is eliminated and the image is recorded crisply.

However, line film is more often used with existing negatives or transparencies, and copied from them either by contact-printing or by enlarging. A high contrast image may be preferable to the original because it is less complicated – the effect is generally that of a silhouette, reducing the shape of the subject to its essentials. A line negative can be used to make prints in exactly the same way as a normal negative.

The line derivative – either positive or negative – can be rephotographed through coloured filters to construct a colour image in the darkroom, and this technique can be used very successfully with a slide copier. More complex is the production of a set of tone separations, in which individual shades of grey can be isolated. Because the extent of the original image that is recorded on line film depends on the exposure, a set of different line negatives can be made from the continuous-tone original; short exposure produces just a small area of density on the line film, while a long exposure gives a dense image over most of the picture area. If a set of line positives is then made from these negatives, different negatives and positives can be combined in various permutations to separate the tones. Finally, different separated tones can be copied onto a regular colour reversal film, using different filters for each. This is an involved process.

Alternatively, a line derivative may be used in combination with a normal negative or transparency to produce a composite image. Fo

Above In a straightforward line conversion, where the intention is to simplify the image, a full-tone original black-and-white photograph of a girl in a yoga position is turned into a silhouette by first contact-printing the negative with Kodalith Ortho film. This line positive, after retouching, is contact-printed with another sheet of Kodalith Ortho. The result is a simplified negative, showing only the shape of the figure, which can then be printed normally.

A more complex use of the same line film is to create a set of positives and negatives, each recording different tonal areas of the original photograph – a black-and-white image of a shell. Different combinations of these are copied onto regular colour film through strong coloured filters, using a slide copier.

1   2

Above A skyline, prepared as artwork, was copied onto line film, and this was then sandwiched with a stock transparency of sky. For images normally seen as silhouettes, line film can be used very successfully, and can be prepared from simple artwork.

Right This photograph involved a complex procedure. A jacket illustration for a book on the subject of migraine, it made use initially of a device that recorded the contours of a human face, in parallel steps. These separately traced outlines were each copied onto line film as black line against a clear background. All of these were then assembled by hand on a lightbox and taped together. The jagged lines on the forehead were added by retouching, and the complete assembly copied once more onto line film, to give a negative image – white lines against a black background. Finally, using coloured filters, this was copied onto colour film.

4

5

Left Line film from different manufacturers have similar but not identical characteristics. Particularly in terms of contrast, their qualities are further modified by the developer. Most developers can be used, but for the highest contrast, with no intermediate tones at all, a special line film developer, such as Kodalith Super Liquid, should be used warm and concentrated. Extended development also increases density. Agfacontour is an equidensity film that produces a high contrast image, as does ordinary line film, but records only the *edges* of tones.
1. Ilford Line Film developed in DPC
2. Ilford Line Film developed in Kodalith Super Liquid
3. Kodak Ortho Type 3 developed in DPC
4. Kodak Ortho Type 3 developed in Kodalith Super Liquid
5. Kodak Ortho Type 3: extended development in Kodalith Super Liquid

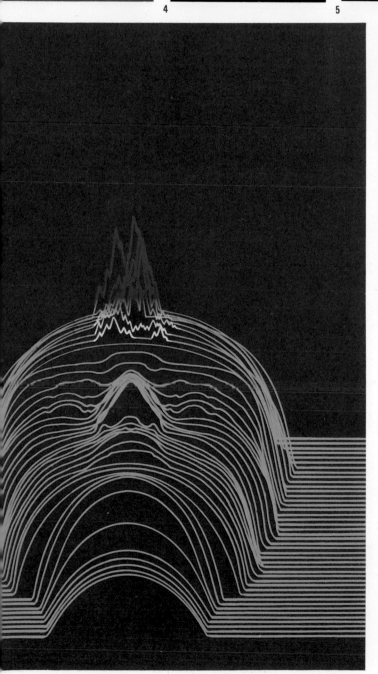

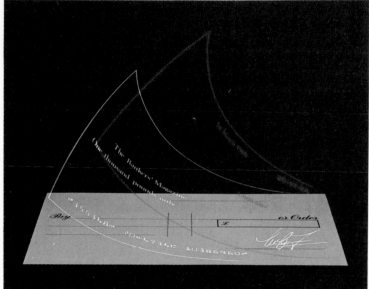

instance, a line image of a skyline, when sandwiched together with a transparency of an area of sky, can produce a convincing silhouette. For the greatest realism, it is better to develop the film in a weak or partially exhausted developer, so that the density is closer to that of continuous-tone film. Audio-visual presentations often make use of line film for titling.

As an intermediate step, line film can also be used to make masks, for special printing or for photo-composites. The original negative or transparency is first contact-printed with line film, and the resulting line derivative retouched with photo-opaque. Then, according to what areas are to be masked, the line film itself can be contact-printed to produce a second generation line derivative. As line images are only black or white, retouching is extremely simple. It is much easier to block in unwanted clear areas, such as pinholes, than to knife or chemically reduce the black parts of the image, so that the best method of retouching is to make a sequence of line images, adding photo-opaque to the appropriate areas at each stage. There is no significant loss of quality or definition at each step.

Above To illustrate the way that bank computers separate the information contained in a cheque, two line film conversions were combined with a full-tone image. This was done by first photographing the cheque in different positions and then, by copying onto line and equidensity film, producing two high-contrast images. The full-tone transparency and the two line conversions were then copied onto a single sheet of ordinary colour film, coloured filters being used for the line images.

Below and right In the photograph below, brightly sunlit areas just outside the picture frame flared the lens, degrading the image slightly. A straightforward duplicate (*right*) made on Kodachrome 25 and using a conventional slide copier, gains contrast, which in this case improves the image.

No special duplicating film is currently available for use with slide copiers, which have an electronic flash light source, and regular films such as Kodachrome always produce duplicate images that have higher contrast than the originals, unless special precautions are taken. Although this can, as in this example, be an advantage, it is more frequently a problem.

1

2

3

4

DUPLICATE TRANSPARENCIES

Duplicating original transparencies is a technique with a number of important applications. Valuable transparencies may be copied in case of loss or damage, or when they are needed for different uses at the same time. Mistakes in the original, such as a colour cast, can be corrected by appropriate filtration. The duplicating process can also be used for various manipulations, such as the later stages of line conversion.

Achieving fidelity is by no means always easy. To begin with, every stage in the photographic process introduces changes, and therefore tends to move away from the image values in the original. More serious, however, are the basic limitations of colour film: because only three colours are used to reproduce a great variety of hues, and because the dyes are not perfect, even the original photograph can be deficient, and, in duplication, colour inaccuracies are often exaggerated. When duplicating, the colours that are being recorded are those of the dyes in the original transparency, not the colours of the subject. For this reason, two transparencies of the same scene on different film stocks, even though they may look similar to the eye, will often duplicate quite differently.

Professional duplicating film, such as Kodak Ektachrome 6121, is balanced for tungsten illumination in an enlarger. Where all the variables in an installation, such as colour temperature and voltage fluctuation, have been thoroughly tested, this film gives good consistent results. However, most slide copiers, which offer great advantages over enlargers for this type of work, use electronic flash, for which tungsten-balanced duplicating film is unsuitable. Regular camera films must be used with these machines, and a few special corrections are needed.

Accuracy in duplicating depends on consistency, and the best way of achieving this is to standardize the procedure, first calibrating the machine and then running a series of tests on one or two stock transparencies. This will establish the basic exposure setting (adjusted by altering the lens aperture) and filtration. A comprehensive set of gelatin colour correction filters will be needed, as different original transparencies and different batches of the film used for duplicating will almost certainly introduce colour casts. For regular duplicating, it is best to stock up with a considerable quantity of a single batch of film.

Duplicating nearly always raises contrast, and although this may improve the appearance of flat transparencies – of scenes photographed in dull weather, for example – with originals that already have quite a high contrast special precautions are necessary. One attachment frequently fitted to slide copying machines is a fogging device, which flashes a weak light over the whole picture area. This is too weak to affect the lighter parts of the picture, but raises the shadow tones; the result is an apparent reduction in contrast, although it is successful only when the shadow areas are relatively small (large shadow areas tend to look weak). Shadow colours can be altered independently of the remainder of the photograph by placing appropriate filters over the fogging device.

Another method of holding down the contrast is to overexpose the film slightly, and then reduce the development; this method cannot, however, be used with Kodachrome, which is factory-processed and responds poorly to altered development. There is, therefore, no clearcut choice of film for duplicating with a slide copier: E-6 films allow good contrast control, but Kodachrome, particularly the ASA 25 type, has such a high resolution that many photographers are prepared to put up with its contrast difficulties. One solution is to use a large format camera for duplicating, to give the best of both worlds – good resolution and a film that can be altered in its development.

Left The photograph (1) was chosen for a duplicating test because it combines two extreme problems: the contrast is very high, and it has a large shadow area. As when photographing the original scene, an average meter reading is inadequate – it would give an overexposed duplicate. Instead, the exposure was set for the sunlit figure. In a straightforward duplicate (2), however, the contrast is so high that all the shadow detail is lost.

By using the fogging device attached to the slide copier, a small quantity of light is flaked onto the whole picture area at the same time the exposure is made (3). This fogs the film very slightly, affecting the darker areas of the image proportionately more than the highlights. This lowers the contrast by lightening the shadows, and because more detail becomes visible, it appears to be an improvement, and closer to the original. However, when the fogging device is used at its maximum, it simply weakens the shadows in an empty way, and the whole image appears degraded (4).

PHOTO-COMPOSITES

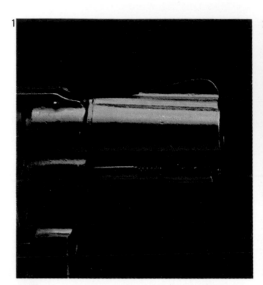

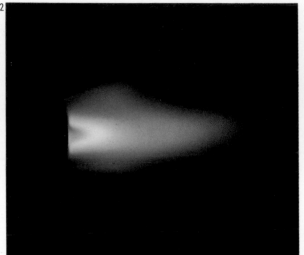

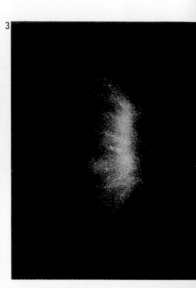

For the complex procedures involved in combining colour images, a slide copying machine is ideal, particularly when sheet film is used and the slide copier adapted for the larger format. In principle, a photo-composite is very similar to the composite print. However, there is much less latitude in the process, partly because tonal control is more difficult and partly because colours need to be matched.

If the first transparency to be copied has a large black area, then another image can be exposed onto this part of the film later without any special precautions except noting the area in the camera's viewfinder. Nevertheless, to align images precisely, some method of register is needed, and this is always easier on a large film format. There are two alternatives: one is to mark the outline of each image being copied on the ground glass screen with a pen. This is uncomplicated but not very accurate. The second method is to attach each original transparency to a spare strip of film with tape, align them on a light box, and punch each with an accurate register punch. Then, by placing each mounted and punched transparency onto a register pin bar attached to the slide copier, near-perfect register is assured without even having to examine the image through the viewfinder. In both cases, every piece of equipment – and the film – must stay precisely in position.

When parts of transparencies that do not have black backgrounds need to be combined, a set of line masks is used. These masks are contact-printed, and a pair used for each image. The negative line mask is combined with the subject transparency, so that only the subject can be seen, against a black background. The positive mask, which blacks out the outline of the subject, is then sandwiched with the background transparency, and this is copied in register. The result is known as a strip-in. Some slight retouching is usually necessary around the edges.

Exploding globe Technical problems and lack of time prevented the use of genuine high-speed photography for this photograph illustrating a feature on global terrorism. The gun barrel was a straightforward photograph *(1)*; the flash was the flame from a gas burner, filtered orange *(2)*; the two bursts of powdered glass *(3, 4)* were airbrushed; the bullet was photographed by tungsten lighting, the camera being deliberately shifted during a long exposure to give a streaking effect *(5)*.
To create the effect of a shattered globe, two transparencies were sandwiched together – one of the globe *(6)*, the other of a light bulb that had first been filled with white paint and cement (to hold the shape), and then carefully broken with a hammer *(7)*. For the flying shards *(8)*, another transparency of the globe was cut and taped behind transparencies of broken, white-painted glass.

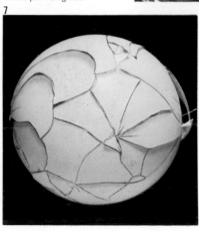

194

5

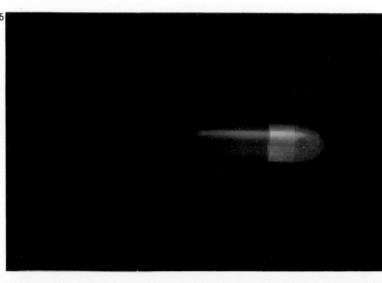

Below From the eight original transparencies, each on 4 x 5 inch (9 x 12 cm) sheet film, the final assembly was also made on 4 x 5 inch (9 x 12 cm) film, using a slide copier and view camera. The use of a large film format made it easy to register each image and kept resolution high, contrast being controlled by overexposing and then under-developing by half a stop. So that each transparency would be copied in exactly the right position, a register punch and bar were used.

DYE TRANSFER PRINTING

For the highest quality colour printing it is necessary to return to one of the most traditional processes – the dye transfer. Just as the old-fashioned platinum print has unsurpassed qualities in monochrome work, so the rather laborious dye transfer process still sets the standards by which all other colour prints can be judged. Unlike the platinum process, however, dye transfer work has not fallen into disuse, because it has one particular quality that endears it to art directors and photographers who work in advertising – it permits the highest standard of retouching and colour control. Because dye transfer prints use pure dyes, which are rolled out individually under normal lighting conditions, undetectable retouching can be carried out using the same dyes. Advertising budgets commonly allow for the high labour costs involved in retouching, and it is normal to make fine adjustments to colour images. As a result, dye transfers are a small but important business for a few professional laboratories; advertising has, in effect, maintained a printing process that would otherwise have become neglected.

Although the procedure is quite different from that involving regular colour emulsions, dye transfer uses a three-colour system. The original, normally a transparency, is copied three times, using three different filters: red, blue and green. The result is a set of three black-and-white negatives, each of which records a separate colour. These negatives are then used to expose three sheets of a special gelatin-image film, and these are finally dyed and used to reassemble the three colours on one print.

There are some underlying similarities between dye transfer printing and screen process printing: in both cases, individual colours are laid down separately, in register, so that the final image is built up from a number of layers. But instead of a finely woven screen, the dye transfer process uses a thick film that carries an image in gelatin. When soaked in a dye bath, this gelatin absorbs the dye in proportion to its thickness – shadow areas are represented by a substantial layer of gelatin, while highlights are practically clear film. This gelatin image-in-relief is carried on what is known as a matrix, and for a straightforward dye transfer print, three such matrices are used: one for cyan dye, another for yellow dye, and a third for magenta dye. The dyes are transferred, via the matrices (which are reusable) to the paper, hence the name of the process.

In any of the three stages of the dye transfer process – negatives, matrices, or printing – many fine adjustments can be made. By varying the exposure and the development of the separation negatives, contrast and density can be altered, and for selected control, weak masks can be made to lighten or strengthen highlights and shadows. Then, the exposure of the matrices can be varied, although this part of the process tends to be standardized. Finally, the composition of the three matrix dyes can be chosen according to the contrast wanted in any particular colour; a small quantity of acetic acid increases the contrast of any dye, while adding a chemical known as triethanolamine lowers contrast.

In skilled hands, many subtle changes can be made to the image that is finally rolled down onto the dye transfer print. The same dyes that were used to produce the finished print can also be used to retouch the print. These blend in perfectly with the basic image. Moreover, by transposing dyes and matrices, or by adding dyes selectively to the matrices by hand before rolling it out on the paper, many special effects can be created.

Making the separation negatives
1. Place the original transparency on a densitometer to assess the tonal range. This check should be carried out at key stages to ensure densities of the separation negatives relate to the original.

2. Punch pieces of scrap film and attach to the transparency as a guide for registration.

3. This, and all subsequent stages, must be carried out in the darkroom. Contact the original transparency with high contrast film, emulsion to emulsion, to retain highlight contrast in the final negatives.

4. Make three exposures through each of three primary filters (red, green and blue) to give three highlight masks: cyan, magenta and yellow. Develop the masks.

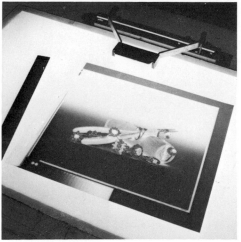

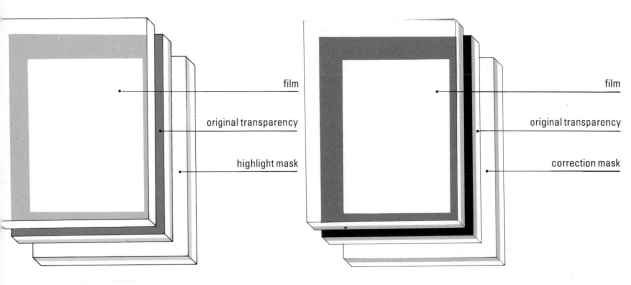

film

original transparency

highlight mask

film

original transparency

correction mask

Above A good dye transfer depends very heavily on the accuracy with which the separation negatives are made. For this, not only must a densitometer be used, but masks are nearly always needed to correct shifts in tone and colour. A mask is a weakly exposed and developed sheet of negative film – the tones of the image that it covers are determined by the exposure, and the colours it records by appropriate filtration. Without such precautions, highlights frequently appear in the print with a slight veil of tone. To correct this, a highlight mask *(left)*, combined with the basic separation negatives, holds back exposure onto the matrix film from the brightest parts of the image. As a result, highlights are cleaned up and give the print brilliance. Similarly, any unwanted colour casts in specific tonal areas can be altered with a colour correction mask *(centre)*. The final product is a set of composite separation negatives, with basic negatives and masks sandwiched together *(right)*. If these are not accurate, later corrections become excessively complex.

Take each highlight mask and contact it, emulsion to emulsion, with the original transparency. Sandwich mask film on the back of the original. Place this sandwich on the lightbox and make three exposures through the appropriate filters to give three correction masks.

6. Contact the emulsion side of the correction mask to the rear of the original transparency. Contact separation negative film to the emulsion of the original. Repeat this, making exposures through three primary filters to give three separation negatives.

Making the matrices
7. Enlarge the three separation negatives to the required format on three pieces of matt film.

8. Place the matt film on the easel of the enlarger and roll it flat, to ensure sharp focus in the final print. Expose through the back of the film. Repeat for each of the three pieces of matt film.

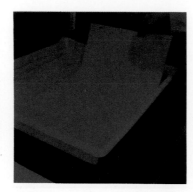

9. Develop, wash, fix (in a non-hardening fixing bath) and wash again each piece of film.

10. Place the three matt films (one at a time) under running water, heated to a temperature of 120-130°C. This forms relief images on the emulsions.

11. Place the three matt films in three separate baths of dye, one for each colour.

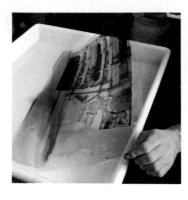

12. Rinse the cyan film in a solution of 1% acetic acid.

13. Transfer the cyan film briefly to an acid rinse holding bath.

Making the print
14. Soak a sheet of plain paper in conditioner and lay it on a glass sheet which has registration pins.

15. Register the cyan film on the paper, roll once and leave it for five minutes to let the transfer to the paper.

16. The relief image of the matrix film holds different amounts of dye, relative to the different densities of colour in the original transparency.

17. Repeat steps 12 to 15 for the magenta film.

18. Repeat steps 12 to 15 for the yellow film, to give the finished dye transfer print.

Left *The Salute, Venice*
This photograph of B. Loghena's church, taken by Dr. Derek Parfitt, illustrates one of the uses of dye transfer printing. The blue in the sky has been almost entirely removed because the photographer considered it unrelated to the colours in the building. The result of this process is startling: the building is highlighted with fine rosy sunlight, the sculptural decorations are clearly defined, yet the sky is a pale, seemingly clouded grey, which does not detract from the typically Venetian beauty of the church. This is only one use of the dye transfer process which is usually made most use of by advertising. There are three principal advantages: improving the quality of the image, combining images, and making a high standard of retouching possible.

CHAPTER 4

USES OF PHOTOGRAPHY

Of all the visual arts, photography is the most widely practised, and the most easily reproduced. As a result, it lends itself to a variety of uses, from exhibitions of individual prints to mass market reproduction. Each use radically affects the ways in which photographers work.

When a photograph is commissioned, it has to fulfil certain criteria. In commercial work, these criteria will be outlined clearly by the client in a brief to the photographer. In editorial work, where the published photograph often must work on its own merits rather than support advertising copy, the brief is usually less restrictive, and more reliance is placed on the photographer's interpretation of the subject.

Any definite photographic use has its own creative standards that the photographer must try to meet, and it is these standards that set commissioned work apart. Producing good photographs to a brief and often a deadline may be difficult at first, but these parameters are more often stimulating than limiting. Knowing what is required, whether for a magazine article, a book jacket or an advertising brochure, helps to direct the creative approach. A large proportion of gallery photography lacks this structure and is often weaker as a result. Even for amateurs it is a good idea to work to a set project to give direction to the photography.

There are three main types of commercial photography: portraits, records of events and photographs that entertain. Portraiture has quietly remained the mainstay of photography throughout its history. To record, photography can be used mechanically to copy flat artwork, or with a great deal of imagination, as in the best photojournalism. To entertain, photography relies heavily on creative skills to make appealing images; these are in great demand for editorial and advertising work.

A major factor affecting the use of photography has been the availability of some means of reproducing pictures. As photographic printing or copying is relatively slow, for the first few decades of photography, audiences were restricted to those who could view original prints or slides in galleries and magic lantern shows. Since then, the development of photomechanical reproduction has exerted a major influence on professional photography.

Right The main vehicles for reproducing photography are the various print media, including newspapers, books, magazines, sales brochures, record covers and product packaging. Although radically different styles of photography may be used, in commercially reproduced print the main function is to sell, by being informative as in the case of the chair catalogue, or persuasive as in record and book covers.

Left The beautiful, considering attitude of this girl was caught by Jean Harvey using a Nikon F2 with an 85 mm lens. The daylight, which was good enough to need no compensation lighting, gave her skin a luminosity and emphasized a medieval quality in her face: the eyes dark and the cheekbones, forehead and long chin softly highlighted. There is delicacy in her pose, and slight uncertainty, which less diffuse lighting might have eliminated. It is a memorable although informal portrait.

Below In advertising and sales literature, one of the most frequent problems is to make quite ordinary-looking consumer products appear attractive. This usually elevates lighting to the most important element in commercial still life photography.

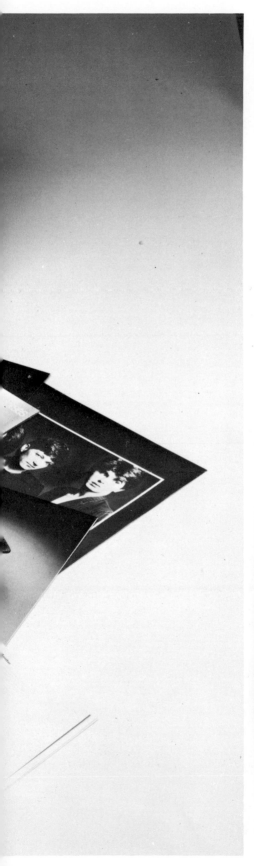

For newspapers, magazines and books, efficient printing methods have made longer print-runs possible; this in turn has meant wider audiences. At the same time, technical improvements have raised the general level of quality of reproduction. In posters, packaging and all types of print media, photography also plays an important role. Television and film make little use of still photography (although when film or tape of a subject is unavailable, as often happens in news reporting, photographs are often used), but a growing medium, which to some extent bridges the gap between stills and motion pictures, is audio-visual presentation.

The development of the 35mm camera prompted photojournalism, and this in turn influenced the design of the new 35mm models. The large format view camera, on the other hand, is in its element where image quality is paramount. Each piece of equipment, each technique and each material has its best application, but all approaches involve some means of reproducing and preserving photographs, from display frames for a portrait or gallery print, to the latest photomechanical process.

SLIDE PROJECTION

Although most photographers who are accustomed to colour transparencies become adept at appreciating them in their original form, a slide is usually only an intermediate stage. Most colour transparencies are too small to be displayed without some means of projection, and while a light box and magnifying glass are useful for making preliminary judgements, slides really need to be enlarged for use. Printing from a transparency loses some of the image's richness and intensity; reproduction in a publication is nearly always dependent on commercial considerations. For many photographers, the best way of enlarging a transparency without losing its best qualities is to project it onto a screen. Modern screens use highly reflective materials, and can preserve the "snap" or crispness of an original transparency. Slide projectors are quite expensive but cost virtually nothing to use.

Slide projectors are available for most film formats, but 35mm is by far the most popular. Designs vary, and the system for storing slides and feeding them into the projection gate range from horizontal or vertical drums that rotate to straight trays that move forward one step at a time. All good projectors have a cooling mechanism that protects the transparencies from the heat of the lamp.

The choice of lens depends on the size of the screen and location of the projector, but 85mm to 90mm is standard for 35mm slides. A longer focal length – 150mm or 250mm – means that the projector must be placed further from the screen to give the same size of image as a standard lens. If the room is large enough, this is often an advantage, as the projector can be sited out of the way behind the audience. When space is limited, a wide-angle lens – usually a focal length of 35mm – increases the spread of the projected image, so that the projector can be used close to the screen. Unfortunately, this type of lens can cause vignetting and poorer image quality towards the edges of the slide. Image quality on the whole depends heavily on the lens, and the advantages of an expensive

modern camera lens are largely wasted if the slide is seen by an inferior projector lens.

Although a white wall, a sheet of paper, or even white cloth can be used as a makeshift viewing surface, only a purpose-made screen gives a bright, rich image. The most reflective screens have either beaded or laminated metallic surfaces and can even be used in an undarkened room. However, these are only effective for people sitting directly in front; from one side, they appear dim. General purpose screens have a matt white surface, which reflects less efficiently but over a greater viewing angle. The final ingredient for a slide show is a well-darkened room. Any light that spills onto the screen from a window or doorway weakens the reflected image.

Assembling a collection of slides into a show that will interest, inform and entertain even a small or informal audience calls for editing skills. The best slide shows are usually short; ruthless pruning of all but top quality material is essential. The slides should be ordered in a logical sequence and in such a way as to capitalize on any visual similarities. In the same way that a designer puts pacing into a photographic essay in a magazine, so a photographer can, in a more rudimentary fashion, organize the sequence of slides to create both harmony and surprise. Similar compositions of very different subjects help to create continuity, while changing from a series of related images – such as a sequence of wide landscape views – to something different – a closeup of a plant, for example – introduces a change of pace. These techniques can lift a slide show from an ordinary collection of pictures to a more coherent presentation.

Beginning the show with a title gives a professional touch. The title should be simple and can be made by using line film. Hand-drawn, Letraset or typeset lettering is usually prepared as flat artwork at a convenient size, and then photographed onto the high contrast line film emulsion. This can then be projected either on its own, or superimposed over the opening slide of the show.

Right Most slide projectors are manufactured for 35mm format transparencies, and the two most common designs use a sliding tray, as in the case of the Leitz and Rollei projectors *(top),* or a revolving magazine, in the case of the Kodak Carousel *(bottom left).* The 2¼ x 2¼inch (6 x 6cm) Rollei projector *(bottom right)* is one of the few models that accept rollfilm transparencies. Most good slide projectors incorporate remote-controlled slide change and focusing.

Below Beaded screens *(left,* which have a surface covered with very small transparent glass spheres, reflect the image very efficiently over a narrow angle, and are suitable for a small audience seated directly in front of the screen. A matt white screen *(centre)* can be seen clearly from a wider angle, but the image is relatively dim. A lenticular screen *(right)* gives both a bright image and good angular coverage, although its textured surface can be distracting if viewed from a close distance.

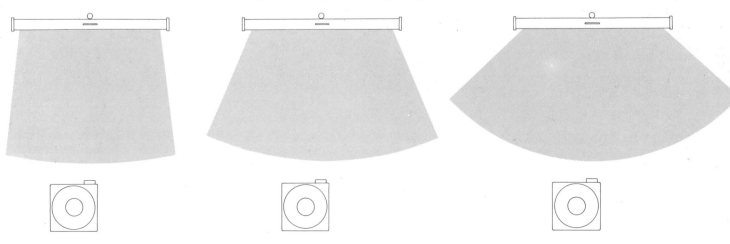

DISPLAYING PHOTOGRAPHS

Superficially, photographs seem to have a great deal in common with paintings, but when display is considered – in an exhibition, or simply on a living room wall – photographs demand a different treatment. The temptation is to assume that the types of frame and lighting traditionally used in art galleries will work just as well for photographs. However, while a painting has certain three-dimensional qualities, which include thickness of paint and texture of the surface, a photograph is essentially an image and as a result calls for a simpler two-dimensional display technique.

Oil paintings and watercolours have surfaces and textures that reflect the processes involved – the layers of paint and brushstrokes reveal the artist's method and are frequently an important dimension of the work. This gives great scope for complementing a work of art or enhancing some aspect of it by imaginative use of frames, which may be ornate or deeply recessed, according to the nature of the work. As a result, the painting's frame can have a considerable effect on the way we see the painting itself.

Any texture in a photographic print, however, is always added and is not a quality of the original image. With any type of picture, it is possible to look *at* it (appreciating its qualities as an object on display) or to look *through* it (seeing it only as an image). The latter predominates in photography and there is therefore a strong argument for keeping the display simple and unobtrusive, restricting the choice of frames to those which attract little or no attention. Unusual shapes and embellished borders nearly always distract the eye and conflict with the basic realism of a photograph. The most common and versatile frames are simple block mountings and plain metal mouldings. A glass or clear plastic covering protects prints from damage and dust, but can prevent the full range of tones from being appreciated.

Like any other work of art, a photographic print must be considered in terms of size, proportions and balance. The size of a print depends on personal taste, as much as on viewing distance and the nature of the image. If the photograph contains bold or recognizable shapes, a simple distribution of colours, or its subject is on a small scale, then it will suit being reproduced quite small. Complicated scenes and expansive views, on the other hand, usually benefit from being a larger size. At the same time, a small print may have the delicate appeal of a miniature, encouraging careful but detached inspection, while a large print whose borders stretch beyond the eye's normal field of view tends to draw the viewer into the image.

The proportions of the frame can also influence the effect of the photograph: a borderless print can seem very direct and unfussy, but with some images it may also upset the balance and composition by forcing attention towards the centre of the picture and allowing the elements at the edges to "fall off". A plain paper or card mount can help to isolate the image from its surroundings. Leaving a wide lower margin in a mount gives a more balanced effect.

The actual position of the print on a wall should also be simple. The best location is at eye level, and where both a clear initial view and closer inspection is allowed. Lighting should be at least as bright as a normal reading level and should not create reflections from the surface of the print. Overhead spotlights or striplights are the best for this purpose, so that the light is at a sharp angle to the print.

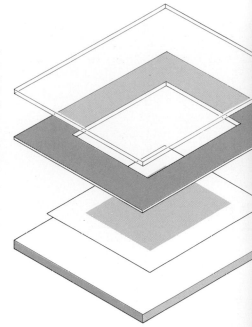

Above One of the simplest methods of mounting a photographic print is a block frame, which can be bought in kit form or, more cheaply, made from scratch. The components are a backing board that will not warp, a sheet of glass of the same size, a mount cut from rag fibre card, and the print itself

Right By varying the proportions of the print to the mount, it is possible to make subtle alterations to the focus of attention. A very wide border emphasizes the edge of the image and its shape, and gives a more deliberate feeling of presentation. A very narrow border, on the other hand, draws the viewer's eye inside the image and reduces the role played by the edges.

Left In this photography exhibition, the prints have been mounted very eccentrically, to offset fairly detailed captions. Identical mounts have been used for all, to impose uniformity on different images from many sources.

STORAGE AND RETRIEVAL

All photographs must be adequately protected, and should be organized in such a way that they are easily accessible. Both film and paper emulsion are relatively soft and easily damaged, while many of the chemicals and materials used in prints, negatives and transparencies are susceptible to contamination and fading. Archival treatment, which is used extensively in museums, aims to ensure that photographs are in as stable a condition as possible; although some of the techniques are too elaborate for everyday use, certain precautions are relatively easy to take. Adequate fixing and thorough washing will do more to preserve self-processed material than practically any other treatment. A short gold toning bath is also a simple, effective way of prolonging the lives of prints.

Storage should protect photographs from

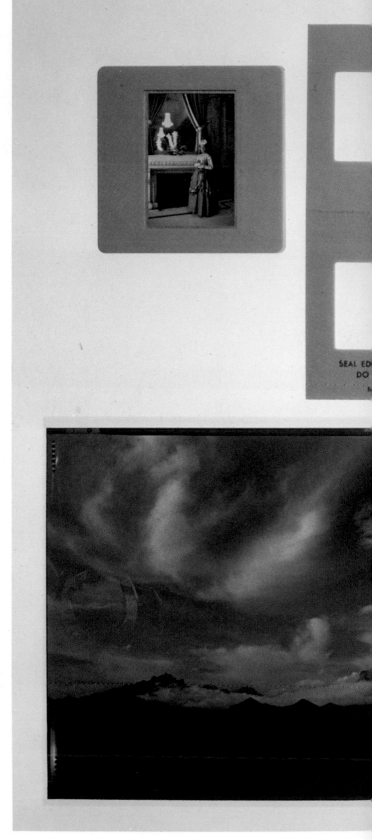

copyright stamp
name stamp
select sticker
frame number
subject information
location stamp
roll number
date stamp

Above Transparencies that the photographer hopes to have used in books or magazines or by other media, need to be captioned carefully, both for identification and to protect copyright. When large numbers of transparencies are stored, stamps or printed labels are convenient for standard information, such as the photographer's name. A typical arrangement of caption information is shown above; on a 35mm mount, space is limited, and only essential information is included.
The standard copyright abbreviation, together with the name of the photographer, is an important safeguard in case of copyright infringement. The stamped, four-digit number identifies the roll of film, while the frame number and date are, on Kodachrome transparencies, such as this, prestamped by the manufacturer.
The country location is stamped for filing purposes, and the essential subject information is noted. Where more details may be needed by a publishing client for a caption, this information may be extended to the reverse of the mount, or logged separately in a caption book. Finally, a red sticker denotes that this is a first select, as a guide for the picture researcher. Photographers who are primarily interested in protecting their transparencies often print the caption information upside-down, so that it can be read when the transparency is stacked in the slide tray.
Right For protection, all transparencies, however used, need to be mounted, or stored in envelopes. The simplest form of mount is adhesive-backed card, for sealing by hand pressure or under heat. It can be written upon, and if the transparency is used for graphic reproduction, a card mount is easily pulled apart or cut open by the separation maker. An acetate sleeve that slips over the mount is adequate protection for most handling.
Plastic mounts that can be closed by pressing together two halves give better protection than card, particularly when they are fitted with glass covers. Some makes, as shown in the mount at lower right, incorporate masks to alter the shape of the frame. Metal mounts, which are hermetically sealed with a special mounting device, give the surest protection of all, but the transparency cannot easily be removed.
Sheet film, which is never protected, is normally stored in a simple acetate sleeve. The film base is thick enough to withstand normal handling.

physical damage such as scratches and creas-
ing and should eliminate fading and staining.
Fading, to which dyes are much more susceptible than silver, is unavoidable if the emulsion
is exposed to strong light for long periods. This
problem can be easily avoided except in the
case of display prints, and even these can be
reprinted if necessary. (A copy negative or
transparency is an essential safeguard in case
the original is lost.)

Staining demands special precautions, as
many seemingly innocuous materials can
affect stored photographs. Over a period of
time, wood, cardboard and brown paper can
release acid compounds that will damage
prints, negatives or transparencies. The glue
used in some envelopes can also be harmful.
To prevent this type of damage, the best materials to use are those designed specifically for
photographic storage. The commercially
available paper sleeves for negatives are acid-
free, inexpensive, and ideal: negatives need
no display, but should simply be visible and
easy to remove, strip by strip, for printing. A
ring-bound file is suitable for storing them or,
alternatively, a baked enamel or stainless steel
filing cabinet (ordinary paint may contaminate
the contents).

Transparencies need individual mounts
and, being originals, often have to stand up to
rougher handling than negatives (when used
for reproduction, they are at risk when separations are made). Card mounts are the simplest
and cheapest, and are usually adequate provided they are surrounded by a clear plastic
sleeve to protect the surface from fingerprints,
spilled liquids and scratches. For heavy use in
a slide projector, however, a more durable
plastic or metal mount may be better. Glass
covers on both sides of the film give even more

Right The three most
common methods of storing
transparencies are in filing
cabinets, looseleaf folders,
or slide magazines. Deep
filing cabinets of standard
office design accept hangers,
which can take up to 24
35mm transparencies, 6 x
6cm, or four 4 x 5 inch (9 x
12cm) sheets. Alternatively,
transparencies can be stored
in either the boxes they are
received in from processing
labs, or in slide projector
magazines.
Other types of filing cabinets
have shelves that are the
depth of a single 35mm
mount. Ringbound looseleaf
books are useful for storing
small quantities of
transparencies, and can be
kept on a normal bookshelf.

protection, although they can also incur other risks – major damage if the glass is shattered, and scratches if particles of grit become lodged inside. One brand of metal mount can be hermetically sealed, which prevents dust from entering. Mounted transparencies are normally stored in slide trays, in boxes, or on hangers that fit into filing cabinets. (Some projector trays, such as those of the Kodak Carousel, double as storage trays, making special preparations for viewing unnecessary.)

Prints are highly susceptible to damage, particularly scuffing of the corners and edges. If the print has a substantial white border, tattered edges can be trimmed off, but this can only be done once or twice before crowding in on the image area. Dry-mounting gives a print rigidity, but also increases its bulk considerably and takes up more filing space. For mass storage of prints, acid-free and unglued card boxes are best. Inside the boxes, or the metal drawers of a filing cabinet if the prints are stored loose, prints should be interleaved with high quality paper or transparent plastic sheets made from cellulose acetate or polyethylene terephthalate.

All photographs should be kept at a reasonable temperature and humidity; heat and moisture are both damaging, and when combined are particularly dangerous. If the conditions are comfortable for living and working, then as a rule they are also safe for storage; ideally, the room should be no warmer than 70°F (21°), and the relative humidity should be between 30% and 50%. Files should never be placed near a radiator or in the basement, which is often the dampest part of a building. As a precaution against humidity, which is not always as noticeable as heat, some photographers keep a desiccant, such as silica gel, in their files – this can also be used to dry out emulsion that has already become softened and swollen through exposure to moisture.

Above When presenting sequences of slides to a client, the order in which they are seen may be important. One simple way of ensuring that they stay in order is to mark the edges with a diagonal line, as shown above.

Above left and below This storage system is used in one of the major international stock agencies, Bruce Coleman Ltd. The storage and viewing room is conventional, with filing cabinets and a large lightbox for visiting picture researchers to make selections, but downstairs a computer terminal gives access to all the transparencies in the files, the information on each shot stored on tape. Rapid location of picture requests is at least as important as the storage.

AUDIO-VISUAL PRESENTATION

Audio-visual presentation is more sophisti-cated than simple slide projection. The addition of a soundtrack (together with other technical improvements) makes it possible to use transparencies in a distinctive way, with greater continuity. Some of the techniques of film editing can be applied, but there remain more differences between film making and audio-visual presentation than there are simi-larities: still images are never perceived in the same way as a moving sequence.

Audio-visual presentations are frequently used when the entertainment value of a story line can be put to good use, or for giving information in a structured way to a captive audience. As training and educational aids they fulfil an important role in schools and sales conferences.

Most audio-visual presentations use a single screen and a standard 35mm format, although ambitious productions may use several screens, each serviced by a different pair of projectors. To avoid the discontinuity of a black screen when one slide replaces another, two linked projectors are used; a dissolve unit fades the image from one projector as the image from the other gradually appears. Mix-ing from one slide to another can usually be done at different rates, from a rapid cut to a dissolve lasting several seconds, and this choice allows the slide programme to be edited to suit the storyline. Fast cutting, for instance, suits dialogue, action and a commen-tary that needs to cover several scenes in quick succession. Slow dissolves, on the other hand, help to create a calmer atmosphere and smooth flow; they are also suitable for match dissolves, when similar shapes are mixed and other sequences where the change has to be almost imperceptible.

The most important extra dimension in audio-visual presentation is sound, synchro-nized to the change of slides. Most commercial tape recorders are suitable, although they should have several tracks so that one can be

Right Audio-visual equipment, whether supplied as a complete kit, or assembled from different sources, generally includes a pair of projectors, linked by a dissolve system, tape recorder and playback, speakers, and handsets for either running the show manually, or prerecording the sequence onto one band of the tape.
The kit shown here, the Kodak AV Presentation Unit, has the added advantage of a 25-watt Dolby sound system. It also includes a light which can be used to point out specific parts of the slide being projected.

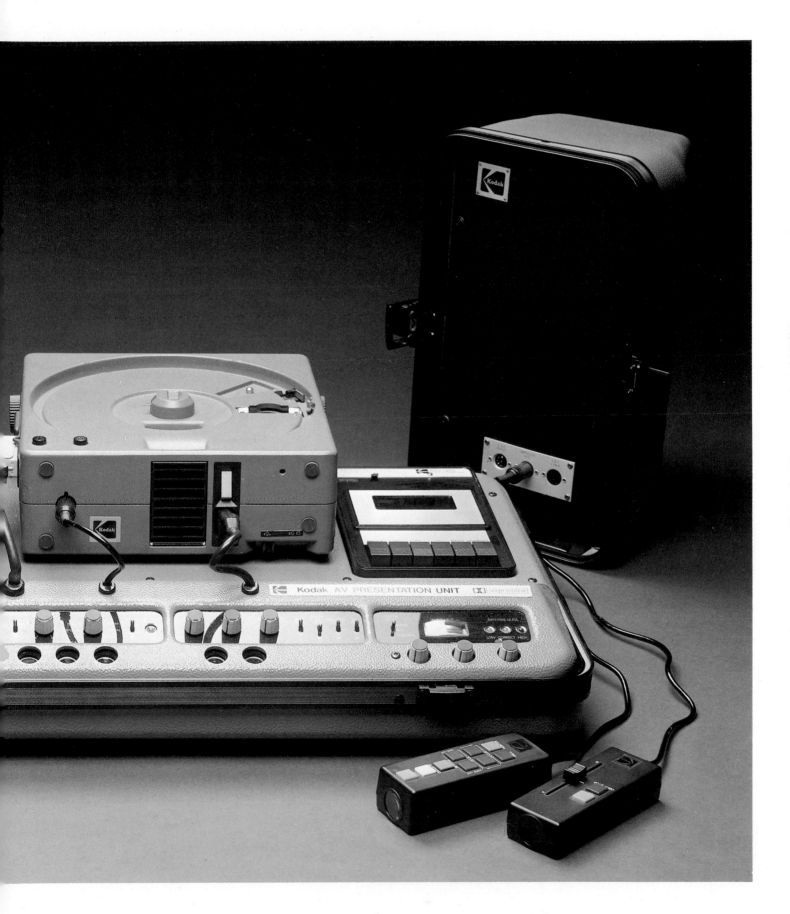

used for programming, and at least two input channels, so that sound effects from another tape machine or a record deck can be recorded at the same time as a voice commentary. During the show, the slides may be changed by hand, using a script and the tape for cues, but a more sophisticated system uses one track of the sound tape to trigger slide changes in the projectors. A slide-tape synchronizer, which is usually combined with the dissolve unit, does this by recording pulses on tape.

The actual recording can be as simple or as sophisticated as the production demands. Good sound quality calls for expensive equipment and a non-reverberant location. Professional sound studios are ideal, but can be expensive. To save recording time costs when such studios are used, slide programmers generally work from a well-prepared script onto a master tape. Editing and making copy tapes is done later. Sound effects are available on records, and all professional studios have sound effects libraries.

The production sequence varies according to the type of audio-visual presentation, but generally follows some sort of pattern. First, a script is prepared and gradually worked up to a full storyboard. Then, the original transparencies are assembled, either from stock or from a special shoot, and selected. These are duplicated in the format chosen for the presentation. Titling and any necessary artwork is prepared and photographed, and the complete slide sequence put in order. The soundtrack is recorded and edited, and finally, the slides and tapes are synchronized.

The presentation is judged on its general appearance by the audience, so the conditions of viewing are as important as the content. A good screen is essential, set up in a well-darkened room at a comfortable viewing distance. Front projection screens normally give a better image than back projection, which tends to produce a brighter image in the middle of the screen than at the edges, although with the former the projection equipment often has to be set up in the audience rather than hidden out of sight. A speaker that is separate from the tape player is essential, and should be behind or next to the screen. Stereo sound is

Right At the stage of production shown here, a storyboard has already been prepared, with script and timing; all that remains is to select suitable photographs. The brief image description on the left of the storyboard is intended as a guide for the picture researcher, and the actual transparencies available may not always correspond closely. If the transparencies are from different sources, or are of different formats, it is usual to make duplicate, 35mm transparencies. In this way, the images can be standardized and, if necessary, colours corrected. Most of the photographs (*far right*) were copied from 2½ x 2½ inch (6 x 6cm), transparencies, which allowed some choice in cropping and composition.

Threatened Rain Forest

No.	Slide	Change	Soundtrack	Time elapsed
1	Panda logo reversed out		Mute	
		Slow dissolve		.00.05
2	Reversed out		Fade in forest sounds: tropical birdsong, cicadas, etc.	
		Slow dissolve		00:10
3	LS Rainforest			
		Slow dissolve		00.15
4	MS Forest interior			
		Fast dissolve		00:19
5	CU bird		Bird call over background	
		Medium dissolve		00:22
6	MS Forest river or lake		Fade in sound of machinery over forest background	
		Medium dissolve		00:26
7	LS Forest		Sound becomes recognizable as bulldozer Volume increases steadily	
		Medium dissolve		00:30
8	LS Single tree		Volume increases	
		Fast dissolve		00:34
9	As 8 + title		Sound of large tree falling Crashes through undergrowth	
		Fast dissolve		00:38
10	CU Bulldozer		Sounds of machinery continue muted, under VO "In the last 12 months…"	
		Fast dissolve		00:42
11	MS Forest being cleared		"…many…square miles of the world's great rainforests have been deliberately destroyed…"	
		Cut		00:47
12	CU Timber		"…to provide timber…"	
		Cut		00:50
13	Clearing undergrowth		"…to make way for farming land…"	
		Cut		00:54
14	LS Transamazon highway		Fades out "…and to create room for human settlement."	
		Medium dissolve		00:58
15	Burning forest		Trees burning (muted) "Yet the destruction of the forest may have serious consequences for the whole planet."	
		Slow dissolve		01:04
16	Earth from space		"At a conservative estimate, rainforest covers…"	
		Slow dissolve		01:08

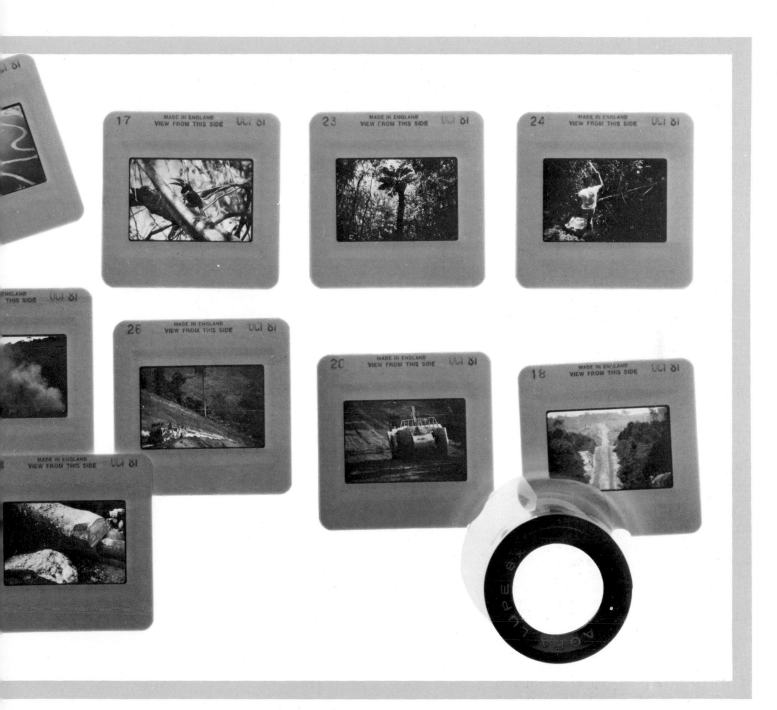

sometimes used, although there is a danger of over-producing modest sequences.

For large audiences and a fairly grand scale of production, three-screen presentations introduce a new element. Not only does the wide screen area make panoramic views possible, but juxtaposition can be used to give different views of a single subject. Used creatively, a three-screen show can provide a sense of spectacle. Because three side-by-side frames in 35mm proportions give a very stretched view, the normal arrangement is to have three square screens. The slide format is normally 1½ x 1½ inch (38 x 38mm), known as superslide, the largest frame that can still be used in a 35mm slide projector. To produce this, 120 rollfilm can be cut with scissors, or there is a film magazine designed specifically for this format for use with a Hasselblad. For a single panoramic view across all three screens, a 120 rollfilm panoramic camera can be used and the transparency cut into three, or a regular camera can be mounted horizontally and swivelled between shots. Calibrated panoramic heads are also available, which are fitted to a tripod.

PHOTOMECHANICAL REPRODUCTION

For all practical purposes, an original photograph, whether a print or a transparency, is a continuous-tone image. That is to say, within its contrast range from dark to light, it can reproduce any intermediate tone, if necessary in a smooth gradient. Under a high-powered magnifying glass, the image can be seen to be composed of individual grains of silver or patches of dye, and the density of the image depends on how crowded these are; but under normal inspection a photographic image appears to be uninterrupted. However, in order to reproduce a photograph on a printed page rapidly and in quantity, inks must be used, and as it is only possible to apply each ink in a single density, some method has to be used to break up the printed image to give th appearance of continuous tone.

For letterpress and lithographic printing this process consists of converting the imag into a tight pattern of small dots, on such a scal that at a normal reading distance the eye car not distinguish between the individual dots bu interprets them as a full image. (Gravure prin ing uses a different method of screening.) Eac dot has the same density, but they vary in size small dots are separated from each other b relatively large white spaces and give the im pression of a light tone, while large dots ar closely packed, giving a dense tone. The re sulting image, in which the tone appears con tinuous even though it is not, is called a halftone

Far right Using a half tone screen for each of the four inks normally used in colour printing – cyan, yellow, magenta and black – the image of the original transparency is converted into an ordered pattern of dots. The success of photomechanical reproduction depends on creating the illusion of continuous tone, and this is achieved partly by using dots that are too small for the eye to see at a normal viewing distance, and partly by arranging them in patterns that are not obvious.
From the colour photograph above, a small section has been enlarged; at this magnification the illusion no longer holds, and the image is broken up.
Right Halftone screens are conventionally formed from two intersecting sets of parallel lines, giving a lattice-like pattern. Details of three such screens show the different ratios of the width of opaque lines to the width of space.

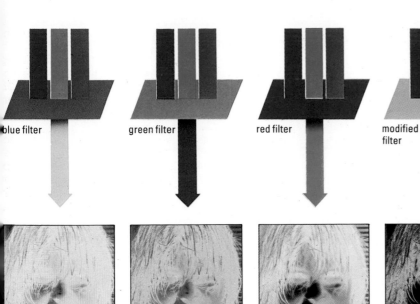

blue filter   green filter   red filter   modified filter

yellow printer   magenta printer   cyan printer   black printer

yellow proof   magenta proof   cyan proof   black proof

yellow proof   yellow plus magenta   yellow, magenta plus cyan   yellow, magenta, cyan plus black

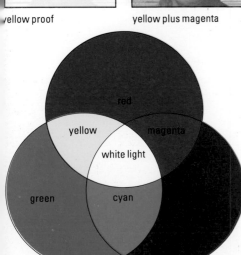

red

yellow   magenta

white light

green   cyan

Left White light is formed by a combination of all the colours of the spectrum. These can be broken down into three main colour sectors – red, green and blue. Since these colours are added together to create white light, they are known as "additive" primaries. If one of the primary colours is taken away, a different colour is produced. Red and green without blue makes yellow; red and blue without green produces magenta; and green and blue without red gives cyan. These three colours – magenta, yellow and cyan – are known as "subtractive" primaries.

Above Just as the effect of a full range of colours in photography is achieved by using three dyes, so colour process printing can reproduce most of the spectrum with a mixture of yellow, magenta and cyan dots. In practice, black is also used, for greater density. The first step in the process is to separate the original image into its yellow, magenta and cyan and black components. Yellow is an equal mixture of green and red, and is created by *subtracting* blue from white light. Hence, the original photograph is copied through a blue filter to make the

yellow printer. In a similar fashion, copying through a green filter gives the magenta printer, and a red filter gives the cyan printer. For the black printer, a modified filter is used. This is the process of colour separation, and may be done in continuous tone, with the halftone screens applied at a later stage, or it may be carried out through a screen, in one step. Colour separations may be made either photographically, using a process camera, or electronically with a scanner.

Its preparation is the first step in the photo-mechanical reproduction.

The traditional method of making a halftone is to use a process camera, which in essence copies the original through a screen consisting of two sheets of glass, each engraved with densely packed parallel lines and bonded together at right angles to make a grid. In closeup, the grid encloses clear surface areas, and it is through these that the halftone is exposed. The screen is separated from the film by a slight gap, which means that while a small exposure of light (from the shadow areas of the original) will develop as a small dark dot on the film, a substantial quantity of light (from the bright, highlit areas of the original) will "spread" to give a large dot on the film. The result is a negative image composed of dots that vary in size; from this negative, the final printing produces a positive image.

The spacing of the lines on the screen determines how coarse or fine the halftone image will be. This is essential because of differences in paper quality and printing processes. A fine quality art paper will absorb only a little ink and so a fine screen, of up to 70 lines per millimetre, can be used without the ink spreading between dots and blurring the image. Newsprint, on the other hand, is cheap and absorbent and may need a coarse screen of perhaps 22 lines per millimetre. As the spread of ink is also affected by how much ink is deposited on the paper, the actual printing process may also determine the size of screen – offset lithography transfers less ink to the paper than does letterpress, for example, and so can take a finer screen.

Nowadays a vignetted contact screen is more commonly used than a ruled screen. The vignetted contact screen carries a pattern of dots that have soft edges. The exposure from the highlight areas of the original penetrates this vignetted fringe around each dot more effectively than does the lesser exposure from shadow areas, and this determines the size of each halftone dot on the film.

Colour originals are converted in the same way, but require an additional stage to separate the image into three component colours. The principle is the same as for making the separation negatives used in dye transfer printing: the original is copied separately through red, blue and green filters to give three records that can later be printed using, respectively, cyan, yellow and magenta inks. In addition, a fourth separation is made, without a filter, so that a black inking can be made to improve detail and shadow density. These separation negatives may be in continuous tone, in which case the screens would be introduced later, or they may be made through a halftone screen in one operation.

In order to combine the four inkings used in colour reproduction in such a way that there is a minimum of interference between the lines of the different screens, each separation is screened at a different angle. This ensures that as each layer is deposited on the paper, the screens intermesh rather than lie on top of each other. If the angles at which the screens are placed are too similar, an interference pattern, known as a moiré effect, may affect the entire image.

Colour reproduction is complicated by the fact that the inks available are not pure, so that they neither absorb nor transmit primary colours completely. As a result, colour correction is essential, and involves increasing or reducing density in certain areas of the image in individual colours. The methods used vary with the process and the equipment.

If the original photograph has a colour deficiency, such as an overall colour cast, this can be allowed for by using the well-developed colour correction techniques available. However, imperfect originals give less opportunity to make standard corrections, and usually give a poorer quality result. Colour transparencies, which transmit a greater range of tones than colour prints, are preferred as originals.

The highest quality colour separations are made with an electronic scanner, and these are gradually replacing process cameras. The original transparency is attached to a rapidly rotating drum. The image is then scanned – in the latest models, with a laser beam – and the information stored and organized by means of microprocessors. Converting the visual information into digital form makes it possible to use computer programming techniques to control the result with great precision. Small-area colour correction is possible without affecting other parts of the image, and the process is rapid.

There are three basic printing processes that are used to reproduce photographs: letterpress, gravure and lithography. In letterpress printing, the oldest of the three, the ink is carried on a raised surface; the dots of the

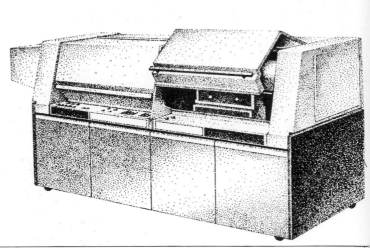

Right Increasingly, colour separation and engraving are performed in one action, by an electric scanner, which replaces the traditional methods of process camera and etching. The original photograph is scanned, and the difference in tone and colour are then translated, by means of a computer, into electrical impulses. These are then fed to a diamond stylus, which engraves the printing surfaces to a greater or lesser degree, depending on density; or, in the case of the latest electronic scanners, to an industrial laser, which performs the same function with a beam that can be varied in intensity.

second colour 75°
black 45°
Two-colour printing

second colour 7
black 45°
third colour 105°
Three-colour printing

yellow 90°
cyan 105°
magenta 75
black 45
Four-colour printing

halftone image are in relief on a plate. In gravure, the dots are recessed into the plate so that they contain tiny wells of ink. By varying the depth of each cell, different amounts of ink can be transferred to the paper, and gravure printing is capable of achieving strong densities by this means. In lithography, the image is not carried in relief, but instead the areas of the plate that will carry it are made receptive to the greasy ink, while the non-image areas are dampened with water to repel the ink. Offset lithography uses the intermediate stage of a rubber blanket, which takes up the impression of the image from the plate and transfers it to the paper. The soft rubber blanket gives a very clear impression, which enables fine screens to be used, although the density sometimes suffers because thick layers of ink cannot be applied.

Above Considerable care needs to be given to the angles at which the pattern of a halftone screen is reproduced on the page. To help the illusion of continuous tone, when a single colour is printed – as in most black-and-white reproduction – the screen is laid at 45°, which is, to the eye, the least noticeable angle. When two or more colours are printed, the screens must be printed at noticeably different angles to each other. If not, the patterns will conflict with each other, and in extreme cases can set up a very noticeable interference, and distracting pattern, known as moiré (above). An angle of about 30° is the optimum difference, so that, when a second colour is added, its screen is positioned at 75°, and that of a third colour at 105°. In four-colour printing, these angles are occupied as follows: black at 45°, magenta at 75°, cyan at 105° while yellow, which is the lightest colour and therefore the least noticeable, can be screened at the most obvious angle, 90°.

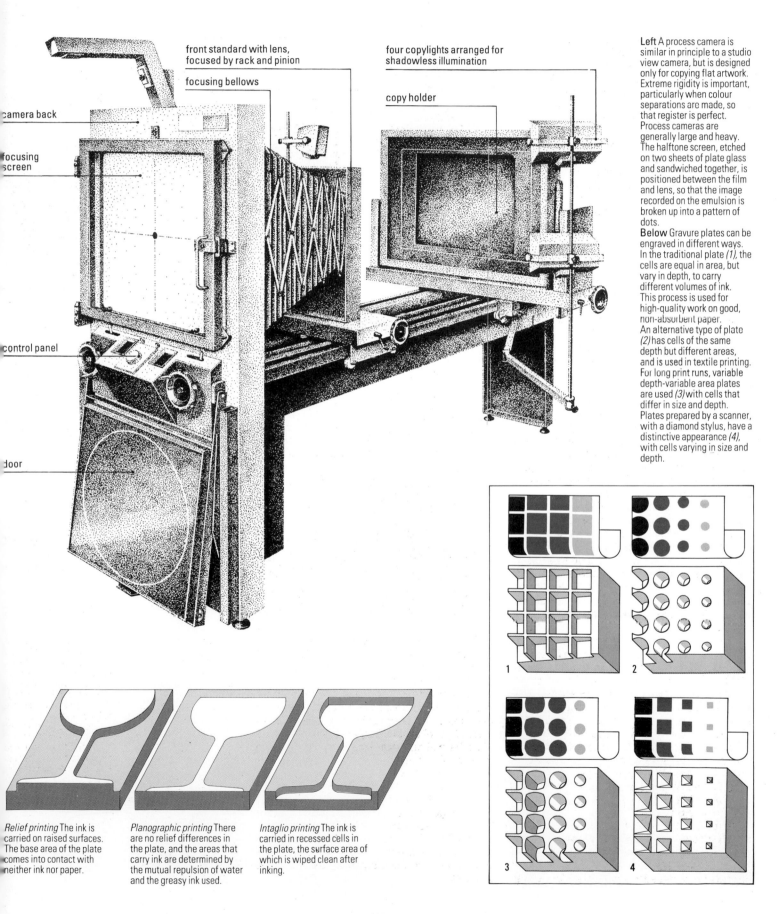

camera back

front standard with lens, focused by rack and pinion

focusing bellows

four copylights arranged for shadowless illumination

copy holder

focusing screen

control panel

door

Left A process camera is similar in principle to a studio view camera, but is designed only for copying flat artwork. Extreme rigidity is important, particularly when colour separations are made, so that register is perfect. Process cameras are generally large and heavy. The halftone screen, etched on two sheets of plate glass and sandwiched together, is positioned between the film and lens, so that the image recorded on the emulsion is broken up into a pattern of dots.

Below Gravure plates can be engraved in different ways. In the traditional plate *(1)*, the cells are equal in area, but vary in depth, to carry different volumes of ink. This process is used for high-quality work on good, non-absorbent paper. An alternative type of plate *(2)* has cells of the same depth but different areas, and is used in textile printing. For long print runs, variable depth-variable area plates are used *(3)* with cells that differ in size and depth. Plates prepared by a scanner, with a diamond stylus, have a distinctive appearance *(4)*, with cells varying in size and depth.

Relief printing The ink is carried on raised surfaces. The base area of the plate comes into contact with neither ink nor paper.

Planographic printing There are no relief differences in the plate, and the areas that carry ink are determined by the mutual repulsion of water and the greasy ink used.

Intaglio printing The ink is carried in recessed cells in the plate, the surface area of which is wiped clean after inking.

INDEX

Heavier **type** indicates illustrations

ACKNOWLEDGEMENTS

All photographs taken by Michael Freeman, with the exception of the following:
6 Joel Meyerowitz; 14, 15, 16, 17 Clive Boden; 19 Henri Cartier-Bresson (Magnum); 22, 22-3(c), 26-7, 28-9 Clive Boden; 33 Ray Daniel; 34(1), 34-5 Richard Cooke; 37,38 (b) Clive Boden; 41 Norman Parkinson (Condé Nast Publications); 42 Clive Boden; 44 Pete Conrad (Space Frontiers); 45(b) Picturepoint Limited; 47, 48-9 Clive Boden; 51 Edouard Denis Baldus (Victoria and Albert Museum); 56-7(b) Neyla Freeman; 58, 59 Clive Boden; 60(1) Harold E. Edgerton (Science Photo Library); 60-1 Science Photo Library; 61(r) Dr Tony Brain (Science Photo Library); 62, 63 Nikon U.K. Limited; 66-7, 68 Clive Boden; 72-3 Snowdon (Camera Press); 76 Clive Boden; 78(bl) Neyla Freeman; 80, 81 Clive Boden; 83(t) William Henry Fox Talbot (Fox Talbot Museum); 83(b) Gustave le Gray (Victoria and Albert Museum); 84 Emil Hoppé (The Mansell Collection); 84-5 Carlton Watkins (George Eastman House); 86-7, 88, 89 Clive Boden; 102, 103 Jean Harvey; 112, 113 Clive Boden; 116-7 Ian Berry (The John Hillelson Agency Limited); 120, 121 Clive Boden; 128 Ilford Limited; 132-3 Clive Boden; 138, 139 Kodak Limited; 140-1, 145, 150 Clive Boden; 151 Paul Joyce; 152 Roger Fenton (The Royal Photographic Society); 153 Roger Fenton (The Science Museum); 155, 158 Clive Boden; 177 Peter Henry Emerson (Robert Hershkowitz); 183(t), 184-5 Clive Boden; 196-7, 198 Jon Wyand; 199 Dr Derek Parfitt; 200 Clive Boden; 201(t) Jean Harvey; 203 Clive Boden; 208(t), 209 Neyla Freeman; 210-1, 213 Clive Boden

Key–(b)below (t)top (1)left (r)right (c)centre